PRAISE FOR
START SMALL,
FINISH BIG

"Reveals many ideas about how to start and fund your own business. Great reading for everyone thinking about starting a business."
—Paul and Sarah Edwards, bestselling authors and
nationally syndicated career columnists

"An engaging narrative that tells aspiring business people things they need to know, without either speaking over their heads or talking down to them....A nourishing read."
—*BookPage*

"DeLuca's approach to entrepreneurship is the stuff that made the American Dream. This book should be put in every high school library in the nation to inspire our future business leaders."
—Don DeBolt, CEO, International Franchise Association

"A book about a sandwich that's a full-course success meal for any entrepreneur. Buy it and devour it!"
—Jeffrey Gitomer, author of *The Sales Bible*

"A great book, loaded with practical ideas you can use immediately to start and build a profitable business."
—Brian Tracy, author of *Maximum Achievement:
Strategies and Skills That Will Unlock Your Hidden Powers to Succeed*

"A masterpiece on how to effectively put together and run your own business."
—Jim Rohn, author of *The Major Pieces to the Life Puzzle*

"The extraordinary thing about entrepreneurs is how tenaciously they pursue their vision....A wonderful read."
—Michael E. Gerber, author of *The E-Myth*

"Pleasant and informative...key lessons...clear and entertaining."
—*American Way* magazine

Books By
John P. Hayes

James A. Michener: A Biography
Franchising: The Inside Story (with John Kinch)
You Can't Teach a Kid to Ride a Bike at a Seminar (with David Sandler)
Philadelphia in Color
Taming Your Turmoil (with Peter L. Brill, M.D.)
Lonely Fighter
Mooney Warther: Life of the World's Master Carver

START SMALL

FINISH BIG

Fifteen Key Lessons to
Start—and Run—Your Own
Successful Business

FRED DELUCA

with John P. Hayes

WARNER
BUSINESS
BOOKS™

Published by Warner Books

A Time Warner Company

Copyright © 2000 by Frederick A. DeLuca and John P. Hayes. All rights reserved.

 Warner Business Books are published by Warner Books, Inc., 1271 Avenue of the Americas, New York, NY 10020

Visit our Web site at www.twbookmark.com.
For information on Time Warner Trade Publishing's online publishing program, visit www.ipublish.com.

 A Time Warner Company

Printed in the United States of America
First Trade Printing: August 2001
10 9 8 7 6 5 4 3 2 1

The Library of Congress has cataloged the hardcover edition as follows:

DeLuca, Fred.
    Start small, finish big : fifteen key lessons to start—and run—your own successful business / Fred DeLuca with John P. Hayes.
        p. cm.
    Includes index.
    ISBN 0-446-52402-6
    1. New business enterprises. 2. Entrepreneurship. 3. Self-employed. I. Hayes, John Phillip, 1949- II. Title.

    HD62.5 .D448 2000
    658'.041—dc21
                                                                                    00-024986

    ISBN 0-446-67756-6 (pbk.)

Book design by Giorgetta Bell McRee
Cover design by Flag
Cover Photograph by Robert Reichert

This book is dedicated to the memory of my dad Salvatore DeLuca who was there for me from the start and to my mother Carmela DeLuca, who still encourages me to follow my dreams.

To Haydee Buck for her support and for my partner Pete Buck. It was Pete who had the idea to start our small business and who had the vision that it would finish big.

To my wife Liz and son Jon—thank you for everything.

Of course, this book is for the members of the Subway family who are the foundation of this business. Each day they make me proud that we continued on our journey toward success—for without them this book would have not been written.

Lastly, to all the up and coming entrepreneurs—may this book help you as you set out to make your dreams a reality.

—Fred DeLuca

All of my earnings from sales of *Start Small, Finish Big* will be donated to the Micro Investment Lending Enterprise (MILE) to assist that organization in establishing chapters across the United States and Canada. MILE is a volunteer-run, non-profit organization that lends money to people who do not readily have access to credit so that they may start their own small businesses. Interest earned from MILE loans to borrowers is used at the chapter level to make more loans to local people in need. No one will make a profit from MILE or the operation of any MILE chapter. For more information about MILE please call 800-888-4848, extension 1636, or visit www.mileloans.org.

—Fred DeLuca, founder,
Micro Investment Lending Enterprise

The resources listed in this book are believed to be reliable by the authors. Such information is current as of December 1999.

CONTENTS

CONTENTS

Contents

FRED DeLUCA'S
Fifteen Key Lessons to Start—and Run—Your Own Successful Business

Lesson One	**Start Small**
Lesson Two	**Earn a Few Pennies**
Lesson Three	**Begin with an Idea**
Lesson Four	**Think Like a Visionary**
Lesson Five	**Keep the Faith**
Lesson Six	**Ready, Fire, Aim!**
Lesson Seven	**Profit or Perish**
Lesson Eight	**Be Positive**
Lesson Nine	**Continuously Improve Your Business**
Lesson Ten	**Believe in Your People**
Lesson Eleven	**Never Run Out of Money**
Lesson Twelve	**Attract New Customers Every Day**
Lesson Thirteen	**Be Persistent: Don't Give Up**
Lesson Fourteen	**Build a Brand Name**
Lesson Fifteen	**Opportunity Waits for No One**

CHAPTER ONE

IT'S AN ENTREPRENEUR'S WORLD

You can become part of it by starting small as a microentrepreneur.

Paul Orfalea doesn't read very well, he has a short attention span, suffers from dyslexia, and he struggled to get through school. But one day, without any business experience and hardly any money, he leased a small space in a garage, leased a copy machine, and launched the business that we know today as Kinko's. Through trial and error, and by following many of the lessons discussed in this book, Paul was able to turn a profit and eventually expand his business. Today, having started with just $5,000, Kinko's has opened more than 1,000 business centers worldwide. I'll tell you more about the development of Kinko's later in the book. For now, let's just say that Paul Orfalea started small and he's finishing big.

Mike Ilitch also started small, and he's finishing big, bigger than anyone could ever have imagined. In his twenties, the only world Mike knew was baseball. He was an amazing high school athlete, so much so that the Detroit Tigers recruited him during those years. After a stint in the Marine Corps, Mike joined one of the Tigers' farm teams. He played well for several years, until he broke his ankle, and soon thereafter his baseball career was history. What would he do now to support his young family? He floundered for several years until he opened a small pizza shop. Even then, lacking experience, he experimented with one idea after another. Success wasn't an overnight phenomenon, but Mike paid attention to the details of his business, he learned one lesson after another, and eventually he opened multiple shops. That was the beginning of the Little Caesar's pizza chain, now known in nearly every community of the United States. Today, Mike Ilitch not only owns Little Caesar's, he also owns several major sports franchises in Detroit—including the Tigers—and many other businesses. But I'll save the rest of Mike's story, too, for later in the book.

Even though the stories of Paul Orfalea and Mike Ilitch sound incredible, they are typical of the stories you'll find in this book. They are typical, in fact, of business stories everywhere. I know because I started Subway with $1,000. My story shares many similarities with the stories of Paul, Mike, and the others who you'll soon meet. We *all* started with small amounts of money, and my overall message in this book is that you, too, may be able to start small and finish big.

At any given moment in the world millions of people are thinking about starting a business. They are people like you and me, motivated by the desire to be their own boss and to become financially independent. Some want the freedom and the flexibility of self-employment. Others want to make more money, and some are tired of making money for others. Some have lost their jobs, some are about to lose their jobs, and many others are simply tired of their jobs. A business of their own, frightening though it may be, sounds like a logical next step. An exciting next step. If only they can get started.

For most of these millions of people, starting a business will remain merely a dream, locked in the depths of their hearts and minds. It's something to think about. Something to talk about around the kitchen table, especially with family and friends who share similar dreams. Unfortunately, few take the first bold step to actually start a business. Few can muster the energy and commitment to begin.

Why?

For a variety of reasons, all of which may be valid. They think they don't have the capital. They think they lack the experience. They think they don't have the education, or they don't know how. They don't feel confident with their plan. They think they need money to make money. And, perhaps more often than not, they never start because a family member or friend told them they couldn't do it: *"You'd be crazy to try . . . play it safe and stick with your job. So what if you're miserable. At least you get a paycheck every week. Small businesses never amount to much of anything anyway."*

Does it sound familiar?

Are you among the millions of people who think about starting a business, but you just never get started? If you are, you'll be glad you read *Start Small, Finish Big*. The lessons and messages in this book are especially for you.

Around the world, and especially in the United States, there are plenty of people like Paul Orfalea and Mike Ilitch who start tiny businesses with less than $10,000 (frequently much less). We call these enterprises *microbusinesses*, the people who start them *microentrepreneurs*, and the organizations that loan them start-up money *microlenders*. These are important concepts to me. Microentrepreneurs are frequently overlooked simply because their businesses are tiny, but many of them contribute significantly to the American economy, and to several economies worldwide. Not to mention the fact that many microentrepreneurs generate sizable personal incomes, and they build businesses that can be kept in the family, or sold as valuable assets. I, for one, plan to do all that I can to focus attention on the phenomenon of microenterprise, and you'll learn more about my interests as you read this book.

Since the beginning of time, people have started businesses with small amounts of money. They begin modestly, without fanfare and often without great expectations. Today, no one knows for sure how many microbusinesses exist or how many are started each year, but the U.S. Small Business Administration reports that first-time entrepreneurs are responsible for 60 percent of business start-ups. Furthermore, the National Federation of Independent Business reports that people under the age of thirty-five launched 1.9 million businesses in 1996, representing nearly half of the businesses started in the U.S. that year. Three quarters of these young entrepreneurs started from scratch, with almost nothing!

Microentrepreneurs come from all walks of life. Male and female. People of color. Able-bodied and people with disabilities. Some have business experience, but most do not. Some may be government dependent, but most are not. Some are young—even preteens—and some are old. Many are retired; they start microbusinesses for something to do, or to supplement their income. Microentrepreneurs are as likely to be high school dropouts as they are college graduates. Formal education is of no significance here. Many of them are employed full-time and start their microenterprises part-time. Frequently they work from home, a basement, a garage, or a truck. Some own multiple enterprises. Some work with partners, especially spouses. But most work alone, at least initially. Microentrepreneurs don't necessarily register their businesses at first, especially if they work from home. They may or may not file for local or state licenses. Most microentrepreneurs, in fact, don't know they are microentrepreneurs. And they may not even care. They think of an idea one day, and the next day they're in business. With the exception of their prospective customers, they don't really have to tell anyone what they're doing.

In their smallest form, microbusinesses feed families, rescue victims from welfare rolls, and replace shame with dignity. Some microbusinesses are intended to supplement a full-time income, or to pay college tuition, or to buy necessities, or even luxuries that would otherwise be out of reach. Many of these businesses remain small, others expand into regional or national operations, and some become international entities. According to the U.S. Agency for International Development, which supports its own Microenterprise Initiative, microenterprises often employ a third or more of the labor force in lower-income countries.

There are few prerequisites for microentrepreneurs. Basically, they need an idea, a little bit of money, and most importantly the desire to get started. There's nothing complicated about what they do. You're not likely to read about them in the newspapers. They don't announce the start-up of their businesses on radio and television, or even the Internet. They simply start. And regardless of how many people these microentrepreneurs employ initially, how much money they generate annually, or how many locations they start with, they all have the potential to grow and finish big. As big as they desire. Sometimes bigger than they can imagine. More often than most people know, as microbusinesses mature they create dozens, hundreds, and sometimes thousands of jobs, and they generate millions, sometimes billions, of dollars in annual revenues.

In an age of corporate and social downsizing, and in an era when people are moving back to smaller towns to simplify their lives, the day of the microentrepreneur has arrived. Or perhaps, more accurately, it has returned. It's a new millennium, and the stage has been set for microentrepreneurs. In the years to come, we can expect to see a proliferation of microenterprises worldwide.

Somewhere right now, perhaps in your own community, there's a microbusiness that's headed for stardom in tomorrow's business press. Perhaps it's your business, or a business that you're thinking about beginning. If so, I believe you've found an important resource in this book.

Conventional wisdom offers little hope to those who dare to try what so many say can't be done. But *Start Small, Finish Big* is a book about hope. For those who dare to take the first step beyond just thinking about starting a small business, this is a book filled with ideas and possibilities. It's a book that helps overcome the excuses. No matter what your situation may be, *Start Small, Finish Big* provides a boost for those who seek the confidence, guidance, encouragement, and the will to get started, or to persist, in a business.

If you're reading this book because you want to start your own business, or expand an existing business, here's what you're about to learn.

The Fifteen Key Lessons. Based on my personal experiences as a microentrepreneur, and the experiences of twenty-one other microentrepreneurs whose stories are included in this book, I'll share with you the Fifteen Key Lessons that will help you start small and finish big.

These lessons are:

1. Start Small. It's better than never starting at all.
2. Earn a Few Pennies. It's good practice before you earn those dollars.
3. Begin With an Idea. There's probably a good one right under your nose.
4. Think Like a Visionary. Always look for the Big Picture.
5. Keep the Faith. Believe in yourself and your business, even when others don't.
6. Ready, Fire, Aim! If you think too much about it, you may never start.
7. Profit or Perish. Increase sales, decrease costs. Anything less and your business will perish.
8. Be Positive. The School of Hard Knocks will beat you down, but not if you keep a positive attitude.
9. Continuously Improve Your Business. It's the best way to attract customers, and generate sales and profit.
10. Believe In Your People. Or they may get even with you!
11. Never Run Out of Money. It's the most important lesson in business.

12. Attract New Customers Every Day. Awareness, Trial, and Usage work every time.
13. Be Persistent: Don't Give Up. You only fail if you quit.
14. Build a Brand Name! Earn your reputation.
15. Opportunity Waits for No One. Good or bad, breaks are what you make them.

Why are these lessons valuable? Because if you follow them, you are more likely to be successful in the development of your business. These are the lessons I learned while building Subway, and they're the same lessons that many other microentrepreneurs have learned and applied, too. If you plan to grow your business beyond a one- or two-person enterprise, there will be other lessons to learn, of course. But these Fifteen Key Lessons will help you get started and keep you focused.

Start Small, Finish Big will introduce you to a variety of microentrepreneurs who, like me, began their businesses on financial shoestrings. Their stories illustrate and highlight each of the Fifteen Key Lessons. Instead of relying only on my experiences, or my interpretation of a particular lesson, you will also gain the richly instructional and personal perspectives of these microentrepreneurs. Their stories usually illustrate not one, but several of the Fifteen Key Lessons, and that's because no one lesson is sufficient to build a successful business. It's a combination of these lessons, if not all of the lessons, that allows you to start small and finish big.

A few of the microentrepreneurs in the book are still in the early stages of building their businesses. You may find their stories encouraging and uplifting. The challenges they battled and conquered, and the challenges they still struggle to resolve, serve as good examples of what you can expect should you choose to become a microentrepreneur.

Some of the other microentrepreneurs in the book have grown their small enterprises into national and international brand names, but they have not forgotten their humble beginnings, and they gladly share their stories in the hopes of helping you accomplish your dream of business ownership. In several cases, you'll immediately recognize their company names, although you may not ever have heard of the entrepreneurs who are responsible for the company's success. These stories, too, should inspire and motivate you as you think about starting a business, or expanding an existing business.

You'll learn about the value of building a brand from Paul Orfalea. Mike Ilitch demonstrates how a couple of bad breaks can lead to great opportunities. Mary Ellen Sheets, a founder of Two Men & A Truck, shares her ideas about the importance of constantly improving a business. Jim Cavanaugh, who built Jani-King, the world's largest commercial cleaning company, shows you what can happen when you look for the Big Picture. And a name that's widely recognized for motivation and inspiration, Zig Ziglar, reveals the down-and-out story of a man who developed a positive attitude and continues to earn his stripes at the School of Hard Knocks.

Then there's the inventor Tomima Edmark, who wondered one day if she could turn a ponytail inside out. That one creative thought sparked the idea for the TopsyTail, and Tomima has been coming up with ideas ever since. Frank Argenbright literally earned pennies before he earned his first dollar, and today his company, AHL Services, Inc., a contract staffing business, generates a billion dollars in sales annually. Tom Morales wasn't ready to start his own business, but one day, annoyed with his job, he decided to resign. After fumbling for a while, he started TomKats, a catering business that serves the movie industry. Tom shows us that even if you haven't done all your planning, you can't take forever to think about your business. Sometimes you fire first, and take aim later.

When she was living in a shelter with her two children, it would have been easy for Cynthia Wake to give up her direct sales business, The Hosiery Stop. In fact, it would have made sense to quit. But Cynthia doesn't believe in giving up, and she'll tell you the price she's paid to persevere as a business owner. Meanwhile, when his economics professor marked an F on his business plan for Campus Concepts, you might have thought Ian Leopold would get a job and forget his idea about launching a series of campus guides. But 100 guides later, and $10 million in annual revenue, is proof enough that it pays to believe in yourself and your business, even when no one else does.

Microentrepreneurs build businesses and people run them. David Schlessinger, who founded Encore Books when he was a college student, explains the wisdom of believing in people if you want to build an empire. Earl Tate shows you what happens when you build an empire and run out of money, as he did twice. The founder of Staffing Solutions, a temporary employment agency, readily admits his mistakes so that you might avoid them.

Terri Bowersock, founder of the world's largest consignment furniture chain, Terri's Consign & Design Furnishings, has mastered the course on attracting customers. Years ago, teachers and friends said Terri couldn't have mastered much of anything. Now she's sharing her mastery with others, and helping them build successful businesses. Ev Harlow, who became a graphic designer while he served Uncle Sam in the Air Force, has mastered the course on generating profits. With no business experience at the time he launched Art Reproduction Technologies, he quickly discovered that a business without profit will soon perish. He didn't waste any time learning the importance of making profit and how to do it.

Whoever said *it takes money to make money* was dead wrong, and the microentrepreneurs in this book prove it. For example, after many years of teaching string instruments in public schools, Paulette Ensign was bored and unhappy. She spent $50 to buy two classified ads in her local newspapers and created Organizing Solutions, a little business to teach people how to organize their lives, their homes, and their jobs. Carlos Aldana was twenty-eight when he left Colombia and arrived in the United States without a job or so much as a penny in his pocket. He worked three minimum-wage jobs before he

9

started his own delivery service. Now he owns a restaurant in New York City.

Michael and Jamie Ford were middle-class Americans before an accident forced Jamie out of work. The family had to move into a travel trailer and collect welfare to exist. If only they could start their own business, they were sure they could get off public assistance and return to their former mainstream lifestyle. When a nonprofit organization that assists microentrepreneurs loaned the Fords $250, it was all the help they needed to start a tiny business selling kettle corn. Since then, the U.S. Small Business Administration has honored the Fords as Entrepreneurs of the Year in New Mexico.

Jeremy Wiener invested little more than gas and phone money to start Cover-It, a business that provides book covers to schools in all fifty states. From so tiny an investment, his business employs ten people and it will soon generate in excess of $2 million annually. Charlotte Colistro Brown, another schoolteacher, invested $200 in materials that she used to make crafts in her home. Her business, Collectable Creations, sells products that retail for $8 to $70 each. A cadre of sixty home-based employees sews and finishes the crafts. The company will soon exceed $2 million in annual gross sales!

Nancy Bombace invested $4,000 to start a honeymoon registry service, an alternative to the traditional department store registry for brides. Now wedding guests can find out where the newlyweds will honeymoon and then pay for the wedding suite, or buy dinner, a bottle of champagne, or a romantic tour. In Alexandria, Virginia, Terri Symonds Grow researched all-natural products and treatments for animals and then invested $1,500 to begin PetSage, a catalogue company that specializes in natural alternative therapies for pets. She's watched her company's sales grow from $30,000 to nearly $350,000!

As you read the stories in the chapters ahead, you'll see that these microentrepreneurs represent a good cross section of the American population. You'll also discover that we share many commonalities. With only a few exceptions, we grew up in lower-to-middle-class homes where both parents had to work. All of us learned how to make money before we were teenagers—a couple started businesses in elementary school. Most of us tolerated school, and several performed poorly. At least three continue to suffer from dyslexia. Five never attended college; four others attended but did not graduate. Six of us began our businesses while we were in college, and five of us started our businesses before we were twenty. Seven of the microentrepreneurs are women, while four of the men started their businesses with help from their wives. Feeling sorry for ourselves, or claiming to be victims of impoverishment and sometimes cruel circumstances, was not part of our routine. The world owed us nothing. Therefore, if we saw an opportunity, we grabbed it. And we still do.

The most interesting common denominator that we share, however, is that we started our businesses with small amounts of money. Two had as much as $10,000. One started with $5,000. All of the others, including me, started with less than $5,000. Ten started with $200 or less! Four got started with loans from microlenders, which are quietly popping up across the United States. (I'll tell you more about microlenders later in the book.) Four borrowed money from family members, and two, including me, borrowed money from a friend. The other half started their businesses with no money, or their own pocket money.

Collectively, I think you will agree these stories weave a fabric of promise and fulfillment, laced with inspiration and possibilities for your own future in business. As you read the lessons and stories in the book, I expect you will find yourself saying, over and over again, *I can do that, too*. You can! It's really only a matter of deciding to do it.

From there, *Start Small, Finish Big* has something more to offer you. My real reason for writing this book, beyond giving people the confidence to start a business, even if they don't have much money, is to support the microenterprise movement that's underway not only in the United States, but in

Asia, Africa, and Latin America. In these countries, people who have no business experience, and no collateral to borrow money, including the poorest of the poor, are able to get capital from several hundred organizations. It's a relatively young movement that's gaining momentum, and as it expands, it can potentially help tens of millions of people.

My introduction to microenterprise occurred in 1989 while watching a segment of *60 Minutes*. That Sunday night, as I sat at home in front of my television, I learned about Muhammad Yunus, Ph.D., an American-trained economics professor who had become a giant among impoverished people in Bangladesh, a country which *60 Minutes* described as "the world's graveyard of good intentions." Dr. Yunus was loaning small sums of money to poor people, who in turn changed their lives for the better. Interestingly, the improvements initiated by Dr. Yunus contradicted the economic theories that he taught in his classrooms. In fact, he told *60 Minutes* those theories—which he learned in America—did not work in Bangladesh. In spite of what he taught his students, economic progress did not occur the way the textbooks promised. Instead of things getting better, they only grew worse.

That's when Dr. Yunus took matters into his own hands. He believed in a bottom-up, rather than a top-down, approach to helping people. If given an opportunity, Yunus surmised that people could do more for themselves than any government could do. So he left the classroom in 1976 and walked into the villages to really study economics. Soon thereafter, he was granting small loans to impoverished people. At the time of the *60 Minutes* report, Dr. Yunus had loaned $100 million to 500,000 people in Bangladesh. The only prerequisites to qualify for a loan were impoverishment and the desire to work hard. The average loan amount was $60. Many borrowers received consecutive loans, renewed annually. (Today, Dr. Yunus's organization has loaned more than $2.7 billion to 2.5 million people. The average loan amount is approximately $180.)

To many people who watched the *60 Minutes* report, this

story may not have made much sense. How could it? What kind of business could you start with $60? Could it become a business of any significance?

Yes! Even in the United States, as you'll soon read, significant businesses have been started with $60 or less. In Bangladesh, $60 is a lot of money. A stool maker, for example, turned a $6 loan into a daily profit of $1.25, up from earnings of just 2 cents a day prior to the loan. With $30, another borrower purchased a loom and eventually earned $1,500 a year—enough money to afford a house and to educate several children. The *60 Minutes* report abounded with these amazing stories of success.

While others looked upon Bangladesh as a classic case study in poverty—people were poor because they did not want to work—Professor Yunus saw something remarkably different. *People were poor because they lacked resources.* They had no money to do anything for themselves. Those who had access to resources were forced to pay outrageous interest rates on a daily basis to local traders. Consequently, people remained impoverished one generation after another. Provide the resources, as well as hope and encouragement, Dr. Yunus reasoned, and people could alleviate poverty on their own.

So he went to work to find money for poor people to help them start their own businesses. He didn't want to provide aid to individuals, in spite of the fact that Bangladesh got plenty of international aid. He wanted to provide credit, which he believed was a fundamental human right. But when he contacted the community banks and suggested they loan money to poor people, who had no collateral, the lenders laughed at his idea. Of course, the reaction would have been the same from banks in the United States. Banks require collateral to make loans, and they rarely grant small loans. That's one of the reasons I'm supporting microenterprise. By establishing microcredit lending groups across the United States, we can help people bootstrap their way into business.

After several banks rejected Dr. Yunus's idea, he established a bank of his own. By soliciting loans and grants internationally, he founded the Grameen Bank, which in Bengali means the "rural bank." Its sole purpose is to loan money to the "poorest of the poor." Impoverishment is the only qualification a borrower needs to do business at the Grameen Bank.

Within a period of a few years, Muhammad Yunus had delivered more hope to crisis-ridden Bangladesh than any man or woman before him. By empowering people with tiny sums of money, and a few skills, he showed them how to help themselves. In so doing, he didn't eradicate poverty, but he helped reduce the ravages of its horrible condition and he helped train legions of people who started grassroots businesses. Years later, President Bill Clinton would honor Muhammad Yunus in Washington, D.C., and state that he should be awarded a Nobel Prize.

While I sat fascinated by Dr. Yunus's story, I couldn't help but connect my own circumstances with the microenterprise movement that he inspired. I was not among the "poorest of the poor" when I started my business. But I had no money at the time, no collateral, and no business savvy. I was a seventeen-year-old kid who needed to find a way to pay for his college education. *I needed resources.* When a family friend offered me a small loan to start a business selling submarine sandwiches, it made all the difference in my life. As I sat there watching how Dr. Yunus changed the lives of people across Bangladesh, I understood how a small amount of money could change a person's life forever. That's when I decided that I would eventually help spread the gospel of microenterprise so that others could benefit from the movement, and perhaps contribute to it, too.

Third World countries were quick to copy Dr. Yunus's somewhat controversial program, but several years passed before a Yunus-inspired organization arrived in the United States. (Other microenterprise groups already existed in the United States, however.) Critics, particularly in the U.S., have said the Grameen Bank doesn't work, in spite of the fact that at least 95 percent of its loans are repaid on time! . . . in spite of the fact that its borrowers have saved more than $100 million, all of it on deposit at the Grameen Bank! . . . in spite of the fact that in nearly twenty-five years of development, the Grameen Bank has helped two and a half million people and spawned profit centers, including fisheries, and a cellular phone business . . . in spite of the fact that the Grameen Bank has demonstrated its ability to help people nourish their self-esteem, and provide for themselves and their families! *"Poor people aren't smart enough to start businesses,"* say the critics. *"If anything, they should be trained for employment. You need big businesses to really help people. Small businesses don't amount to much."* Perhaps a few of the stories in this book would change their minds.

Fortunately, the critics have not discouraged Dr. Yunus, or his legion of admirers and supporters, who continue to help people start their own businesses. In recent years, the Grameen Bank, and organizations similar to it, have won favorable attention from major media, including the *Wall Street Journal*, the *Washington Post*, *Forbes*, *U.S. News & World Report*, and *The Economist*. Support for these various organizations has come from numerous groups and corporations, including Citicorp, Arthur Andersen, AT&T, NationsBank, Microsoft, Discover Card, the Ford Foundation, the Charles Stewart Mott Foundation, J. P. Morgan & Co., BP America, Rotary Clubs, and Kiwanis Clubs.

More support is needed, of course, if the microenterprise movement is to flourish in North America. Much of the support will have to come from individuals who are committed to the success of small enterprises. I committed the time to develop this book because I want to be counted among those individuals. I have also provided initial funding for the Grameen-Subway Micro-Credit Initiative, as well as the non-profit Micro Investment Lending Enterprise (MILE). MILE is a *community service franchise* that loans money to people who do not have access to credit, but who want to start a business.

All of my earnings from *Start Small, Finish Big* are being contributed to the microenterprise movement, and specifically to MILE. In case you're wondering, neither I nor anyone associated with MILE earns a profit from MILE. All interest earned on MILE loans is recycled back to MILE so that the organization has additional money to lend. I hope that after you read this book you'll want to get involved with me in supporting microenterprise, and specifically, MILE. But more about that later.

Today, approximately 100 organizations in the United States loan small amounts of money—rarely more than $5,000—to people who are ready to join the world of the microentrepreneur. (You'll find a partial list of these organizations in the back of this book, along with information about MILE.) Many, but not all of these organizations require their borrowers to be low-income. Once you know how to access these organizations, some of them may be willing to assist you, not only with money, but with business training, too. Also, many of these organizations rely on volunteers to help them work with their borrowers, representing yet another opportunity to get involved with microenterprise.

Before I tell you the story of how I started Subway, and then share with you the Fifteen Key Lessons, I also want to tell you what you won't learn in *Start Small, Finish Big*. This isn't a book about writing business plans or about how to get your idea funded by investment bankers. This isn't a book about business strategies or cutting-edge research. It's not about breakthrough developments or technical prowess. It's not about styles of management. It's not about franchising your business, although it includes information about franchising. It's not about my "clever strategic plan" to build Subway—because such a plan never existed—or my "incredible business skills"—because they were minimal when I started my business.

Start Small, Finish Big isn't about building a multinational company, or even a big company. The size of the business doesn't matter. The BIG in the book's title may mean a part-time venture, a home-based business, or a kiosk at the mall. It could also mean a chain of stores, or an international corporation. BIG is however big or small *you* define it to be. It may simply describe the incredible feelings of accomplishment and pride that you derive from your own business, no matter how big it gets.

Some people may find it hard to believe that you can start a meaningful business with a little bit of money. I don't blame them. Roll-ups, international buyouts, industry consolidations, and dot-com companies are the meat and potatoes of the business press these days. There doesn't seem to be much opportunity for the small enterprise. And yet, it exists. Small businesses abound. The small business is the backbone of the American economy and it will continue to be the future of this country and many others. Small businesses create more jobs every year in the United States than do big businesses. As many as 40 million Americans now work from their homes, and the majority of them are small business owners. In the age of the megadeal, there's still room for the small businessperson. All you've got to do is look for it, then reach out and grab it.

When I started Subway in 1965, no one told me that I couldn't succeed with just a little bit of money. Of course, at the time, I was just a teenager, recently graduated from high school. I really didn't know much about running a business. I knew nothing about making sandwiches, nor the food industry. I knew nothing about franchising. One day, when a family friend encouraged me to start a business, I became one of those millions of people who think about starting a business at any given time. But I also became one of the few who took the first bold step. Fortunately for me, and for an ever-increasing number of people worldwide who are part of the Subway family today, I didn't know that you couldn't start small and finish big.

Now that I have, let me help you get started!

CHAPTER TWO

———

———

THE FIFTEEN
KEY LESSONS

How I discovered them and implemented them, and
how they helped me start small and finish big with
Subway!

Before I tell you my story, and the stories of the other microentrepreneurs in this book, and then get into the substance of
the Fifteen Key Lessons, it's important to explain how I discovered each lesson and how the lessons contributed to Subway's
growth, and to my current way of thinking about building any
business. I wasn't looking for these lessons when they became
evident to me. Chances are you've already learned some of
these lessons on your own, but you haven't recognized them as
lessons. Several of the lessons escaped me until I was well into
the development of Subway. But eventually they all appeared—
some from my childhood, some from my business associates, and
others from trial and error. Each lesson proved to be invaluable
to me, and I believe they'll be important to you, too.

Lesson One: Start Small. I learned this lesson while owning
two newspaper routes. In my estimation, a newspaper route is
one of the greatest training grounds for business. It's a really
small business, and yet it provides a vast array of experiences
with all the fundamentals of business represented. You have to
buy a product, deliver the product, provide a good service to

customers, and of course you have to collect your money. It goes almost without saying that you'll have to work hard to make a profit. Through rain, snow, hail, and on sunny days when you'd rather be doing something else, you've got to deliver your papers! A paper route is a great way to be introduced to the world of business, but actually, any small start serves the same purpose.

Some people have the idea that a small business doesn't amount to much unless it delivers a sizable income, or it expands into an international enterprise. But I don't agree. Just because it's small doesn't mean the business can't grow. And while it is small you will have the time to learn the lessons that are essential to your future success. If you want to finish big, starting small is the best way to begin.

Lesson Two: Earn a Few Pennies. I learned this lesson at age seven when it was important to have pocket change. Collecting discarded soda pop bottles and redeeming them for pennies was an important lesson. Buried in *the process* of collecting bottles and redeeming them for a couple of cents was a lesson that said: *It's not how much you earn at first, it's learning to earn something, even a few pennies.* Exchanging bottles for money taught me the importance of the transaction in business. It set me up for bigger things to come. At the time, of course, the lesson didn't interest me. I spent the money on baseball cards, comic books, and other things that kids enjoy. Little did I know that this was my first real lesson in economics.

Lesson Three: Begin with an Idea. This lesson was introduced to me at a family picnic when I was seventeen. Family friend Pete Buck suggested that I open a small sandwich shop. He saw a need for one, and that was the idea for Subway. We spent a few hours talking about the idea, and later that day Pete and I became business partners. The idea was so simple that we got started the next day.

Take a look around you. What needs to be improved? Where is there a void? Ask others for their opinions. Eventually you'll find a good idea.

Nowadays, it seems all the big business ideas are coming from the recent technology of the Internet. Talk about starting small and finishing big, some of these dot-com businesses have created overnight billionaires! But even many of these companies started with a simple idea.

Lesson Four: Think Like a Visionary. After Pete and I agreed that we would start a sandwich business together, he then suggested that we set a long-term goal. That's when I first realized the importance of creating a vision for your business. Pete suggested that we open thirty-two stores in ten years, a rather incredible goal, but big enough to capture my attention and commitment. That goal would help keep us focused during the difficult times that awaited us.

It's not enough to have an idea. It's important to look beyond the idea. If you implement the idea, then what? It's really important to ask the "what" questions. What will result after we open the business? What can it become? What value can it provide? What good will it do for me emotionally and financially? What is it about this business that will capture my commitment, my energy, and money?

From those questions come the answers that will help you create a vision for your business. Think big when you create that vision! Give yourself the opportunity to get excited about your idea and the future.

Lesson Five: Keep the Faith. I learned this lesson within six months of getting into business. That's when Pete and I realized our first sandwich shop was an economic failure. At that point, it would have been so easy to give up the belief in our idea, and our vision, and close our business. Fortunately, we didn't take that approach.

Building a business is a challenging commitment and the challenge never ends. Many days the future of your business will look bleak. You'll run short of money, you'll lose customers, vendors will disappoint you, employees will sometimes take advantage of your business. Many things can go wrong. When they do, you can expect at least some of the people around you to say that you should forget your "crazy idea" and do something else, like get a job! But during these times you cannot lose faith in yourself or your business.

Starting a business as a teenager was actually a blessing for me. It never occurred to me that I couldn't succeed, and people didn't discourage me because, after all, I was young. There was always time for me to rebound. Consequently, on those bleak days that come with every business venture, I might have been disappointed, or emotionally down, but it never occurred to me to give up faith in what we were doing and what we could accomplish.

Lesson Six: Ready, Fire, Aim! I learned this lesson by opening the first store without any experience. In other words, I learned it by doing it and not just thinking about it. With clarity about the idea for Subway, and at least a glimpse of the vision, I went to work the next day! Someone else might have taken time to plot out the job requirements and to write a business plan, but doing those things may have prevented me from actually starting. There's a good chance the planning process would have consumed my energy. Or I would have decided that what I thought was a good idea wasn't such a good idea after all.

As I've discovered on many occasions since starting Subway, it's better to fire in the general direction of where you want to end up and then adjust your aim, than never fire at all. Get started. Move in the general direction of where you want to go. Make course adjustments along the way.

Lesson Seven: Profit or Perish. Early in Subway's development I found out that it's easy to make a lot of sales and still not make a profit! That's when I learned about profit or perish. One day my accountant congratulated me for generating annual sales in excess of $1 million for the first time. But in the next breath he also explained that unfortunately I had lost $100,000 that year! How could that happen? It didn't take me long to figure out there are only two ways to make money: increase sales and decrease costs. Believe me, this is a lesson worth learning as soon as possible. It's a lesson that we teach our franchisees at Subway.

Lesson Eight: Be Positive. I learned this lesson in the midst of building the first few Subway shops. From an economic point of view, those first shops were disastrous. In the process of locating and building those shops, I made many mistakes, as might be expected of someone who was inexperienced and had no real plan. The early failures could have boxed me into a negative mind-set where it might have been nearly impossible to solve problems and make real progress. Fortunately, that's not the path I chose. I'm sure it helped that I was young, and I also had a business partner who set a positive example. Where there were challenges, we sought solutions. And even when one solution didn't work, we sought another and another until we worked through the challenge. It's a lesson that I continue to practice every day that I'm involved in business.

When you're faced with seemingly insurmountable obstacles, it doesn't help to be negative. Keep a positive mind-set.

Lesson Nine: Continuously Improve Your Business. This is a lesson that may not become apparent until you're faced with competition. Businesses do not stand still. They may fall behind some times, but those that succeed do so by continuously improving their operation. Progress requires that they introduce new products, new ways to serve their customers, new ways to market, new ways to get ahead of everyone else. This is not a once-and-done experience. It's continuous.

Even today, when we introduce new ideas at Subway, our competition won't be far behind. The only way to stay in business is to continuously make these improvements.

Lesson Ten: Believe In Your People. One of the greatest assets in any business is people. That's been reinforced for me over the years, but even so, I learned this lesson the hard way. You'll enjoy the story that follows if you've had to learn this lesson the hard way, too.

One night I walked into a Subway shop and found a mess behind the counter. There was food everywhere. I read the riot act to the employee who was working alone. "You've got to keep this place clean," I demanded of him. I helped him clean up and then sternly said, "Don't let this happen again." And I left the store.

The next day, much to my surprise, I discovered that store had set a new sales record for the most sandwiches sold in the shortest period of time. That's when I realized the place was a mess because our single employee was working hard to serve our customers. As I looked further into the matter, I discovered he had experienced a rush of business just before my appearance at the store. He never had a chance to clean up the mess, and I never gave him a chance to explain.

That night I went back to the store to apologize to our employee. But he told me not to worry about it. He said it was okay. Intuition told me it wasn't okay, so I coaxed him to open up. "Are you sure?" I asked. "I feel bad about what happened."

He then admitted that he was angry with me, and he wasn't able to get his work done because he was thinking about how badly he had been treated. An hour or two later, he said he was *still* angry! That's when he decided he had to do something to work out his aggression. "After you left the store," he said, "I went in the back room and poured a gallon of oil down the drain." That's when I learned that you better believe in people . . . or some of them might get even with you.

Lesson Eleven: Never Run Out of Money. I learned this lesson as a kid, and I bet you did, too. Almost all of us have played the game of Monopoly. On a cold winter's night, or a rainy afternoon, mom or dad would pull down the Monopoly box, spread open the board, count out the money, and set us up to play the game for several hours. It was a lot of fun . . . so long as you didn't run out of money. As long as you had money, you remained in the game with everyone else. But if you ran out of money, your game was over. You'd have to watch television while everyone else continued having fun playing the game!

Consequently, since then I've realized that you must never run out of money. You can make mistakes, you can have a bad day, a bad week, even a bad year. You can get low on money, but you must never run out of money!

Lesson Twelve: Attract New Customers Every Day. As I was preparing to open our first Subway shop I learned the importance of attracting customers every day. That first shop, as well as every additional shop we opened, was surrounded by potential customers. However, that fact didn't guarantee us a successful business. One day it occurred to me that we couldn't grow unless we could continue to attract new people to our location. That's when I began to understand the theory of Awareness, Trial, and Usage. It became important to me to make people *aware* of our shop and then invite them to *try* our product. Then, we had to turn them into regular *users* or customers. Once I understood this lesson, it became my job to attract new customers every day.

Lesson Thirteen: Be Persistent: Don't Give Up. Many days it would have been easy to throw up my hands and walk away from Subway. I often remember thinking, "How will we make it? We don't have enough money." But in the back of my mind there was this almost self-evident lesson that said: *If you quit, you fail. If you give up, you're out. If you stop playing, you can't play anymore.*

Not giving up requires something more than keeping the faith and maintaining a positive attitude. It's all about persistence. If you don't have faith in what you're doing, or faith in yourself, and if you can't think positively about your situation, it's nearly impossible to be persistent. Some days you're going to feel like your business is rejecting you, or you may feel like separating yourself from the business. On those "blue Mondays"—which surely will occur—you must always find a way to persevere. It's perseverance that enables people to keep going so that they can become successful. I think we can all look back on something in our lives that we gave up on too soon. Had we remained committed to a plan, a goal, or a vision, had we persevered in spite of the obstacles, things may have turned out differently. In business, it's important to work through the issues, no matter how difficult. Otherwise you could find yourself giving up and never finishing big. People who give up ultimately have to go back and start all over again. Never give up!

Lesson Fourteen: Build a Brand Name. Like most adults, I learned this lesson at the supermarket. Let's say you want to buy a carton of cereal. At the supermarket, you'll find an entire aisle with many brands to select from. There's cold and warm cereal. Sugar-free cereal, protein-enriched cereal, and high-fiber cereal. There's cereal with fruit, cereal that's crunchy, and cereal with famous sports figures on the box. And look, there's generic cereal, too!

If we compare the labels of these various cereals we'll find that the brand name products are pretty similar to the generic products. In fact, the only real difference appears to be the price. The generic cereal costs less. So what are we going to do? More often than not, people will spend a little more and buy the brand name.

The fact is, branded products sell, and they sell for more than unbranded products.

Lesson Fifteen: Opportunity Waits for No One. When my business partner, Pete Buck, who you'll soon read more about, invited me to go into business with him, I had the choice of saying yes or no. If I had said no I don't know what I'd be doing today, and there's a chance Pete would have offered the same opportunity to someone else. Of course, it was easy for me to say yes because of the circumstances. First, I had nothing better to do, and second, Pete was investing the money. Nonetheless, when you're faced with opportunity it's important to be prepared to say yes before the opportunity goes elsewhere.

This is not to say that I believe in taking every opportunity that comes along. But you've got to say yes to something if you want to start and build a business.

* * *

There you have them. Now that it's clear how I learned these Fifteen Key Lessons, and what they mean, let's move on. I'm going to tell you my story in the next chapter, and then, through the resourceful research and writing of my co-author, John Hayes, I'll tell you the stories of other microentrepreneurs who collectively have implemented all of the lessons in their businesses. You'll find these stories in Chapters 4 through 18. Finally, I'll conclude the book with some ideas and information about how you can apply the lessons that I'm sharing with you. You'll also find more information in the Appendixes about microenterprise, microlenders, and how you can start a Micro Investment Lending Enterprise in your city.

Besides the help these Fifteen Key Lessons gave me, I truly believe they can help most people who start small. Thirty-five years ago, just out of high school, I planned to be a medical doctor. One day Pete Buck, a family friend, suggested that I open a tiny sandwich shop to earn my college tuition money. What I didn't know—what no one knew—was that Pete's idea would lead to the creation of Subway, the world's largest chain of sandwich shops, and for many years, the world's fastest-growing franchise company. Even in my wildest dreams I couldn't have imagined how this opportunity would change my life, or how the resulting business would impact the lives of thousands of people worldwide. Now, with more than 14,000 stores in more than seventy countries, and annual sales in excess of $3.5 billion, even I admit it's an incredible story.

But beyond the importance of the Fifteen Key Lessons, there's a valuable take-away message that I want to be sure you understand before we go any further. You can adapt these lessons to your business, either one that already exists, or one that you plan to start. You can use these lessons to build an exciting and rewarding business. You can use these lessons to start small and finish big. I've done it, others have done it, and you can do it, too!

CHAPTER THREE

MY STORY

**How a seventeen-year-old kid from "The Projects"
started Subway with a microloan of $1,000.**

This story could have happened to almost anyone, anywhere.
Carmela Ombres and Salvatore DeLuca just so happened to
live in Brooklyn in the 1940s. One day they met, and not long
thereafter they were married. In 1947 they had a son, and that
was me.

For the first several years of my life we lived in the basement apartment of a two-family house. It was a humble, low-
rent apartment, something that newlyweds could afford.
When I was five, we moved to the Bronx to a new development, which everyone called "The Projects." It was public
housing, one of many similar developments built after World
War II. For the DeLuca family, it was a step up!

When I was ten, my dad's employer, Empire Devices,
moved its manufacturing facility 120 miles upstate to Amsterdam, New York. Since my mother had just given birth to my
sister, Suzanne, and since my father's job was fairly secure—he
was the foreman of a small production line—we left the Bronx
for a small apartment in Schenectady, near Amsterdam. And
that's where we met Pete Buck and his wife, Haydee, who soon
became close friends.

It was an unlikely friendship in my estimation. Pete was a
brilliant scientist who had earned a doctoral degree from Co-

27

lumbia University. My dad was a high school dropout who worked in an electrical factory. It didn't seem the two could have much in common, but they became pals—bow hunting was among their favorite pastimes—and they frequently brought their families together for picnics and parties.

The family friendship was briefly interrupted in 1964. Empire Devices moved again, this time to Bridgeport, Connecticut, and once again we followed dad's job. Much to our delight, Pete called several months later to say that he was switching jobs and moving his family to Armonk, New York, about forty miles from Bridgeport. One Sunday in July 1965, after nearly a year's separation, we were invited to visit the Bucks' new home and enjoy a family barbecue. That was the day Pete and I formed a business relationship that would eventually make a huge impact in the fast food industry.

I had just graduated from high school and my only real concern was to figure out how to pay my way through college. While I was growing up, my mother instilled in me the value of an education. She not only told me how important it was to go to school, she also gave me the confidence to believe that I could graduate from high school, and college, too. But in the summer of 1965 there wasn't much hope that I could get through college because my family simply didn't have the money. I worked at a local hardware store as a stock clerk earning $1.25, the minimum hourly wage. It was a good job for a kid, but it wasn't going to provide the money I needed for a college education.

The more I thought about college, the more I wondered about how I could find the money. As we pulled into Pete's driveway it occurred to me that I might ask Pete for some advice. The Bucks lived in a large white house built on three quarters of an acre, which to me seemed like a sprawling property. I was really impressed when I saw the two-car garage with *two* cars parked inside! *Pete must have landed himself a great job, one that paid a lot of money*, I thought to myself.

It was late afternoon when I saw the opportunity to talk privately with Pete in his backyard. His young children were

28

playing in another part of the yard with my sister. My parents and Pete's wife were sitting at the picnic table not far from the house, still catching up with each other's lives. As Pete and I stood in the middle of his green lawn I said, "Pete, I want to go to college, to the University of Bridgeport, but I don't have the money. And I was wondering if you had any ideas about how I might get the money to pay my way through school?"

When I asked that question I had a secret hope that Pete might offer to loan me the money and tell me to pay him back after I graduated. After all, he had known me for half my life and he liked me. Pete used to get a kick out of the way I thought through problems. He'd challenge me with mathematical games and I amused him by spitting out the answers in rapid fire. Pete knew that I was a hard worker, and while I wasn't a straight-A student, I was competent and dependable. Once he heard how badly I wanted to go to college, and that I wanted to be a medical doctor, I thought there was a good chance he might help me financially.

But Pete looked at me, and without hesitation he said, "I think you should open a submarine sandwich shop."

What?

Of all the possible answers, this was *not* one I expected. What an odd thing to say to a seventeen-year-old kid, especially one who came from a modest home where no one had ever owned a business. Sure, I had my own paper route and I participated in Junior Achievement where I learned a little about business, but I was just a kid! I didn't know what to say. Fortunately, my natural curiosity took over, and before I could say yes or no, I heard myself asking Pete: *How does it work?*

Pete explained the submarine sandwich business very simply. He said that all I had to do was rent a small store, build a counter, buy some food, and open for business. Customers would then come into the store, put money on the counter, and I would have all the money I needed for college. To Pete, it was just as simple as that, although Pete had never owned a business nor run a sandwich shop himself.

Thinking now about our conversation it's almost unbelievable. We were just two guys at a Sunday afternoon barbecue, speculating, really, about something we knew little to nothing about. Under similar circumstances I can imagine a teenager thinking Pete's idea was *impractical*, or *impossible*. Or another teenager might easily have shrugged him off and quipped, *"Good idea, Pete, but not the idea I was looking for."*

The more Pete talked about the sandwich shop the more I could see myself opening such a shop. Pete recognized my enthusiasm and eventually said, "Fred, you sound like you're interested in this idea. If you want to do it I'm willing to be your partner."

Pete's offer caught me by surprise, but it didn't take me long to figure out it was a great opportunity for a kid from "The Projects." *Of course I was interested!* Besides, I didn't have any other ideas, or any better offers to choose from, so I said, "Sure."

Next thing I knew Pete walked into his house and returned with a clipping from an upstate New York newspaper. It was that clipping, I would soon understand, that got him thinking about the sandwich business. We moved from the yard to the picnic table to include the other adults in our conversation. We all listened as Pete read an article that a year or so earlier featured Mike's Submarine Sandwiches, a familiar name to all of us because when we lived upstate we had frequently enjoyed Mike's sandwiches. The story explained how a hardworking entrepreneur named Michael Davis opened thirty-two restaurants, mostly submarine shops and a few roast beef sandwich stores, in ten years. He started with almost nothing and created a mini-empire in upstate New York. The reporter related some of Mike's struggles as well as his many triumphs as king of submarine sandwiches in his part of the world. When Pete finished reading the article he looked up at us and wondered: "If Michael Davis can do this, why can't we?"

I now know that the question didn't come out by accident. Pete wanted to set a long-term goal beyond the opening of one store. When no one could think of a reason why we couldn't perform as well as Michael Davis, we began discussing what we could accomplish. That's how we set a goal to build thirty-two submarine sandwich shops in ten years!

The importance of that goal didn't immediately register with me. I was still thinking about how to open the first store. I just wanted to get through college. I didn't really plan to make a career of the sandwich business. But nonetheless, we set our long-range goal, and eventually the significance of those numbers would become meaningful.

During that night we also spent several hours discussing our menu. We thought Mike's menu was a good one. It consisted of seven foot-long, cold sandwiches, and we decided to offer a similar menu. However, Pete then told us about Amato's, his favorite sub shop in his hometown of Portland, Maine. Pete thought Amato's sandwiches had a better taste profile than Mike's. At Mike's, they only put onion, lettuce, and tomato on their sandwiches, along with meat and cheese, but Amato's included pickles, peppers, and black olives, without the lettuce. We talked about visiting Amato's in the near future.

Amazingly, we even established the prices for our sandwiches! Like Mike's, our prices ranged from 54 cents to 69 cents. It just never occurred to us that it didn't make sense to set these prices before we knew a thing about our food and operating costs.

As we were getting ready to leave the Bucks' home that evening, Pete asked us to wait for a second. He then pulled out his checkbook and he wrote a check for $1,000. That was his investment in our new venture.

On the drive back to Connecticut with my family, little did I know that if I succeeded at opening a submarine sandwich shop I would accomplish more than funding my college education. Success would mean financial independence and everything that comes with it, not just for me, but for many other people around the world. Success would mean adventure and excitement on a nonstop roller coaster that would eventually be called Subway. But on this particular ride home, I wasn't looking very far into the future. I was thinking about the next morning when I would set out to find our first location.

GETTING STARTED

When I tell people about my backyard conversation with Pete Buck, explaining that I had agreed to open a submarine shop even though I didn't know how, they frequently ask me, *Weren't you afraid of failing?* Failing never entered my mind. If other people had opened submarine sandwich shops I thought there was a reasonable chance I could do the same thing.

The next morning I drove my dad to work so that I could borrow his car. Pete said the first step was to find a small store, and while I really didn't know how to do that, it didn't take me long to find exactly what I *thought* we needed. It was right around the corner from United Hardware, where I was employed as a stock clerk. I called the landlord and arranged to inspect the shop on Saturday, when Pete could join me. That afternoon I reported to work at the hardware store as I did every workday until we rented the first store.

It would take a few months before Pete and I realized that I hadn't done a very good job of finding our first location. When I looked for available shops, I just drove up and down the familiar streets without even considering other parts of town. I simply didn't know any better. I didn't know there were certain characteristics that made one location better than another. Consequently, I didn't know what was wrong with the location we were about to inspect, and neither did Pete. I had worked at the hardware store for several years and never noticed the location before. I should have realized that if I hadn't noticed the location customers would have a difficult time finding it, too.

On Saturday the landlord met us at the shop shortly before noon. We walked inside and found approximately 450 square feet of space. Pete and I were impressed: The store was clean and neat and we wouldn't have to do much to get the place ready for business. The ceiling and tile floor were in good shape. We would have to add a counter for making sandwiches, and build a partition to block off the storage space in the back of the store, but we had already figured as much. Otherwise, the shop looked acceptable to both of us.

"What do you think, Pete?" I asked my partner in earshot of the landlord.

Pete said, "How much is it again?"

"One sixty-five a month," the landlord responded.

Pete nodded yes. He liked it.

"Okay, let's have a lease drawn up," the landlord continued.

"Lease? What's that?" I asked.

The landlord explained that the lease was a legal document that spelled out the terms of our agreement and would establish the rent at $165 a month for two years. It was a protective measure for both of us, he said, adding that it would cost about $50 to hire a lawyer to prepare the document. "We'll split it," he said.

Neither Pete nor I knew anything about leases, and all I could think about was the $25 that we'd have to pay the lawyer. That was 2.5 percent of our capital, and that was more money than we could afford.

"I think we'll just take it without a lease," I responded.

The landlord didn't object. Of course, he was a guy with a crummy location that he needed to rent. On the spot we paid him $330, the first month's rent and a month's security deposit. He handed us the keys, and that's how we rented our first store. It took about five minutes.

As soon as the landlord collected his money he was on his way and Pete and I were left to design the store. That took us another five minutes. We knew we needed a spot for the cash register, space to prepare the food, a partition to block off the storage area, and a counter for customers to lay down their money. I would recruit a friend from high school to help me with the construction. Pete reminded me that we'd also need an outdoor sign, a cash register, and some miscellaneous equipment, and that was it, perhaps another five minutes spent discussing store design before we left and locked the door behind us. We ate lunch together, discussed some other ideas, and Pete drove back to Armonk.

It's easy now to say that we rushed into the deal, or that we were carried away by the excitement of our new enterprise. I certainly should have conducted a wider location search and I probably should have signed a lease. However, we were just getting started, and college was opening soon so it was important to take action. Rather than sitting around making plans for the rest of our lives we decided to just go ahead and do it. Pete and I were, and still are, the type of guys who like to make decisions without belaboring things. From my perspective today, taking action is a good quality and I'm glad we took that first location. Sometimes, knowing less and actually doing something is far better than knowing everything and never doing anything at all.

THE SUBMARINE SLEUTHS

Funny thing, until I was face-to-face with our first customer, I had never made a submarine sandwich. Nor had Pete. We enjoyed eating them, and we knew they consisted of meat, cheese, vegetables, oil, and bread, but we had absolutely no experience making them. So it was important that Pete took the time to drive my mom and me to Portland, Maine, where we decided to research the fine art of making submarine sandwiches. Although we were familiar with Mike's in upstate New York, we needed to experience another taste profile, and also watch the process of making sandwiches.

Pete had grown up eating submarine sandwiches at Amato's Italian Deli, and he remained fond of their product, so he suggested that we visit his parents in Portland and spend some time hanging out at Amato's. My mom decided to join us, and we appreciated her company, especially because she knew much more about food than we did.

We arrived in Portland in time for dinner and decided to begin our research the next day around noon. From outside Amato's front window we gained a vantage point from where we could watch the action behind the sandwich counter. After a few minutes we decided to go inside to gain the experience of being a customer. We ordered our sandwiches, paying attention to the entire process of ordering and making the sandwiches. We then took our sandwiches outside and resumed peeking through the window. We paid particular attention to the process of cutting the bread, laying in the meat and cheese, and applying the oil. One of the things we noticed was that Amato's people poured oil onto each sandwich from a gallon can. Our trio, in spite of our inexperience, thought that was clumsy. We immediately decided it would be better to transfer the oil into smaller containers, the size of a small pitcher, then pour from the containers onto the sandwiches, thus making the operation a little easier. Later we discovered our idea also added expense and created inconsistency!

There was only so much we could learn from Amato's. They only sold two variations of sandwiches—ham and salami—so we decided to visit several other sandwich shops that day. We bought sandwiches at each shop, observed their operations, and evaluated what we perceived as the pros and cons. Between visits we compared notes.

Within twenty-four hours, our research, sparse and unscientific though it was, provided what we thought was sufficient information to make some key decisions. Essentially, we had two prominent profiles to consider for our business: Amato's and Mike's. The two had little in common and that was a plus because it gave us different perspectives. Mike's variety of sandwiches included cheese and tuna. Amato's sold only the two sandwiches. We liked variety, so we stuck with our earlier decision to sell seven different cold sandwiches.

We preferred Amato's taste profile, but we also preferred Mike's bread. Amato's used a nine-inch soft roll, but Mike's was a foot long, and that sounded good to us. Amato's added a larger variety of fresh vegetables to their sandwiches. Mixed with oil, the fresh vegetables added flavor to the sandwich, so we decided to include them. The foundation of an Amato's sub was like an Italian salad without lettuce, and that was very much to our liking. We decided to imitate Amato's sandwich and put it on a foot-long roll, but we would sell a greater variety of sandwiches, just like Mike's.

Even though we didn't know anything about costs, we stuck with Mike's pricing scheme. After all, as good as it was, there was only one Amato's, but there were thirty-two Mike's! We figured Mike's must have been doing the right thing with pricing, but the fact that Mike's combined thirty-two restaurants' worth of volume and had far greater buying power wasn't even a consideration for us. What did we know about volume?

That was the sum and substance of our research. It was really simple. Could we have done more? Certainly. Would it have made a difference? Probably. Observation is a terrific tool, but when you don't know any better, you can see something that's obvious and not know what it means, or you can miss a critical component. Something like pouring oil on sandwiches is a good example. When we watched Amato's people poke a small hole in the top of a gallon can and lift that heavy can each time they wanted to pour oil on a sandwich, we thought there had to be an easier way. That's why we decided to use small pitchers. However, the secret to pouring the oil from a gallon can with a small hole in the top is control and consistency. By making the hole a certain size, Amato's

36

could control the amount of oil per sandwich. With our pitcher, we had *no* control. The amount of oil we poured on each sandwich depended on how far we tilted the pitcher, and for how long. Consequently, our oil costs and product quality varied from sandwich to sandwich. But that's not something we would have understood simply by observation. We had to try it ourselves before we realized there was method to the madness.

Intuitively, we realized that to really understand our business, we would have to begin to work it. It didn't matter if we chose Amato's pricing instead of Mike's, and Mike's taste profile instead of Amato's. If we made mistakes—and we did—we could correct them as we progressed. We realized that we were starting a *small* business. It was a tiny investment of money. We didn't have much to lose. If there ever was a time to experiment, it was now. Indeed, other people were already operating similar businesses, and it was so easy to go see what they were doing. Why would we spend our limited time and capital on research?

Today, however, it's a different story. For example, to introduce something as simple as a new cookie formula in our Subway stores, we invest months of time and tens of thousands of dollars in the research. We might send researchers into five or six regions in North America to hand out cookies and ask detailed questions to gather information about perceptions and preferences from consumers. We then hire experts to correlate mounds of data in anticipation of finding the perfect cookie for our customers. And with 14,000 stores, if we spend $70,000, a modest amount of money for this kind of research, that works out to just $5 per store. What a bargain! When we were just getting started, we couldn't get much research for $5, and we couldn't have afforded much more than that. Therefore, we did what we could as quickly as possible without getting hung up on what we didn't know.

And there was plenty we didn't know.

PREPARING THE STORE

On the way back from Maine we targeted Saturday, August 28, 1965, for the opening of our store. That meant I would devote all of August to preparing for the big event. With some help from my parents, and my high school friend Art Witkowski, who wasn't doing anything that summer, I purchased equipment and supplies, contacted vendors, built a counter and an outdoor sign for the store, and drummed up future customers by handing out promotional flyers.

Oh yeah, Pete and I also came up with a name for our business. As we looked at the stores adjacent to our shop, there was Ann's Bakery, Judy Blair's Dance Studio, and Suzie's Yarn Shop. All of the businesses were identified by a person's name, so we arrived at the logical decision to call our business Pete's Submarines, but we decided to glorify the name by adding the word "Super." Thus we became Pete's Super Submarines! Occasionally we had to shorten the name to the less glorious Pete's Submarines to make it fit on our outdoor signs.

However, we later discovered the name wasn't easy to communicate. When people heard the name Pete's Submarines over the radio, they often thought they heard the words "pizza marine." When consumers who had never been to our stores began asking me "What kind of pizza do you have? Is it seafood pizza?" I knew we had a problem.

I was driving in my car one day thinking about our name and what to do. I wanted a name that was short, clear, and difficult to mispronounce. I wanted to use "sub" in the name because it was a crisp, short way to say submarine. And suddenly, the word "subway" popped into my mind. We changed the name to Pete's Subway, and eventually to Subway, but not until after opening several stores.

While my buddy Art helped me get the shop ready for opening day, my mom helped me line up the various vendors who would provide the bread, paper goods, meats, vegetables,

and cheeses that we would need. Without anyone to guide us
in these matters we consulted the local Yellow Pages and my
mom and I were sort of like the blind leading the blind. With
a name and an address in hand, off we'd go to tell our story to
any vendor who would listen. I'm sure these vendors had
never witnessed anything quite like it before. A pretty, little
Italian woman and her lanky teenage son show up with plans
to open a sandwich shop so he can afford to go to college.
They say their goal is to open thirty-two stores in ten years! It's
not a story they heard every day.

We must have been a convincing pair, however, because no
one turned us away. I am sure they took me more seriously because mom was with me, but the process was fairly simple. I
think it's the type of thing that anyone could have done in almost any community. In nearly every town there are suppliers
and most, if not all, of them need more customers. And even
if mom and I seemed a bit unusual, and our business a bit risky,
the suppliers were willing to work with us. We registered our
most complicated request at the bakery. We wanted our rolls
custom-made. But the baker said even that wasn't a problem.
Everything was cut-and-dry. After all, what's to buying vegetables, meats, cheeses, or paper products? The suppliers simply
sold us what they had in stock.

Of course, we had absolutely no purchasing power, but we
never worried about it, either. We simply had to pay high
prices for whatever we needed to buy, but any small business
faces a similar predicament. There wasn't anything we could
do about it. However, the vendors didn't require payment in
advance. They gave us credit on the spot! We could have
shopped around and looked for better deals, but that would require more time. It was more important to line up what we
needed, buy it, and figure out how to get it cheaper at a later
time.

Now that I wasn't working at the hardware store, I had no
income, so time was a major issue. Every day that our store was
closed I was losing money, and so was the business. There was

not only the cost of ongoing rent and utilities, but also the lost opportunity. If the store wasn't open, we couldn't sell anything. If the store wasn't selling anything, I couldn't get paid. My singular focus was to get the store open.

Of course, the store couldn't open without equipment, so while my mom helped me find suppliers, my dad helped me scour the newspaper classifieds every day for used equipment. We needed a cash register, a refrigeration unit, a commercial sink, a meat slicer, and some countertops and shelves. We found it all, even on our shoestring budget. Most of it was obsolete, but it was functional and it lasted for many years. My most unusual purchase was a big, brass cash register. When we pressed the number keys, two or three of them simultaneously, the price popped up with a "cha-ching" in the top of the cash register, and the drawer opened automatically. It was so old that the highest dollar amount it could ring up was $2.99. That wasn't a problem, though, because our highest-priced sandwich was 69 cents. For the purpose of collecting money and making change, that piece of junk was all we needed.

OPENING DAY

On Saturday morning, Art Witkowski and I had no idea what to expect when we opened the store at nine to prepare for customers. One of us cut up the vegetables: onions, tomatoes, green peppers, and even olives, while the other sliced the ham, cheese, and salami, a half pound of each. A half pound seemed right to me because that's the amount mom would ask me to buy when she sent me to the store for our family.

By 9:30 we were ready for business and patiently waiting when a young neighborhood girl rode up to the store on her bicycle. We smiled as she walked in and ordered the first sandwich. This was a critical moment in the history of Pete's Super Submarines, but not for the obvious reason.

Yes, it was our first sale, but now I had to teach Art how to make a submarine sandwich. Even though I planned to go into the sub business, and I traveled to Portland to watch Amato's, and I rented and built the store, bought the food and equipment, I had yet to make a single sandwich. And that wasn't the worst of it. Within an hour I had to leave Art in charge of the store. Coincidentally to our opening day, the University of Bridgeport scheduled an English capability exam at 11:00 A.M. for entering freshmen. I had to take the test, and that meant I had to leave Art alone in the store for a couple of hours. Pete, his wife, and my parents planned to help out later in the day, but until they arrived, or I returned, Art would have to handle things on his own. That meant he had to know how to make sandwiches.

Actually, making sandwiches didn't seem to be too difficult. By the time we had left Maine a few weekends earlier, we had thoroughly discussed the details of how to make our sandwiches. We talked about how to cut the bread, how to layer the meat and cheese, the vegetables, the oil, and the seasonings. As Art watched me that morning, he didn't think it was much of a challenge, either. Good thing, because our first customer was our last customer before I left the store. Art was on his own with one sandwich worth of training.

At approximately 12:20 P.M., the English exam now a successful but distant memory, I returned to our store parking lot and it was packed. As I glanced over at the shop I couldn't believe my eyes. Not only were customers crammed inside, they were standing in line outside! It was the noontime rush, and all I could figure was that a lot of people had come to the store, or the service was very slow. As it turned out, it was a little of both.

Walking across the parking lot I spotted my partner. "How you doing, Pete?" I said with a measure of excitement in my voice. I noticed he was carrying a brown bag. "What do you have?" I asked.

"Knives," he responded. Pete had arrived earlier at the store and discovered that we only had one knife for slicing vegetables and making sandwiches. "We can't serve all of these people with just one knife."

Having worked at a hardware store I knew there were many types of knives, all priced differently, some cheaper than others. Pete had purchased two knives at $3 each and I cringed. That was going to put a crimp in our budget, but there was no time to do anything about it. We rushed into the store and went to work, furiously taking care of customers.

Since we didn't know anything about establishing an operational system, we didn't have one that first day, or for many weeks thereafter. Consequently, we had a continuous line of customers and we were behind the eight ball. It didn't help matters that our tiny store was designed as a one- or two-person operation and there were now six people working in it: Pete, his wife, my parents, Art, and myself. As best we could, we each found a place to work. Art had transferred his masterful sandwich making training to the others, so they were busy behind the sandwich counter. I walked to the back room where we had several bushel baskets of green peppers. I turned over one empty basket for a place to sit and used two full baskets to support a piece of plywood that served as a table where I could cut vegetables. Then I went to work replenishing the vegetable supply at the counter.

The line out front never gave out and every so often I took a curiosity break to see who was in the store. Occasionally a friend came out of the line to congratulate me, and I immediately took advantage of the opportunity. "Let me give you a tour," I'd say. Then I'd proceed to explain, "This is the counter we built. Here is the cash register. Over here is the partition we built to hide the back room, and"—pointing now to my makeshift work station—"here's where I'm cutting vegetables. Why don't you have a seat here and help cut some vegetables?" I recruited five more people out of the line to help us that day.

By 5:30 in the afternoon mom told me we were nearly out of food. We had sold almost all of the rolls, twenty-five dozen, and we were low on meat and cheese. So I ran out to an Italian deli to buy more supplies. It was late in the day, however, and I returned with only another dozen rolls. Within an hour, we ran out of food, but fortunately, we also ran out of line at the same time. We had planned to remain open until 11:00 P.M., but at 6:30, having sold 312 sandwiches, we closed the doors. What an unbelievable day!

When the last customer had left, and our group started cleaning up the store, Pete and I moved outside to sit on the curb at the edge of the parking lot. We had that exhausted-but-satisfied feeling that athletes experience when they win a big victory. As we reviewed the day, we could hardly believe our success, and our anticipated good fortune.

"If all of these people showed up today," I said exuberantly, "and hardly anyone knows we exist, imagine tomorrow!"

"They'll all come back and the next time they'll bring their friends. We're going to do great. We're going to be million-aires!" Pete said confidently.

Reveling in the glory of our opening day success we couldn't help but think the customers loved our store. All we had to do now was build more stores and attract more customers.

Of course, it wouldn't work quite that way. There was a challenge around every curve, and the first curve was just ahead. We soon discovered that while we sat on the curb that day, we had committed the sin of counting our chickens before they hatched!

MONDAY NIGHT QUARTERBACKS

Several days after we opened Pete's Super Submarines, I entered the freshman class at the University of Bridgeport as a commuter student, and possibly the only student who owned a small business, although that meant nothing to me at the time. Even with a full load of sixteen credit hours, I managed to arrange my schedule so that I attended classes in the mornings, worked in the shop in the afternoons and early evenings, and studied at night. Some days it was possible to study in the shop, but I didn't look forward to those days because it could only mean that business was slow.

Mine was a busy schedule, but not especially difficult. Every day presented a new challenge or opportunity. Mondays, however, became particularly important in my routine. Following our research trip to Maine, when there was a lot of work to be done, Pete and I began meeting weekly to assess our progress and evaluate our plans. Now that our shop was open for business, a weekly meeting continued to be a good exercise to monitor our development, review our progress, and plan for the future. Each week we met at the same place—World Headquarters—also known as my mom's kitchen table.

On Monday nights Pete left work at about five and drove from Armonk to our co-op apartment in Bridgeport. Right after six he would walk through the back door into our kitchen where my mom was minutes away from serving a spaghetti dinner, including homemade sauce and meatballs. I was there waiting for him, anticipating his first question, which he asked religiously upon arrival: "How's business?"

I always answered with the number of sandwiches sold by 6:00 P.M. that day. A few minutes before Pete's arrival I would call the store for an update from our employee. Pete didn't want to know dollars and cents, only the number of sandwiches sold. If the number was high, Pete smiled. If it was low, he frowned. After I announced the number, Pete joined my family at the table and we enjoyed mom's dinner. We made a point not to talk about business while we ate.

After our meal, as the table was being cleared, Pete would open a three-ring binder that he brought with him to every meeting. Like the good scientist that he was, Pete kept a journal to track our progress. He charted our weekly sales on a graph in his notebook, and he recorded observations that he

44

considered important. We talked about every aspect of the business—sales, products, customers, employees, marketing ideas, and even the bills we had to pay that week. My parents participated in these meetings because they were involved in the business, even though they had other jobs. My mom knew all of our suppliers and both she and my dad helped out in the shop, particularly when I couldn't be there.

We didn't know it at the time but we were at a tremendous disadvantage during these Monday meetings. We were like travelers without a roadmap, or scientists without measuring tools. The purpose of our get-together was to observe, calculate, project, and analyze the business. But we were painfully slow arriving at good conclusions. More sophisticated businesspeople would have had a variety of reports and an occasional financial statement from their accountant to measure their progress, and enlighten them. But we were years away from having these tools. We didn't have an accountant. We kept our own books, and we didn't know how to produce a financial statement. Without business experience, we really didn't know what to observe, calculate, project, or analyze.

For example, when we spoke about serving the customer, or the quality of our product, we weren't able to make a good assessment of how we were doing. Obviously we wanted to serve a quality product and keep our customers happy, but we didn't know enough about what customers wanted to adequately discuss the components of those issues. We simply didn't know the right questions to ask.

Funnier yet, none of us necessarily had answers! Pete didn't show up on Monday nights with all the answers. Sometimes, frustrated by slumping sales, tight cash flow, or a problem we just couldn't solve, Pete would jump out of his chair, run to the back door of our apartment, and shout, *"What's wrong with you people here in Bridgeport? Get over to our store and buy some subs!"* As business neophytes, we were all inadequately trained to understand the business.

Nonetheless we plodded forward, somehow sensing that

we were doing a good thing by meeting every Monday night, taking a step back from the business to conduct these conversations. And, of course, we *were* doing a good thing. We didn't make great strides from week to week, but over a long period of time the cumulative knowledge we gained about our business was invaluable. Without a network of savvy advisers, or even one who had owned a sandwich shop, these meetings yielded the information we needed to build our business. The meetings presented an opportunity to learn and to prepare, to try and to try again, and to continually improve. No matter what challenge we faced, Pete and I were proactive. We looked for solutions, and we were always ready to give it another try. That was another major benefit of the meetings. They fostered a successful partnership by giving Pete and me time to calibrate our thoughts. We didn't always agree, and we were often frustrated by the various challenges we faced, but there was never tension between us personally. There were no loud, knock-down battles or arguments of any kind. If Pete's Super Submarines was going to succeed, we had to depend on each other to come up with the solutions and get the job done.

THE PLUMMETING GRAPH

After a month or two of Monday night meetings a pattern emerged on Pete's sales chart. The shop was busiest on Fridays and Saturdays and slowest on Mondays and Tuesdays. Sunday was an odd day. Business could be dead until 4:00 P.M. and then we'd get a surge of customers until 7:00 P.M., and then it would be dead again until we closed. The more interesting pattern emerged after several months, however, and it was neither pretty nor encouraging.

With each passing week since the opening, we sold fewer

sandwiches. In other words, our sales chart was headed down-hill! That record of 312 sandwiches sold on opening day had quickly faded, not to be seen again. By November, 100 sandwiches sold was a big day, but it was far from adequate. All the more disappointing, and worrisome, the numbers continued to fall.

One Monday night in late November our "brain trust" decided the store lacked exposure, so we invested in the Jingle Bell Special, an advertising promotion sponsored by a local radio station. It cost us $550, an enormous sum of money, but an insignificant amount if the special could improve our December sales. The radio advertising rep convinced us that people would be out Christmas shopping all month and they'd hear our promotion and stop by for a sandwich. Indeed, people were out shopping, and certainly they heard the radio spots for Pete's Submarines, but they didn't stop for a sandwich. Our sales continued to fall in December, and January, too. The low point didn't occur, however, until one cold, dreary Monday in February.

"How's business?" Pete asked when he arrived at World Headquarters on this particular day.

"Seven," I said.

It didn't take the genius of two Monday night quarterbacks to know that Pete's Super Submarines was in trouble. Even at our top price of 69 cents, sales of seven sandwiches wasn't enough money to pay our employee for seven hours' work, let alone cover the cost of food and rent for the day. Anyone else probably would have closed the business that night. In fact, that was the first option Pete considered, but not until after dinner.

As we began that night's meeting, Pete picked up his notebook and I watched him print the letters: LTDATATK.

"That's our first option," he said.

"What does it mean?" I asked.

"Lock the door and throw away the key," he responded.

But as soon as he said it we both decided it was a bad idea.

Closing the store wasn't what we wanted at all. It was only six months old and it was too soon to give up on it. No, there had to be other options, and there were, of course.

"We could advertise the store," Pete said.

However, as we talked about that option we remembered the Jingle Bell Special. If anything, that was proof that we didn't know *how* to advertise effectively.

As our discussion continued, and we evaluated various options, we eventually settled on an idea that most people would have said was absolutely crazy.

We were pretty sure the problem was the store's location, and so we thought we ought to move it. We batted around the idea of finding another shop and relocating. But the more we discussed that strategy, the less we liked it. The shop was losing money. Moving it didn't make sense. Let's close it, we said, and just find a new location and start all over again. But that strategy didn't appeal to us, either. If we closed our first location before we opened a second location, we might never get started again. Now that we knew the challenges of operating a submarine sandwich shop, we might not be as brave the second time.

Our meeting was running late and we thought we had exhausted our options when Pete suggested that we keep the first store *and* open a second shop. I'm sure that if we had consulted an accountant or a board of directors they would have said Pete's suggestion was outrageous if not irresponsible. We had not proven that we could operate *one* successful submarine sandwich shop. And now we wanted to operate *two?*

Why?

For several reasons it made perfect sense. If we moved the current store we'd have two investments. We'd have the expense of leasehold improvements in the new shop while we abandoned the leasehold improvements we had already paid for in the first shop. And then there was the equipment. It wasn't worth moving our old equipment, especially if we had to pay to install it a second time. If we had to buy equipment all over again to relocate, then why not buy it for a second shop?

And there was more. A second store would give us the opportunity to experiment and compare results. We could accelerate our learning curve in the business by keeping one store as a control unit for measurement purposes. Plus—and this was a major benefit—two shops in the same market would be like advertising. People in Bridgeport might get the idea that we were so successful we were expanding, and that alone would help sales rise again. We even joked about creating a promotional flyer that said, *"Thank you Bridgeport for making us so successful. We're now opening our second store!"* We figured no one would know we weren't successful because hardly anyone was coming into the store!

The one negative thing about our decision was continuing to carry the burden of the original, unprofitable store. How much would that detract from the success that we might achieve in our second store? It was an unknown, but in the final analysis, we decided the second store was worth the risk. As it turned out, it was one of the best decisions we ever made.

BLESSED BE THE VENDORS

We needed little more than $1,000 to open a shop, and strange as it may seem, money wasn't an issue when we decided to find a second location. Sales had plummeted in February, but due to the help of our vendors, which I'll explain in a moment, we were not out of money. We weren't flush with cash by any means, but I held tight to the purse strings, a practice that helped us then and has helped us many times since.

Since we didn't have much money to start the business we never allowed ourselves to build up big expenses. We avoided buying anything that required a hefty payment on a weekly or monthly schedule. After paying the rent, the utilities, and a couple of employees, our only expense was the cost of supplies, primarily the paper goods, plus the meat and cheese, vegetables, and bread that we used to make our sandwiches. Of course we also sold soda and chips, and we paid for these products when they were delivered to our store.

My salary was skimpy and I didn't collect it all at once. As management, I earned $1.35 an hour, 10 cents over the minimum wage. That worked out to $67.50 for my usual workweek of fifty hours. However, after I quit my job at the hardware store, I calculated that my personal expenses amounted to only $13 weekly. So when we opened the first shop I told Pete that the business should pay me a weekly allowance of $13. Then, when tuition was due at the University of Bridgeport, about $600 a semester at that time, the business would pay that, too.

As part of the routine during our Monday night meetings we subtracted my allowance and any tuition payment from my accumulated earnings and most weeks the business owed me money. This may not sound very attractive to someone who's thinking about starting a business, but in reality most new business owners can't collect all of their salary at the time it's earned. Our microbusiness remained open partly because I was willing to stick with it, to figure out how to make it work better, to work for a low salary, and at the same time delay collecting my salary. There was always the risk, of course, that the money would never be there, but that was part of the gamble in starting a business.

The real reason we didn't run out of money, however, had less to do with delaying my salary than with the special relationship we developed with our vendors. Every Friday morning I would look at the bills to be paid and, depending on the amount of money in our checkbook, I would decide how much we could afford to pay each vendor. In the early days, we could never pay as much as we owed, which is why bills started piling up. But I always wrote a check for each of the four main vendors. Then, instead of stamping envelopes and mailing the checks, which would seem to be the efficient thing to do, my mom and I visited the suppliers with payment in hand. It was an unusual procedure. Somehow, though, it felt better visiting the suppliers, and it was good that we did because otherwise we would not have been in the position to expand.

It took about two hours for mom and me to visit the vendors, and we got a terrific return on our investment of time. Since they were all small businesses, there was a good chance the owners would be on site when we arrived and we'd have the opportunity to talk with them. We always started with a quick update about our business. *Sales were slow this week, the big snowfall hurt us. But overall things are going great. And here, we brought you a check for $100.* I don't think the vendors were particularly interested in our story, but we told it anyway. Then we'd give them some unsolicited feedback about their product. With years of experience handling food, mom was particularly good at this. *The bread formula was perfect this week, keep making it that way . . . Be sure we always get this brand of ham, it's really high-quality . . . These paper products didn't hold up. Can we try something else?* Ten minutes and we were finished. However, we had one other critical point of business to handle. We didn't leave until we placed the next week's order, which was usually for more than the check we had just given the vendor.

By the time we decided to open a second store, we owed our suppliers several months' worth of bills, altogether amounting to more than $3,000. It was rare that we owed them less than two months' worth of invoices on any given Friday. In spite of that, none of the suppliers ever pressured us for money. I can only assume this had something to do with our track record. We never failed to give them at least a small payment every week. We never missed a week, and we were always up front with them. If nothing else, we had earned credibility in the eyes of these suppliers, and consequently they were willing to do more for us. As it was, we financed the construction of our second shop, and even subsequent shops, with the credit supplied by our vendors. Blessed be the vendors!

THE EXCITEMENT MOUNTS

I had a good feeling about our second shop in neighboring Fairfield, Connecticut. It was just as bad as our first location, with poor visibility, but the rent was only $85 a month, and no sooner than we had agreed to take it, sales began to climb at our original shop. I took that as a good omen. We opened the shop on Saturday, May 21, 1966, and once again a record crowd turned out to purchase Pete's Super Submarines. Within a few weeks sales were so strong in both of our shops that we patted ourselves on the back for the fortitude to not only remain in business, but to expand our business. The fact that the seasons of the year had more to do with our increased sales than the opening of a second shop had not yet occurred to us!

One Monday night three weeks later, as Pete and I reviewed his impressive sales chart, which was now climbing uphill, we agreed that two shops were better than one. That led us to the logical and immediate conclusion that three shops would be better than two. That night before Pete left for home, we decided to open a third location.

I found a third shop at 1212 Barnum Avenue in Stratford, Connecticut. Two vacant storefronts were next to a parking lot and I had the choice of renting the inside storefront for $85 a month, or the more visible outside section for $100 a month. The lower rental fee was tempting, since we didn't have a penny to spare, but I decided to pay the additional $15 monthly just for the visibility. Since we had no visibility in our other locations I had a hunch visibility was worth the extra money. Fortunately, I was right.

So on July 22, less than a year after we had opened our original shop, we opened our third location, which initially was as successful as our first two. For the next six weeks, through early September, we had a thriving business, and the mood of our Monday meetings was even more high-spirited than usual. Sales were up at all three locations, proving our theory that it was better to have more stores than to have fewer stores. We were far from thirty-two stores, but we still had nine years to hit that goal.

But then, one Monday in late September, that ugly downhill pattern that had appeared the year before on Pete's sales chart showed up again. Sales in all three stores had begun to follow the first-year pattern of our original store. September's sales were lower than August's. And the downhill trend was back in force. By the winter of 1967, instead of owning one low-volume, money-losing shop, we owned three of them!

That's when we suspected the seasonal effect to our business. Had we known anything about the fast food business, we would have anticipated the dramatic swings that occurred in sales between summer and winter. Eating out in the 1960s was not yet an everyday occurrence, and with cold weather and several holidays that consumed energy and money, people were more likely to eat at home. Consequently, winter's sales levels might amount to just 60 percent of summer's sales. But we had no way of knowing this at the time. All we could do was wait it out. "By spring, sales may pop back up again," Pete said one winter night. Thank God he was right.

A TURNING POINT

We opened a fourth low-volume location on Park Avenue in Bridgeport in 1967, and then one Monday night in April 1968, I surprised Pete with the news that I had just rented our fifth shop. He was excited and he wanted to know where it was located, but I was saving that information until after dinner. "It's in Bridgeport. We'll drive over to see it after we eat," I said, building a little suspense.

I was nervous about showing Pete our fifth location, and for several reasons. We had yet to sign a lease for any of our shops, but I had signed one this time. It probably wasn't legal because I was underage, but the landlord wasn't about to do business without a lease. When he told me to report to his office to sign the document, I did. I then immediately began construction on the shop. That might not have been an issue except that I also made a dramatic change to our standard decor without consulting Pete. Worst of all, however, Pete had actually seen this location two years earlier and had rejected it because there was no parking space for customers! This was the first time I had made bold business decisions without seeking Pete's approval, and I didn't know how he would react.

After dinner we headed toward the location in my car. Pete wasn't very familiar with the streets in Bridgeport and I purposely drove the back roads to confuse him even further. I approached the shop from a direction that I hoped he wouldn't recognize. "There it is," I said, as we turned the corner from East Main Street onto Boston Avenue. "It's already under construction, and we'll be open in May."

Pete looked at the shop for a moment and said, "Haven't I seen this location before?"

I admitted that he had, and that he had rejected it.

However, I was excited. The store's visibility was incredible, so much so that I didn't really think parking would be an issue. The store was its own billboard, particularly after dark. People coming down Boston Avenue, a heavily traveled road, could see the shop for half a mile. Tucked into a large residential neighborhood, the shop was the first commercial business for three quarters of a mile and my experience told me that was powerful! Parking didn't matter, I was sure of it. Customers would figure out where to park.

In the two years since Pete had rejected the location I

couldn't get it out of my mind. I drove by it every day because my girlfriend, Liz, who is now my wife, worked half a mile down the road at a German delicatessen owned by her parents. Every time I stopped for the light at the corner of Boston and East Main, I would look at the location that could have been. So when the florist who rented the store failed, I decided to grab it and deal with the consequences later.

"Pete, I think it's going to be our best location," I said tentatively.

Pete wasn't happy. "Without parking," he grumbled, "customers aren't going to come to this shop. That's a problem." And he wasn't happy about the extensive decor changes, either, but he didn't interfere.

Opening day sales of our fifth store dwarfed each of our previous first-day sales. Just as I had hoped, the terrific visibility overpowered the parking problem. Customers parked wherever they could. They parked in the bus stop and they drove over the curb to park on the sidewalk immediately adjacent to the shop, and they also parked across the street in a no-parking zone. Basically, everyone parked illegally, but no one complained. As for Pete, he was no longer annoyed once he saw how much money the store generated for us.

At about 4:00 P.M. on opening day, when the store wasn't supposed to be busy, I was installing floodlights on the roof to illuminate our sign. As I looked to the ground and watched the steady flow of customers coming into the shop it reminded me of our original opening day when Pete and I sat on the curb counting our chickens. This time, however, I was counting customers, and I was certain this shop would become our strongest producer.

In fact, the Boston Avenue shop often doubled the sales of our other locations. The shop made a profit its very first day and never slid backward. Within a matter of months Pete and I knew that Boston Avenue was a turning point in the development of our business. Without it, our company might not have succeeded because our earning stream was tenuous, and we may not have survived many more winters. Until we rented this shop, our mix of locations was not really profitable, and it was getting old making money in the summer only to lose it in the winter. But now, with Boston Avenue onstream we had some stability and we could weather the tough times. We probably could have kept this one store and closed the others and made as much money as with the five. However, the goal of thirty-two stores was important, so we kept them all. As proof of the staying power of the Boston Avenue store, after thirty years it still exists. After we began franchising, Pete and I sold it to one of our employees, Rosa Perillo, who to this day continues to benefit from its bustling location.

RAPID EXPANSION

After we started Subway in 1965, I devoted most of my time to the business. However, I didn't really think of myself and the business as companions for the long term. I attended classes, I studied, and while no one would have called me a party animal, I had fun. I joined a fraternity, I dated Liz, and I had a good time in college. As important as the business was to me, I always thought of it as a means to an end, and nothing more. It wasn't a lifelong commitment, and it wasn't intended to support me forever. It existed to get me though college. I didn't expect the business to end after I graduated, but I didn't think that far ahead, either. I was committed to opening thirty-two stores in ten years, but that didn't mean I couldn't do something else simultaneously. I liked dual roles. Once I graduated from college, I assumed I would pursue my *real* career, and like Pete, I'd also be involved in the business. I didn't view a profession and the business as mutually exclusive. However, through the mid- to late 1960s, I was a college student first and foremost. My mission was to go to school and graduate with a degree. Only one thing had changed since I started pursuing my mission. I no longer planned to be a medical doctor.

By my junior year I changed my mind about premed when I discovered that I didn't like laboratory classes. They required much too much detail over a lengthy period of time, and my mind didn't work that way. I thrived on a variety of stimuli and skills. Like a kid with a huge toy box, I wanted to play with several things at once, but only for short periods of time. I liked choosing a topic, studying it for as long as I was interested, then putting it down and moving on to something new. If I had to, I could concentrate on the same project for half a day, but that wasn't my style. So by 1968 I switched my major from premed to psychology. Actually, I didn't want to be a psychologist, either, but that department was willing to accept all of my science credits, and that was important because I didn't want to take additional course work. *All I wanted to do was graduate!* Then I would figure out my true profession.

DECIDING TO FRANCHISE

Meanwhile, I concentrated on expanding Subway. After eight years in business we had opened only sixteen stores, and it wasn't likely that we could double that number to hit our goal within two years. In fact, we were certain it wouldn't happen and our only hope of hitting the goal was to find a strategy other than opening our own stores. We didn't have the money to expand any faster than at our current rate and we didn't have the management skill to run stores well at a great distance. Plus, the more stores we added, the more challenging it became to manage them all.

One Monday night in 1974, rather than meeting at World

Headquarters, Pete and I met in the office of attorney Mario Rubano where we wanted to discuss the future of our business. Mario was a family friend who occasionally handled some legal work for us. As we evaluated our options we talked about franchising, particularly because McDonald's and Kentucky Fried Chicken were opening a lot of franchised units in the Bridgeport area at that time. As we left Mario's office, we agreed to think further about franchising.

We knew nothing about the topic although we had discussed it previously. A couple of years back my uncle John DeLuca asked if he could buy a Subway franchise to open in New York. After thinking it through we turned him down, explaining we didn't think franchising was for us. He went to another small submarine sandwich chain, bought a franchise from them, and then sold it a couple of years later when he realized he didn't like the fast food business.

We thought franchising was for bigger companies that built free-standing units, like McDonald's, so we didn't think it made sense for our little take-out business. At the time we did not include tables or booths in the stores. So the first couple of times we discussed franchising, we rejected it without much more consideration than that. However, now, because we were behind schedule, we were willing to look into it again.

One Monday night, after weighing the pros and cons, we decided that franchising was the best way to get from sixteen to thirty-two stores. We could recruit people who would invest their money and use our management system to open and run Subway stores in their neighborhoods. Maybe franchising wasn't just for big companies, we told ourselves. Maybe little companies could franchise, too. What we didn't know at the time was that there were many other small businesses that used franchising as a method of expansion.

Rather than go out and hire consultants and lawyers to prepare us for franchising I figured that the simplest way to get started was to find a franchisee. That's when I spoke to my friend Brian Dixon. Our wives both worked as nurses at the

West Haven Veterans Hospital. Occasionally we got together to play cards or go to a hockey game, and I knew Brian wasn't happy with his job and I thought Brian would do a terrific job with one of our stores.

One night between periods at a hockey game in New Haven I made Brian an offer he couldn't refuse. I told Brian about our franchising plans and offered to loan him the money to buy our store in Wallingford, Connecticut. I even said that if he didn't like the business for any reason he could return the store to us and not owe us a penny.

He refused! Even though he didn't like his job, he explained that he got paid every Thursday and he didn't want to risk going into business. On several other occasions I tested Brian's interest in becoming our first franchisee and he repeatedly turned me down. So I continued to devote my time to managing our existing stores and decided to worry later about franchising. Expansion would have to take care of itself.

But then one day Brian changed his mind—later you'll read how it happened—and after he did, we changed Subway. We rented office space, hired my aunt Lucy DeLuca as our first secretary, set up shop as a franchisor, and began advertising our opportunity in the classified sections of newspapers throughout Connecticut. We set our franchise fee at $1,000—that was the amount of money a franchisee would pay for the use of our name and management systems, as well as initial training—and our ongoing royalty at 8 percent of the store's sales. Leasing space, buying equipment and supplies, signage, inventory, and other site-specific components required an additional investment.

Since Subway was already well known in Connecticut, the response to our tiny ads was immediate and steady, and the sales process was straightforward. People called us, I provided them with information, and if they were interested we met personally. Within a few months we sold franchises in Danbury, Middletown, and Waterbury. That first year, we didn't advertise outside Connecticut and we didn't open stores outside the state because our new franchisees had the fear that *people were different out there!*

GOING BEYOND CONNECTICUT

However, we quickly broke through the boundary barrier when my wife's brother, Marty Adomat, graduated from college and decided to open a store in Springfield, Massachusetts, in 1975. Almost simultaneous to his decision, my aunt and uncle, Tony and Louise Scotti, opened a store in Staten Island, New York. Both locations were ninety minutes from our office, still a manageable distance for our fledgling franchise operation.

But then, in 1976, Aunt Louise introduced us to Jerry Smith, who was a customer in her store. He and his brother, Jim, wanted to open Subway in Baltimore, Maryland, where they had grown up and where Jim still resided. Baltimore was a four-hour drive, and I thought it would be difficult to provide adequate service to a franchisee so far away. By this time, I had learned that frequent communication and guidance was an important element of franchising. Also, I knew that as we franchised further from home it would be more difficult to service the stores, just as it was more difficult to operate company-owned stores that were far away from our home base. In addition, I was concerned that the Baltimore unit would be all by itself in a big city and until we could sell additional stores in the area, and have someone nearby to service those stores, it didn't make economic sense to expand to Baltimore.

But then I considered another approach. I told Jim that we would agree to sell him and his brother a franchise, but to do so we would need someone locally to take on more responsibility. I suggested that Jim should be that person, and I said if he was willing to do so, we could work out a deal. Jim *was* willing and it took only a day or two for us to work out the details. That's when we created the position of Development Agent, a person who would help us build and service stores in a specific territory. Jim liked the idea, and that's how we planted Subway's flag in Baltimore.

Right after we developed this new servicing concept the Scottis became Development Agents in New York and my brother-in-law, Marty, became a Development Agent in Springfield, Massachusetts. Later, Brian Dixon became a Development Agent for Rhode Island and New London County, Connecticut. All of these pioneers are still Development Agents and store owners today.

Marty, however, is now in Houston, Texas. During one family vacation in Florida Marty and his wife, Lasha, told me they no longer wanted to live in the snowbelt so we talked about Subway opportunities in other parts of the country. Houston sounded interesting to them, so on the ride back home from Florida they turned left to check it out. Soon thereafter Marty traded his territory in Massachusetts for Houston, and due to the size of that city, he teamed up with a partner, Bill Horner.

SETTING ANOTHER BIG GOAL

As we celebrated Subway's tenth anniversary in 1975, the fact that we were several stores shy of our goal wasn't much of a disappointment. We knew it was only a matter of time until we would surpass that goal and set a new one. We opened our thirty-second store in 1976; in two more years we opened our 100th store; and by 1982 we doubled our network to 200 units. The rapid growth created numerous challenges that required the resolve of our talented home office team. Subway was no longer a tiny operation. It was on track to expand far greater and faster than Pete and I could imagine.

So now what do we do? How were we doing? Was 200 stores a lot or a little? What else was possible? If we set another goal, what would it be? After conducting a market study of the fast food industry in 1982, sizing up other chains and their growth, and considering Subway's growth, I decided our new goal would be 5,000 stores by 1994. It was an aggressive goal. Most of our employees were stunned when I announced it, and some of them thought I was absolutely crazy. *We only have 200 stores. How are we going to open up 4,800 more?*

From the perspective of many of our team members it seemed impossible to grow Subway twenty-five-fold! But from my perspective it looked like an extremely challenging objective, but not much more challenging than opening thirty-two stores in ten years from an investment of only $1,000.

After all, we had already spent nine years learning how to run our company stores, and another eight years refining our franchise organization. We had developed terrific control systems, we had a network of experienced franchisees, and we were beginning to put Development Agents in place around the country. We had seventeen years of experience to rely on, and to my way of thinking, we were going to keep doing what we were already doing, but we would just do lots more of it.

There was no doubt in my mind that if we worked hard and did lots of things correctly the goal was achievable. Despite any misgivings about the goal, everyone on the team focused on the objective. We made further improvements to Subway and by 1991, a full three years early, we surpassed the 5,000-store goal!

We were growing so quickly that by that time I had already revised our goal to 8,000 stores by 1995 and we even surpassed that goal two years ahead of schedule. In fact, in the ten-year span between 1988 and 1997 we added over 10,000 stores to Subway, and for most years during that period we held the distinction of being the world's fastest-growing franchise company.

How did we expand so quickly? What most people don't

know is that our existing franchisees who were in an expansion mode opened about 65 percent of our new stores each year. We have many talented, ambitious, hardworking franchisees in Subway and they fueled our spectacular growth. Once they learned the details of the business and how to succeed with a single unit, many would return to invest in additional stores. Having succeeded once with Subway, they wanted to succeed over and over again. Even to this day, about 65 percent of our new franchises are sold each year to existing owners who are reinvesting in the business. By keeping the operation simple, the investment in our stores low, and by discounting the initial fee for existing franchisees who are expanding, we made it desirable for our franchise owners to open multiple units.

When we passed the 8,000-store mark we decided it was time to publish a different type of goal. Now, rather than measuring how many stores we opened, we decided to concentrate on cents per capita in North America. Our goal is for every man, woman, and child to spend 50 cents per week at Subway by 2005. We have a long way to go to hit that mark, but we're up for the challenge.

INTERNATIONAL EXPANSION

In terms of store counts we now have to think of expansion on a global scale. We recently opened our 15,000th store—it looks to me like a large fast food company will be able to operate more than 100,000 outlets worldwide by 2050. I'm fairly confident McDonald's, with over 25,000 restaurants currently in operation, will be first to hit that number, but we haven't as of yet set a worldwide store count goal. Right now we're working on our international infrastructure and if we continue to do a really good job we might be able to reach 100,000 outlets, too.

Where will we open all of those stores? Outside North America, for the most part. We've operated in international markets since 1983 when we opened a small store in Bahrain, in the Persian Gulf. Shortly thereafter we had a false start in the U.K., and in 1986 we opened in Canada where today we operate more stores than McDonald's.

However, it's only been in the past few years that we've begun to make big strides on the international scene, thanks to the persistence of Don Fertman, who heads up our international division. Today we have more than 2,000 stores outside the U.S., making Subway the fifth-largest international fast food franchiser after McDonald's, KFC, Pizza Hut, and Burger King. But there's still lots of work to do.

Even though we're now located in more than seventy countries and in most every region of the world, including countries like Japan, the United Kingdom, Australia, Venezuela, South Africa, Israel, and China, in most places we have just a tiny presence. Actually, Subway today feels a lot like 1982 when we had only 200 stores scattered across the U.S. We've got a good start but there's a lot of growth to look forward to.

Our international plan is to follow the same basic formula that has worked so well for us in the U.S. We're looking for dedicated franchisees to operate stores in their neighborhoods, and just as we did when we expanded to Baltimore, we're looking for Development Agents to lead the expansion in local markets around the world.

While our terrific team has accomplished a lot in the past thirty-five years, there is still much work and many challenges ahead. Today we must put the pieces in place for Subway to become an international powerhouse. But like every big objective that we've faced in the development of Subway—many of which you'll read about in this book—our team is up for the challenge.

What I never expected, and what Pete Buck never expected, was that we would build such a large company from such humble beginnings. For two guys who knew almost nothing about business, the food industry, and franchising, our thirty-five-year-old partnership has led to our personal success as microentrepreneurs. More significantly, we've touched, and in many instances changed, the lives of people worldwide. For a kid from "The Projects," it's been a fabulous journey. I hasten to add that these accomplishments have less to do with me, and Pete, than they do with our associates at Subway World Headquarters, our Development Agents, and most importantly, our incredible franchisees. These are the folks who continue to make the journey exciting and rewarding.

Come along now, and I'll explain each of the Fifteen Key Lessons in more detail, and I'll introduce you to twenty-one other microentrepreneurs whose own incredible stories emphasize the value of these lessons.

CHAPTER FOUR

START SMALL

These microentrepreneurs are certain of one thing: Starting small is better than never starting at all! Regardless of money, circumstances, and experience, these microentrepreneurs will show you how to get started.

My story sounds a little improbable, doesn't it? After all, who could go to a barbecue one day without any intention of starting a business and wind up with a plan, a partner, and the seed money to get started? And what seventeen-year-old ever started a business before, anyway? And who can start a business with only $1,000?

Actually, I think most people would be quite surprised by the number of businesspeople who start on a shoestring and their array of improbable beginnings. You don't even have to scour the country to find them. For a real eye-opener, survey ten local businesspeople in your own community to learn how they got started and how much money they started with. My bet is that at least two of them, and perhaps as many as five of them, will tell you an interesting story of the tiny business they started long ago with less than $10,000.

Most people think that starting a business is a complex proposition. Dynamic entrepreneurs with big plans and lots of resources are the type who start businesses. They have special training, brilliant ideas, unique strategies, and a cadre of sophisticated advisers at their beck and call. Most people don't think that regular folks with ordinary ideas and limited resources can make much happen. Boy, would they be surprised at the way the real world works.

This book is all about regular people who start small businesses in ordinary ways. As you read the stories in this book you'll see that my story is similar to the way many others have started. *What can you do with a thousand dollars?* people often ask when I tell them that's all the money I had to start Subway. Of the many entrepreneurs I meet every year, more than a third of them started their first businesses with less than $10,000 and some of them with far less than $1,000. But the amount of money doesn't really matter, as you'll see in the stories that follow. In this chapter I'll quickly introduce you to several of these "regular folks," then in the next fourteen chapters I'll introduce you to more of these same kinds of people in greater depth. More than the money, getting started is what it's all about, and all of these microentrepreneurs will tell you that it's better to start small than never start at all.

Jeremy Weiner, for example, never hesitated to start small. He was suffering from boredom in the summer of 1995 between his sophomore and junior years in college. He attended Babson College in Wellesley, near Boston, well known for its entrepreneurial program, but he spent the summer at home in California. He was supposed to be working at two different brokerage firms in Beverly Hills, preparing to become an investment banker after graduation. By midsummer, however, he discovered that he hated the business. With several weeks remaining before returning to Babson, Jeremy quit both of his jobs. For a couple of days he hung out on a friend's boat, but then the reality of his empty bank account struck him, and he decided he better earn some money before he returned east to school.

Jeremy learned to make money when he was just ten years old. In the fourth grade, with an Apple 2GS computer that his parents purchased for him, and a software program called

Printshop, he started his first business. "I was just a kid, but I figured out how to make banners," he says. "When my mom took me to the mall I sold banners to the retailers. Five bucks a page! It was great revenue. I'd be lying to you if I told you I knew what I was doing."

As a high school student he and a friend worked in concessions at a movie theater frequented by Hollywood stars. "We saw an opportunity to sell more popcorn and drinks if we had a cart to push through the theaters," says Jeremy. "We noticed that the stars weren't standing in line to buy stuff, and a lot of other people didn't want to stand in long lines, either. They'd just go into the theater and sit down. So my friend and I convinced the manager to let us start a cart. We sold a lot more popcorn that way."

They also added handsomely to their earnings!

"The tip money was really good," says Jeremy.

However, the theater's managers soon put an end to the cart because it created more work for them. "Even though we were selling more food and drinks, the managers didn't like it because the cart was another register that they had to close out at the end of the night. We didn't have any say in the matter, they just told us to stop. I should have known then that I'd never want to work in a corporation. Bureaucracy isn't something that I could ever get used to."

In his sophomore year at Babson College, Jeremy started a student directory, for which he sold advertising. If there was one thing he could do well, it was sell. That's why he pounced on an opportunity to sell ad space in those remaining weeks of his summer boredom. One day he visited his former high school, just to say hello, and to rib the principal about a B that he thought should have been an A. While he was there, he got an idea. He noticed that the school needed covers for the students' textbooks. He asked the principal if he could provide the covers, and the principal agreed. He contacted three other area schools and asked if they needed covers. They all said yes. Then he contacted local businesses who wanted to reach the school market. Within a couple of weeks—with no investment other than gas money and phone calls—he raised $10,000 in ad revenue! Printing the book covers for all four schools cost $1,000. "With $9,000 net," says Jeremy, "I still had a week to spend on the beach before I had to go to school."

At first, Jeremy had no plans of repeating the book cover gig, at least not by himself. He did it to make money. He made the money. End of story. However, the next summer he explained to his brother, Brian, and a friend, Michael Gleeson, how they could continue operating the business. He taught them how to contact schools and sell advertising. While the guys got busy, Jeremy accepted a summer job working directly with the president of a toy company in Boston. He thought it was an ideal opportunity to learn about running a business. By midsummer, Brian and Mike had signed up fifty schools, but they had spent little time generating sales. So Jeremy took a leave of absence from the toy company to sell the advertising.

With only a few weeks remaining in the summer, Jeremy worked the phones and through sheer persistence sold a major deal to JanSport, the leading manufacturer of backpacks. The company bought the front cover for $24,999. Two additional spots on the back cover netted another $13,800, and included a recruitment ad purchased by the Los Angeles Police Department. With gross sales of $38,800, Jeremy anticipated earning a modest profit, but it didn't work out that way. Instead of purchasing covers for five schools he purchased for fifty schools. The printing bill jumped to $30,000. With delivery costs, phone bills, and miscellaneous expenses, the summer enterprise lost $2,700!

Undaunted by the loss, Jeremy and Gleeson teamed up in a senior field studies course about entrepreneurship and wrote a business plan for what they now called Cover-It. Their primary motivation for writing the plan was not only to operate the business, but to compete for the prestigious John H. Muller, Jr., Business Plan Award, which included a $5,000 prize, and Babson's Student Initiative Award, worth $1,000. In spite of tough competition, including more than 100 submissions for the Muller award, the entrepreneurial pair won *both* awards in April 1997. They split the $6,000, which more than covered their losses from the previous summer.

Following graduation from Babson amidst a flurry of media articles about his successes, Jeremy was offered numerous jobs. However, he turned them all down. He decided to pursue his future with Cover-It. At first, his partner was going to join him, but at the last minute he decided not to. He turned over his interest in Cover-It to Jeremy, who set up shop in a printer's office in Boston and went to work. JanSport renewed its contract for $70,000, and the L.A. Police Department renewed, too. Jeremy expanded the number of schools in his distribution network from a mere 50 to 16,000, reaching 12 million students in kindergarten through twelfth grade. How he accomplished those numbers is a trade secret. "One of the toughest things about this business," he explains, "is to sign up schools." Once the selling season ended, and Jeremy distributed the book covers, he ended up with approximately $30,000.

By the next year, he expanded Cover-It's distribution to 26 million students (distribution would eventually climb to 30 million). Instead of printing one cover for all the schools in his network, he printed five, creating five front covers to sell instead of one. By 1999, with ten employees, three offices—Boston, Chicago, and Los Angeles—and distribution in all fifty states, Cover-It exceeded $1 million in sales. Jeremy projected that his year 2000 gross revenue would exceed $2 million.

At age twenty-four, Jeremy says he's still figuring out how to run his business. "Every month," he says, "there are thousands of challenges." But given the choice of working for someone else, or owning your own business, Jeremy says there is *no* choice—especially when you can start small and finish big.

Paulette Ensign of San Diego, California, is another microentrepreneur who started a business with almost no money invested. She taught string instruments in public elementary schools in New York and Connecticut. In 1981, with a master's degree, she was earning just shy of $18,000 annually. After ten years, she decided she had had enough. Nothing was working in her life. She was unsatisfied with the teaching, she wasn't earning enough money, and her marriage wasn't working. She needed a change.

While she was an excellent teacher, and a better-than-average violinist, neither of those qualities interested her anymore. Oddly enough, perhaps as a response to the turmoil in her life, she felt like cleaning up. She was good at organization. Drawers, cabinets, checkbooks, desks, schedules—all of them yielded to her expertise. She never spent time looking for things because in her world everything had its place, and she never permitted anything to be out of place. "My personality," she says, "is one of being naturally organized. If a pile gets to be more than two inches, I'm uncomfortable and I need to have those things find their homes." So when a neighbor lady, who was well aware of Paulette's organizational skills, and equally aware that she was looking for work, offered to pay her to organize her house, it was a perfect match.

"We each had something the other one needed," says Paulette, who hasn't surrendered her throaty New York accent to San Diego, where she's resided for several years. "She needed help organizing a lifetime of accumulation in her home, and I needed money." After several days of digging through the contents of her neighbor's home in April 1983, Paulette found a business.

"I was enjoying the gratification of working with this woman, creating order out of chaos. The gratification fed a need of mine, and it was good. I got the idea that I could make a business out of this. There was an exchange of money for service, and it was a service that others needed. So even though it was a financial stretch for me, I threw a $25 classified ad in the *Scarsdale Inquirer* and another in the *Westchester Women's News*. My ads said something to the effect of create order out of chaos. It was down-and-dirty simplistic, and it didn't take long for my phone to ring."

However, it also wasn't long before the phone was about to

be cut off. "My husband and I had hit rock bottom in our relationship," Paulette explains. "We didn't have enough money to pay our bills. Everyone was at our door to collect. We had a backlog of six to seven months of bills. We had no money in reserve. Friends were sending us food. My family was incredulous. *How could you allow yourself to get into such a mess?*" Within a year the couple separated and divorced.

As requests for Paulette's organizational skills started to build, she increased her hourly fee from $10 to $25, and that relieved some of her financial strain. "I was bright enough to target my advertising to affluent communities," she explains. "Some folks hired me to come into their homes once or twice a month to write checks for them. Others hired me for a day or two a week. I was soon making about $1,800 a month, and the money was like manna from heaven."

For the next eight years, Paulette organized homes and offices. In 1986 she incorporated her business under the name Organizing Solutions. Eventually she purposely priced herself out of the residential market and focused on the commercial market where she could earn up to $125 an hour. Later, a major New York City–based bank hired her to conduct a workshop entitled Managing Multiple Priorities. At the height of her business, she was earning $100,000 a year!

But by the early 1990s, the economy shifted and suddenly the workshop business went soft and managing priorities was no longer such a big issue. Companies decided against sending their employees to workshops that cost money. "I was down and out," says Paulette, "and my bills were beginning to backlog again. The cash wasn't flowing and I still hadn't learned how to save or invest money. I had no cushion for myself— saving money is a missing cell in my brain! I needed to do *something* fast."

That's when she remembered a booklet that she had received several months earlier. She had placed it in a desk drawer thinking she might return to it someday. It was a book of tips about how to make business presentations, and when

Paulette read it she thought, "I could do better." Now was the time to do it.

She spent several days writing *110 Ideas for Organizing Your Business*, a booklet that, once printed and bound, could be mailed in a business-size envelope. All of the information in the booklet was based on material that Paulette taught in her seminars and used in her consulting sessions. Once she finished typing the manuscript, she located a printer, agreed to pay him $300 over a period of ninety days, and he produced a supply of the booklets. Meanwhile, with no advertising money to promote her product, Paulette sent excerpts from her booklet to magazines, newsletters, and newspapers, and invited the editors to publish her material in exchange for mentioning how readers could purchase a copy of the booklet. During the next six months, she sold 15,000 booklets at $3 each! Later she increased the per booklet price to $5. Five thousand sales came from one source, a newsletter called *Bottom Line Personal*. "They ran only nine lines of text about my booklet," says Paulette, "and when I went to the post-office I found a pink slip that said: *See Clerk*. They could not fit all of the envelopes in my mailbox!"

Since producing her booklet in 1991, Paulette has sold more than half a million copies in three languages without spending a penny on advertising. She also has licensed several companies to reproduce her booklet for their own promotions. Lillian Vernon offered the booklet free to customers who purchased from the company's catalogue. After Paulette established a Web site and began communicating in cyberspace, she sold 105,000 copies of her booklet to a firm in Milan, Italy. "To this day we've never spoken," she explains. "We've done all of our business by electronic mail."

In addition to booklet sales, Paulette now generates revenue by teaching others how to write, produce, market, and sell booklets. She has created a videotape and workbook package that she sells via her Web page, www.tipsbooklets.com. She teaches many seminars by telephone, consults privately with clients, and also teaches public seminars.

"Along the way," Paulette says, "I'm learning how to make money. When I started my business, I had to dig out of a hole. I was making decent bucks, but I had to work my way up to zero. I don't think that's an unusual situation. But as I started to own my intelligence, I got smarter. For example, I said why sell booklets for $3 when it's a lot easier to pull a $5 out of a wallet? When I realized that I'm an intelligent person and I was just missing some information, and all I had to do was get it, business became easier. In the meantime, I've got plenty of enthusiasm and the ability to talk endlessly."

And with those qualities, who needs much money to start a business?

Michael and Jamie Ford of Los Lunas, New Mexico, near Albuquerque, have yet another story to tell about the virtues of starting small. They were once a middle-class family living in Oklahoma with their three young children. They decided to move to New Mexico in 1991 to be near Michael's grandmother, who was ill. Little did they know that the move would nearly destroy them financially. In a short period of time, they went from middle-class to living off public assistance. It wasn't until they managed to borrow some money to start a business that they got back on their feet again.

The Fords had no trouble finding jobs when they arrived in Albuquerque. In fact, Jamie was hired to manage the office of a psychiatric firm that paid higher wages than her previous employer, and Michael went to work as an installer for a cable television company. The family settled temporarily in an apartment not far from Michael's grandmother. They were thinking about buying a home. "It seemed to us," says Jamie, "that we had the world by its tail." And then she slipped and fell in a grocery store, injuring her shoulder and neck.

The injuries required long-term rehabilitation and even then Jamie's mobility would be permanently impaired. After an extended absence from work, she lost her job. "We couldn't live on Michael's income alone," Jamie explains, "and I couldn't find another job. Then I got depressed and things got worse.

Our car was repossessed, we had to move out of the apartment complex, and our credit was destroyed. We found a battered, two-bedroom travel trailer for rent and that's where we ended up living. It was awful. To see my kids needing things like shoes and clothing. It's sad to live like that."

In her doctor's opinion, Jamie would never be able to manage an office again, and she would have to live with the migraine headaches that sent her to bed whenever they attacked. Public assistance came to the family's rescue with a $300-a-month food allocation and another $400 for living expenses. The trailer rent alone was $425 a month.

"Psychologically," continues Jamie, "it was devastating. We came from upper-middle-class families where we always had plenty of everything. We ate out in restaurants and at Christmas we got things that we really didn't need. I never imagined something like this could happen to us. It was like I fell into a sleep for a long time and woke up 100 pounds heavier. I lost my drive. I didn't want to get out of bed or off the couch. I thought my life was ruined."

It might have been, too, had it not been for Michael. He hated what had happened to his wife, but he sized up the situation in a hurry and decided he had to get the better of it before it destroyed his family. "I accepted our circumstances," Michael explains, "but not permanently. We were up against a challenge, and I kept telling Jamie and our children that we would work our way out of it." For several years, however, Jamie's rehabilitation monopolized the family's energy.

By the mid-1990s, life hadn't improved for the Ford family, but Michael had a plan. Before his wife's accident, they had often talked about going into business together. "We've always worked well together," says Michael, "and I knew that if we had a business it would be good for Jamie. It would keep her mind off her injury, and it would keep her from falling into depression again." Of course, the family had no money but that didn't stop Michael. He and Jamie had once visited with a man who sold kettle corn, a sweet, salty popcorn which was a favorite at fairs and specialty stores. Michael decided he and Jamie could start a similar business. All they needed was a kettle, a propane tank and burner, some popcorn, and a recipe. Michael thought it would be a good idea to write a business plan, too, if for no other reason than to keep Jamie busy.

"I've always been good at research," Jamie explains, "and it took me about six months to get our plan together."

Once it was completed, they intended to use the plan to request a loan. "We knew it was a long shot to get money for a business," says Jamie, "but we thought it was worth the try, particularly if we had a good business plan. The only damaging thing on our credit report was the car. If we could show someone that we were trying to get off public assistance, even though we didn't have collateral, we thought they'd help us with a loan."

In the meantime, Jamie and Michael also decided to enroll in a local community college to study business. They applied for a grant to cover the cost of tuition and books. By sharing the textbooks, they were able to save some money to buy a kettle. During the early months of 1996 they experimented at their trailer with various recipes and learned to make the popcorn in several flavors including red chili, cheese, and barbecue. With some help from friends, they accumulated their equipment and supplies, including a screened tent that allowed them to make their product under cover. In July 1996 they reserved space at a flea market, dressed up like pioneers, and put on a show for the local community. "We got a few strange looks from people," recalls Jamie, "but as we handed out samples and people tasted our popcorn, everyone wanted more. It was something new in our area and it was a big hit."

The Fords soon discovered, however, that the cost of reserving space was prohibitive. Some fairs required as much as $400 for a weekend. "That's why we needed some capital," says Michael. "We had a good product, we knew it would sell and we could make money off it. But we needed the upfront money to reserve our booth space."

In late summer of 1996 the Fords had completed their business plan for M&J Pioneer Popcorn and they intended to submit it to a company in Albuquerque that specialized in small business loans. Meanwhile, their contact at the Division of Vocational Rehabilitation, one of the public agencies that assisted Jamie, told them about ACCION International, a microlender that had recently opened an affiliate office in Albuquerque. Established in 1961 to help impoverished microentrepreneurs in Latin America, ACCION expanded to the United States in 1991 and began offering business loans to low-income people. The Fords submitted their plan to ACCION and almost immediately received a loan for $250.

"ACCION was what we needed," says a delighted Jamie. "They not only provided financial assistance and business advice, they also helped us network with other members who owned businesses. Another ACCION client was an interior decorator who worked in both the residential and commercial markets. She was trying to get new clients so she bought bags of our popcorn and presented a gift to her prospects and clients when she called on them. Another client owned a restaurant in Old Town Albuquerque and he invited us to display our product there and sell it. These connections were extremely helpful. In times when we were bummed out, it was good to go to an ACCION workshop and sit with people who were full of ideas and energy. It was like a revival!"

With assistance from ACCION the Fords expanded their enterprise and were soon appearing regularly at special events in the Albuquerque area. "Our first year in business," says Michael, "we earned about $10,000 net income, but we had to plow a lot of that money back into the business. We needed a $3 million insurance policy to get into the big events, and that alone required a $1,900 premium." They were able to use a small amount of the money to supplement their public assistance.

An additional loan from ACCION helped the Fords purchase labels imprinted with their phone numbers to apply on the bags of popcorn. Now customers could reach them in between events to buy their products. The Fords also purchased a bag sealer, which guaranteed the shelf life of the popcorn and provided the opportunity to sell their products in convenience stores.

After two years of operating M&J Pioneer Popcorn, life improved dramatically for the Fords. They worked their way off public assistance. "We never wanted it," says Jamie, "and we were ready to get off it, but it truly helped us through a bad time." Eventually they moved from that tiny trailer to a family-sized trailer situated on an acre of land. "It's still only two bedrooms," explains Jamie, "but it's like a mansion compared to what we had."

Michael, always a fisherman, bought a book about fly fishing and taught himself to tie flies. For months, Jamie, who had benefited for so many years from Michael's encouragement, told Michael that the flies were beautiful enough to sell. "One day," Jamie says, "Michael got up the nerve to call around locally to see if any of the stores wanted to buy his flies. The next thing we knew, he had five accounts, and a week later he had orders for 500 dozen flies! Then he started getting so many orders that there just wasn't time to run the popcorn business."

By 1999, Michael was tying flies full-time and taking orders faster than he could fill them. "You need a lot of patience to tie flies," says Michael, "and it's not something that a lot of people want to do. Depending on the pattern, it takes between thirty and ninety seconds to make one fly. You've got to do it just right or the fly won't fool the fish. I'm a perfectionist so it's something I can do very well." Michael sells the flies a dozen at a time at a cost of $7.50 per dozen.

"It's better money than popcorn," he says, "and there are no big insurance premiums required. The materials are kind of expensive. I need animal fur, rubber legs, and a few synthetic parts. Chicken hackles and the hooks are very expensive. I use a lot of feathers, too, but now we're raising chickens so I've got plenty of feathers." A $2,200 loan from ACCION helped Michael purchase a large quantity of materials, as well as a computer. He also changed the name of his business to M&J Pioneer Merchants.

As the Fords made the transition from selling popcorn to tying flies, Jamie found herself with little to do. She wasn't inclined to operate the popcorn business on her own, so she decided to look for a job. In 1998 she was hired at a local Blockbuster Video where she became an assistant manager. "I attribute everything to Michael," she says. "He snapped me out of my situation. He said he couldn't do it alone, he needed my help. He told me, and our children, what to do, and that's what saved us."

In all, the Fords estimate they invested about $2,000 to start their popcorn business. At the time, it was a huge amount of money to them, but a pittance when they considered what it bought them. By starting small, Jamie and Michael Ford became the architects of their own success. They not only earned some well-needed money, they also built up their self-respect and took back the dignity they had lost when they were struck by financial devastation. Ultimately, the experience led them to a second business, and it put them back on the road to their former middle-class lifestyle. "We needed something to do," says Michael, "and starting a business was the right thing. It kept us going. It made us think that we can make a difference some day. I get a lot of encouragement from that, and from what we've accomplished together."

In 1998, the Small Business Administration honored Michael and Jamie Ford as New Mexico's Entrepreneurs of the Year.

In addition to Jeremy Weiner, Paulette Ensign, and Michael and Jamie Ford, the list of people who started small goes on and on.

In Mill Valley, California, Nancy Bombace was a newlywed when she invested $4,000 to start HoneyLuna, a honeymoon registry service. Rather than registering at department stores for china and toasters, brides can register with HoneyLuna for airline tickets, hotels, meals, and activities that can be used during their honeymoon.

In New York City, Carlos Aldana emigrated from Bogotá, Colombia. He shared an apartment in Washington Heights, a huge Hispanic community north of Harlem, with several other men. Carlos planned to start his own business, but he had no money. He took on three jobs to build up a savings. Starting at 2:00 A.M. he delivered newspapers for the *New York Times*. Then he delivered late-arriving luggage for the airlines at JFK, La Guardia, and Newark airports. He also delivered orders for a pharmaceutical company. Many weeks he worked without a day off. Eventually he started his own delivery business, delivering "anything for anybody." In the early 1990s, Carlos discovered ACCION's New York office. He borrowed a little money to purchase a second car so that he could hire an employee for his fledgling delivery business. For several years Carlos continued saving money, and by the mid-1990s he and a partner could afford a down payment on a tiny restaurant. In 1995, Carlos bought out his partner and began selling *arepas*, traditional Colombian cornmeal patties. By 1999, with a $15,000 loan from ACCION New York for equipment, Carlos had quadrupled his output and he was selling his popular *arepas* to 175 retail accounts in New York, New Jersey, and Connecticut. His business was grossing more than $700,000 annually. Eleven years earlier he had arrived in the United States without as much as a penny in his pocket.

In Portland, Oregon, a former teacher with $200 in start-up money, and a talent for designing and producing unique collectibles, launched Collectable Creations. Charlotte Colistro Brown's endearing line of soft, stuffed snowmen, Santas, angels, rabbits, and hares sell out quickly in retail shops across the United States. The company's unique Sparkle Snowman eventually appeared on the covers of Harry and David's Christmas catalogue and *Country Folk Art Magazine*.

"I never thought about starting a business," explains a soft-spoken, but enthusiastic Charlotte. "I took a year off from teaching and I was going stir crazy. So I made an angel. People wanted to buy it and I just wanted to fill up time. I got bitten by the creative bug. Things slowly snowballed. The next thing I knew, I was working fourteen hours a day! I couldn't keep up with all the activity, so I asked my sister, Judy, to help me." Eventually, the sisters became partners.

"Every year we doubled or tripled our volume," Charlotte continues, "and people just went nuts over our designs." The first three years, though, Collectable Creations didn't make much money. "By our third year, we grossed $45,000, and we decided we needed more volume to make more money. Otherwise I was going back to teaching school. That's when we decided to contract with sales representatives nationwide, and we went to our first gift show. The markets then really began to open up." By 1997, Collectable Creations grossed $1.5 million, and in 1999 the company was on track to sell more than $2 million of products. All from an investment of $200!

Across America and other parts of the world there are countless fascinating stories about people who started small. They get an idea, they capture a vision, and they begin. Frequently nowadays, many of these microentrepreneurs borrow money from the microlending organizations that are popping up throughout the world. This presents an opportunity for even more people to start businesses, and that's one of the reasons why I think microcredit is such a good idea. It's a reason why I think microcredit deserves my attention, and I hope the attention of many readers.

In the next fourteen chapters you'll meet more microentrepreneurs who will show you how they've implemented the Fifteen Key Lessons that I describe in this book. Most of these microentrepreneurs, in fact, have implemented more than just one or two of these lessons. As you read their stories, see if you can identify the lessons they've utilized.

But, of course, you don't have to read a book or look far to find these microentrepreneurs. They're in your community, your neighborhood, your family. And in the future, there will be many more of them. In the future, I hope *you* will be one of them! All you need to do is start small.

CHAPTER FIVE

EARN A FEW PENNIES

**By earning pennies first, dollars second, Frank Argen-
bright learned how to make money. He's used that ability to build a billion-dollar, multinational enterprise in
the contract staffing industry.**

If anyone had asked for my résumé at the time I started Subway, it would have read like this:

Finding soda pop bottles in New York City and collecting
a refund of 2 cents per bottle . . . Bartering comic books and
baseball cards with friends . . . Baby-sitting the neighborhood kids for 50 cents an hour . . . Building a newspaper
route, delivering the papers, and collecting every two
weeks . . . Working for minimum wage at a hardware store.

At age seventeen, that was the sum total of my work experiences and credentials prior to becoming a microentrepreneur in the real world. It wasn't much of a track record that
would impress anyone. No one would have hired me based
on that résumé and I certainly didn't have any of what might
be called the "normal" qualifiers for a career in business,
franchising, or the food industry. And yet, these small beginnings weren't a bad way to learn about all three.

Of course, business wasn't my goal. As a kid, I never
looked for the lessons in doing odd jobs. I picked up soda
pop bottles and tossed newspapers for pocket change. That's
what kids did when I was growing up. When we needed

money—and no one in my crowd ever had enough money—we discovered ways to earn a few pennies. It was simply part of our culture.

The size and scope of the jobs, the hours devoted to the jobs, and the money earned from the jobs didn't matter. Oh, it mattered when we didn't have enough money to buy another package of baseball cards, or go to a movie. But what mattered most is that we learned the relationship of work and money, and that we participated in the process of exchanging products and services for money. Even though we were just kids, we were making transactions. Not big transactions. Not life-changing transactions. Not even transactions that would feed us or clothe us. But transactions that earned us a few pennies, and eventually a few dollars.

For me personally, those odd jobs laid the foundation of my career. Whether it was Subway or some other business, or an entirely different profession, the value of my childhood work experiences cannot be underestimated. I believe that's true for most people who start a business and succeed. Even though I wasn't aware of it at the time, those odd jobs provided the foundational knowledge that I would need to take the next step toward building a real business.

My experiences are no different than those of other microentrepreneurs. Maybe they didn't trade in soda pop bottles, or sit for the neighborhood kids. But they sold something, either a product or a service, and they earned a few pennies before they earned any dollars. They may have sold Girl Scout Cookies. Lemonade. Magazines. Candy. Gift wrap. Or any number of other items.

As a child, Zig Ziglar, whose story appears later in this book, says he sold vegetables from his mother's garden, and later he peddled sandwiches to college students. Long before he founded Jani-King, the commercial cleaning giant, Jim Cavanaugh, who you'll meet later in this book, sold pennants and peanuts during college football games in Norman, Oklahoma.

I would guess that most successful entrepreneurs

learned the process of making money by earning a few pennies and then learning how to make a few dollars. It's a valuable lesson.

Frank Argenbright is a good example of a microentrepreneur who turned pennies into dollars, and ultimately into a billion-dollar business. Frank is the chairman of AHL Services, Inc., an Atlanta-based contract staffing company, with ninety-six offices in the United States and another sixty-seven in Europe. AHL's 40,000 employees staff many of the security checkpoints at major airports, and they also work in factories, including those of Mercedes and BMW in Europe. Some AHL employees provide skycap services, wheelchair and cargo services, and they operate shuttles and fueling stations for airports and universities. This is a story of courage and imagination. But it's mostly a story about a man who learned how to make real money, big money, by earning pennies first.

Listening to Frank Argenbright's story, no one would ever have guessed that he could build an international business serving Fortune 500 companies. He grew up in a small country town, Madison, Florida, with his mother, a schoolteacher, his father, a salesman at a feed company, three brothers and a sister. They all lived in a two-bedroom house with one bath. "I'm probably too materialistic today because of that experience," says Frank.

While growing up, Frank dreamed about becoming an agent for the Federal Bureau of Investigation. But there were a number of challenges in his path, beginning with his performance in school. It wasn't good. "I did poorly," he admits. "I graduated from high school with a 1.9 average, that was a D-plus. As a senior I took my mother's history course and got an F. You'd think she could have rationalized a D for her son, but I deserved an F and she gave it to me. Even so, my mother was my sole source of encouragement. When I brought home bad grades, she'd say to me, 'Frank, you have more potential than anyone I know.' Later I figured out she was really saying that anyone with a D had a lot of potential to improve! But my mother never gave up on me."

Other teachers, and his classmates, were not as kind. Teachers placed him in the back of the room, and often told him that he was stupid. "It was no secret that I was a D student. Teachers told me to get a skill. 'You'll never get to college,' they said."

His mother said otherwise, however. She had earned two master's degrees and she told her son, "You'll go to college." After high school, Frank's parents borrowed money to send him to college prep school for the summer. The program was especially for children with high potential and low grades. The school prepared Frank to enter North Florida Junior College the next fall. Two years later, armed with an associate's degree, Frank transferred to Florida State University. "Once I earned the associate's degree, FSU had no choice but to accept me," he explains. Even so, he spent his first quarter on academic probation.

Still hoping to join the FBI, he selected criminology for his major. But scholastically his performance remained shoddy. Years later, Frank would discover the real reason for his academic problems. He was dyslexic. On top of that, he suffered from attention deficit disorder. Unfortunately, neither malady was detected before he graduated from college.

"I ended up with a 2.0 grade average, but it was art that pulled me through," he explains. "I was good with my hands. I could draw, and if I had a clump of clay, I could turn it into a pot. They called that art. And for that, I got an A. I took as many art courses as I could to balance out the Ds and Fs that I earned in criminology classes."

With a degree in hand in the early 1970s, Frank called on the FBI, but at the time the agency was hiring only accountants and lawyers. He thought about joining the military—he had completed an ROTC program during college—and while he waited to decide his future, he found a job selling cameras at Eckerd, the drugstore chain. It was his first real job, but it wouldn't be the first time he earned money.

"I was always an entrepreneur," Frank says, "and frequently it got me into trouble. When I was in the fifth grade you could buy bubble gum that included a wrapper with a water-soluble tattoo. The tattoos were pictures of comic strip characters, like Popeye. You could place the wrapper on a part of your body, usually the back of your hand, or an arm, rub it with water and the cartoon character would stick to you like a real tattoo. The store closest to my home sold the bubble gum for a penny, but I didn't have any money. However, my friend had 50 cents, so I convinced him to buy the gum and let me resell it to the farm kids at school for double the price. That's what we did. And we split the profits.

"But one of the kids stuck the tattoos all over his body and a teacher sent him to the lavatory to wash them off. He demanded to have his money back and I said no. Next thing I know I'm sitting in the principal's office and my mother is called in for a conference. I was frequently an embarrassment to her. They said I was making money during school hours and that was forbidden."

From then on, Frank says he always found something to sell, though not necessarily during school hours. During his high school years he ran a trap line. "I'd get up early and go out on the riverbanks where every day I set traps to catch raccoons and opossums. I used steel traps, which are frowned upon now, and they were very effective. In the early morning hours, I'd gather up whatever my traps had caught the previous day and night. I'd take an assorted collection of animals to cold storage, go to school, and then return that afternoon to sell them to poor people in town. All the time I was in school, I needed to make money. I grew up with the feeling that I wasn't as good as everyone else, and that gave me a lot of desire. It also gave me the drive to set goals and get ahead."

At the prep school he attended the summer before college, Frank sold fireworks to the other students. He drove his motorcycle home on weekends, loaded his backpack with fireworks, and then returned to school ready to do business. "These were all rich kids," he recalls, "and they either didn't know that I had tripled the price of the fireworks, or they didn't care."

As he got older, he got more creative. He discovered that Florida State offered a program to study art in Europe for a semester, and he wanted to go to Europe. However, the program was specifically for art history students who maintained a grade point average of better than 2.5. Frank didn't qualify, but he figured out how to get accepted for the program. He switched majors just for that semester! And when seventy-five females and only twenty-five males applied for the program, Frank explains, "FSU decided to make an exception for my poor grade point average because they needed every guy they could get on the trip."

Once he arrived in Italy and moved into a villa with the other students in the program he applied his entrepreneurial skills to generate the spending money that he would require. "I bought a little motor bike, the kind you frequently see in Europe, and I got into the pizza delivery business. I was the only student who had transportation. So I would drive into the city to buy pizzas and then sell them to my classmates. The pizzeria gave me a 20 percent discount, and that's how I earned a little money for myself."

In addition, he became a tour organizer. "We attended classes Monday through Wednesday, so we had long weekends to travel. I organized trips for all of us, and by doing so I earned free tickets and spending money. That's how I got to stay at numerous resorts in Europe, and that's how I supported myself that semester."

He never made a lot of money, of course, but by making small amounts he learned the all-important *process of making money*. His moneymaking abilities didn't go unnoticed, either. "My mother's best friend was our school's English teacher and I was even worse in English than I was in history. When you're dyslexic and you have ADD it's hard to make any progress in English. This teacher called me Frankie, and she always commented about how I could make money. 'You have a knack for it,' she'd say, 'and someday I expect you to make a lot of money.' However, she also told me to hire a good secretary since I wasn't any good at English. I took her advice, because if I wrote you a letter, even now, you wouldn't be able to read it."

When Eckerd offered Frank a job, it was customary for the company's employees to take a polygraph exam. When the polygraph examiner discovered that FSU had recently graduated Frank, with a degree in criminology, he asked the obvious question: "What are you doing selling cameras?" Frank explained his situation, and the examiner asked him if he had ever thought about going to polygraph school, to become an examiner. It was a good business, the examiner explained. But it wasn't until he said, "You can charge by the hour," that Frank *really* paid attention.

"In my hometown," says Frank, "only the professional people could charge by the hour. The doctors and lawyers, the people who lived in the brick houses. The rich people. If a polygraph examiner could charge by the hour, *I* was interested."

So while Frank went to work selling cameras for Eckerd, he applied to polygraph school, and he eventually became a commercial polygraph examiner. By January 1979, he was twenty-nine years old, and he had managed to save the grand sum of $500. It was time, he decided, to start his own business. He set a goal for himself: to build the largest polygraph company in the country. And so he went to work.

The entrepreneur that he was, he approached the Sheraton Hotel near the Atlanta airport and offered to provide free polygraph tests for the hotel's employees in exchange for an office in the hotel's basement. He then called an attorney to incorporate his business and that's when he made his first mistake as a businessman. "I found this lawyer in the Yellow

Pages, called him and told him that I needed to incorporate my business. I asked him what it would cost. He asked me how much money I had and I told him $500. He said, 'That's exactly what it'll cost you to get your business incorporated.' "

Frank paid the attorney and went to work administering free polygraph exams during the day for the Sheraton Hotel. He also devoted what time he could to promoting his polygraph services to potential customers. To earn money, he worked nights as an undercover investigator for a guard company, and he also worked in security for a trucking company. "For about three months I had to work one twenty-four-hour day every week. From 8:00 A.M. to 5:00 P.M. I was a polygraph examiner. Then I went to work at night as an undercover agent. And at 4:00 A.M. I reported to the trucking company," he recalls. "Finally, to do the polygraphs, I hired another examiner to free up my day."

Meanwhile, Frank diversified into security- and transportation-related businesses. However, he didn't lose interest in the polygraph business, which he still intended to build into the country's largest company of its kind. With an examiner on board to help him during the day, he intensified his marketing efforts. "I started by going to every restaurant and club in Atlanta and asking them if they had a shrinkage (employee theft) problem. Of course every one of them did. I offered them my polygraph services, but very few people believed in it, or they didn't want to go to that extreme. So I came up with a deal no one could refuse. 'I'll polygraph ten of your employees,' I said, 'and if I don't get confessions from eight of them, you don't owe me a cent. But if I do get the confessions, you owe me $250.' Everyone accepted my offer, and I never lost. In restaurants and lounges, everyone does something wrong, and it would be easy for the test to expose it." Common confessions included waitresses who gave away drinks, and bartenders who charged twice for drinks and kept half the money. "One of the best scams was refilling Perrier bottles with soda water and selling it for Perrier!"

Within eight months of working his marketing plan, Frank had most of Atlanta's major nightclubs and finer restaurants under contract. As he continued to expand the polygraph business he hired additional examiners, and within three years of launching his company he employed sixty-five examiners. With Frank's help, they generated annual sales of $3 million! Suddenly he realized he had fulfilled his goal. He owned the world's largest polygraph business. "But no sooner than I realized it, I decided it was no big deal," he says. "It was only $3 million. And that wasn't much for a guy who supposedly had a knack for making money."

The big money was yet to come.

However, it wasn't going to come from polygraph exams.

Even before he hit the $3 million mark, Frank suspected the polygraph industry was headed for its demise. "The labor unions were making rumblings that they were going to rally against the exams," he recounts. And by 1986 that's what happened. The practice of screening job applicants and employees using a polygraph was legislated almost totally out of existence. "We still do a little bit of polygraph work today," Frank explains, "but by the end of the 1980s, our business was focused on outsourced contract labor."

And that's where he would fulfill his English teacher's prediction. Frank was destined to become successful by providing labor to other companies and industries.

In 1986, AHL Services, Inc. generated $14 million in annual revenues from outsourcing staff and some polygraph work. One day Frank called his management team together and told them it wasn't enough. He planned to build a $100 million business, and he set a goal to hit that number in ten years. "They didn't believe me, of course. Didn't believe we could do it. But they didn't dare say so, at least to my face. They worked for me, so what could they do?"

He was surprised, however, when his banker didn't believe him, either. "I applied for a $10,000 loan, but before I was approved my banker asked me the standard questions: 'What are you going to do with the money?' and 'What are your goals?' I said we're going to grow to $100 million by 1996. And he said, 'Frank, that is stupid. You can't grow internally to $100 million by 1996.' Well, he was right about that. I didn't. I made it in 1993!"

Late that year, the $100 million goal already past-tense, Frank called his management team together once again. It was time to set another Big Picture goal. "But when you're not good with numbers, which I'm not—I'm a motivator, I'm a driver—and when you're 'stupid' and you're doing $100 million, the next logical goal is not $200 million, or $500 million. It's a billion. At least that's the way you see it if you're not smart," Frank says with a chuckle.

So in 1993 he told his management team to plan on hitting $1 billion in annual revenue by 2003. "Once again they didn't believe me. In fact, the top guy in the team, the president of the company, didn't believe me. Behind my back he called me a buffoon for thinking that we could become a billion-dollar business. That's when I realized he wasn't a smart guy. The smart people figured out that once I set a goal, I'm like a blowtorch burning toward it."

Not surprisingly, Frank made a change in his leadership team. He then did something that everyone told him was impossible. He recruited and formed a partnership with Ed Mellett, who had been president of Coca-Cola USA and Europe. "No one believed a guy of that caliber would want to join my company," says Frank. "He's as smart as they come. But I am smart enough to know how dumb I am. That's why I have surrounded myself with very bright people. I believe in paying them well, and turning them loose. I'm not afraid to pay an executive more than I earn, especially if he's smarter than me."

Simultaneous to forming a partnership with Mellett, Frank organized an impressive board of directors and he became chairman of the board and co-CEO with Mellett.

In the mid-1990s, AHL's new leadership refocused the multinational company to provide contracting and outsourcing services for Fortune 500 companies worldwide. "And then we were off to the races," says Frank. Federal Express, Coca-Cola, Mercedes-Benz, BMW, BellSouth, Georgia Power, and Nike expanded the company's impressive list of Fortune 500 clients.

In 1997, the business that Frank Argenbright started with $500 became a public company. He retains approximately 50 percent of the business. His English teacher would be very proud.

"We're not going to hit a billion dollars in revenue by 2003," Frank admitted in 1999. "We're on track to hit the billion-dollar run rate in late 1999, four years ahead of schedule."

As he was interviewed for this book, Frank said he wasn't prepared to make any more predictions, except to say that he expected to see multibillion-dollar revenue years in the new millennium.

And to think that it all began by earning a few pennies.

CHAPTER SIX

BEGIN WITH AN IDEA

Tomima Edmark says: If you want an idea, look around, find a problem, and solve it. She's made a fortune doing just that!

The first step in starting a business is to get an idea of the type of business you're going to own and operate. For many people this turns into a huge step because they become overwhelmed trying to figure out complicated answers to rather simple questions. In other words, they make the process of coming up with an idea more complicated than it needs to be.

As people think about ideas for a business, they tend to simultaneously evaluate or judge each idea. Is the idea big enough? Small enough? Good enough? Original enough? At first blush, the answer to each of those questions is: No. It's easy to find something wrong with every idea. Consequently, many people never do much more than talk about going into business. Coming up with the right idea is a hurdle they can never get over.

Too often people wait to start a business because they want to come up with a novel idea, something never done before, or something that will set the world on fire. But novel ideas are rare. Besides, novel ideas frequently don't work, or they don't work fast enough. Some people have said that "the leading edge is the bleeding edge," meaning that people who pioneer new ground often have to pay a heavy price before they gain a reward.

When it comes right down to it, most businesses are copies of other businesses. Look around you and what do you see? Barber shops, ice cream shops, carpet cleaning companies, plumbing companies, gasoline stations, car washes, restaurants, donut shops, computer stores, furniture stores, dress shops, maid services, catering services, travel agencies, advertising agencies, and on and on. These are all businesses that we need today, and we will continue to need them in the foreseeable future.

Very often people get into business after seeing a business that they like. They decide they'd like to operate the same or a similar business. It's something they feel confident they can do; something they'd enjoy doing; something that would make them proud over a period of years. As a result, people often start businesses that are similar to already existing businesses. It's not plagiarism or trademark infringement because they operate under another name and they present their goods and services in their own unique way. Of course, some businesses require special skills training, but for the most part, if people are willing to apply themselves to the tasks at hand, they can learn how to operate most any business. People who don't want to use a great deal of their energy inventing a business from scratch often make the decision to become franchisees or licensees of already proven concepts. That way, they can focus on learning the operating system, building a customer base, and enjoying the economies of scale that many franchises provide.

If there's a business in your future, the idea for that business is probably right under your nose. I suggest you start with a familiar idea, one that you like and know that you can do. The simpler the idea the better. Make sure it's an idea that arouses your interest, and an idea that will make you proud. Then, go do it.

Don't focus too much on evaluating the idea. If you're

confident you'll enjoy the business and you can envision your long-term future in the business, and you know it's a business that customers will patronize, then it's time to get started. Until we got started with Subway, and we were able to assess the business and make improvements over time, we never really knew how good the idea was. The bottom line is this: Find a need, fill it, and be careful not to analyze the idea to death before you have a chance to test it. If you overanalyze it, you may never get started.

According to Tomima Edmark, an inventor in Dallas, Texas, and a very successful businesswoman, coming up with ideas isn't a special skill. It's a matter of looking around, finding a problem, and solving it. Tomima practices what she preaches, as you'll see in her profile. Her story isn't typical of the other stories you'll find in this book, but her approach is interesting. I think you'll agree that she adds a different twist to coming up with ideas.

Tomima Edmark didn't know how good her idea was until *Glamour* magazine publicized it in 1992. She thought of the idea one night in 1989 while accompanying her mother to a movie theater to see *When Harry Met Sally*. "A woman walking in front of us was wearing a French twist in her hair. I turned to my mother and said, 'I wonder if you can turn a ponytail inside out?'"

That was an odd, albeit creative question to ask. What causes someone to think about turning a ponytail inside out? Tomima admits it's a bit unusual, but explains, "It's a dyslexic type of thought, and I'm dyslexic." Rather than stifling her thought process, dyslexia spurred her creativity that night in the movie theater. She believes her impairment helped her consider a solution to a problem faced by millions of women. In fact, within several years her idea led to a product that aroused the fashion industry and eventually generated sales in excess of $100 million worldwide!

Tomima called it the TopsyTail, a device that helps women fashion their hair in a variety of styles, quickly and conveniently.

"After the movie that night," Tomima explains, "I went back to my mother's house and started playing with my fingers to create a loose version of what the hairstyle might look like." Using a circular knitting needle, and some masking tape, she fashioned a prototype for the yet-to-be-named TopsyTail. For the next several months she created new hairstyles using the prototype in her own long hair. She also looked for an opportunity to take the prototype to market. She didn't have a business at this time, and really didn't know much about starting one. She was especially good at coming up with ideas, though she didn't assign much value to that talent.

"People think coming up with a good idea is a gift," she says, "but I don't think so. A good idea comes from a need to improve something. People in search of ideas only need to look around them. What works and what doesn't work in your daily life? What frustrates you? Once you figure that out, you can think of a way to make it better or easier. You don't always have to invent something. Creativity takes many forms. If you're a housekeeper, come up with a way to be more efficient, or find a way to make better use of a common cleaning device. If you use tools, think of ways to use them more efficiently. Look at ways to improve your productivity, no matter what service you provide. To me, coming up with ideas is all about everyday life and making it better."

The TopsyTail wasn't Tomima's first invention, nor her last. "I was raised with five brothers," she explains, "so I wasn't afraid of fixing things or figuring out how they work. My dad was a gadget guy and I was his assistant. I can take a toaster apart and see what's wrong with it. I can look under the hood of the car and not be overwhelmed. In college I used to fix the girls' hair dryers. I can think outside of the box, and that's helpful when you're trying to come up with ideas."

At the time she invented the TopsyTail, Tomima was working for IBM as a marketing representative. "I had earned an MBA and I expected to rise to the top tier at IBM and become a big executive. But I soon found out I wasn't going anywhere with the company. I was going to be a marketing rep and that was it. Not that a marketing rep isn't a good thing. The money was great, but for me it became a trap. With a nice lifestyle and money to pay the bills it was hard to give that up and start a small business. But personally, I wasn't satisfied. I was an achiever and I wanted something more. I expected something more."

The TopsyTail distracted her from the numbness of her job. "It was my sanity," she claims. "Developing the TopsyTail helped me feel like I had a future. I worked on it at night and during the weekends. I didn't want to be married to IBM. With the TopsyTail, IBM wasn't in control of my life, I was."

By October 1989 Tomima consulted an attorney and applied for a patent to protect her TopsyTail design. Up until this time, her idea hadn't cost her any money. By December, however, she would need $3,500 to pay her patent attorney, and she didn't have the money. Fortunately, she was working on a major sale, and if it came through, she would collect a large commission check by year's end. "I decided that if I got the sale, I would invest my commission money in myself," she explains. The sale closed on schedule and Tomima collected more than enough to pay the attorney.

"There were many other things I could have done with that commission money," she recalls. "I had been working on that sale all year, so it was a major deal. I kept a tight budget waiting for my commission check. I didn't buy new clothes. I made lots of personal sacrifices. I didn't have the money to buy Christmas presents that year. I wasn't impoverished, but my lifestyle had maxed out my income. Things were tight. But I realized that if I wanted something more than what I could get out of my job, I had to make sacrifices. Too often people think they can have it all and not make sacrifices. But it doesn't happen that way."

Paying for the patent was just the beginning of the sacrifices, Tomima was soon to discover. With the product legally protected, she could now manufacture it. But that would require an injection mold to produce it. And the mold would cost $5,000—more money that she didn't have. But she wasn't discouraged. "When God closes a door," she says, "somewhere he opens a window. I have never run up against a wall in the development of my product. I've been frustrated. And there have been roadblocks. But I've never failed to find a solution. There's always an answer. That's my attitude. I keep searching until I find a solution."

Her solution for coming up with $5,000? Write a book! Another unusual idea, especially considering her dyslexia, and not to mention that she had never before written a book. "Actually I got the idea for the book before I thought of the TopsyTail. But now, because I needed the money, I decided it was time to move forward with the book." Even the subject of the book was unusual. It was about the art of kissing.

While she was in graduate school, she went out with a man one night and at the end of the evening she kissed him. "I didn't think the kiss was anything special," she says, "but *he* did! He said I was a great kisser." Rather than savoring the compliment, Tomima got to thinking about kissing. "I wondered what makes a great kiss," she says. "So I went to the library, where I spent most of my nights studying, and during a break I looked for a book about kissing." To her amazement, there wasn't one. "There wasn't anything about kissing," she continues, "and it was exciting to find a subject no one had written about. That meant I could become the self-proclaimed expert on kissing!" And that's what she did. Originally she didn't plan on writing the book herself. She thought she could find someone to write it for her, but when she sought the help of a writing teacher, the teacher coaxed her to do the writing on her own. She devoted weekends—"more sacrifice," she explains—to writing an outline and sample chapters of the book. Several months later she prepared a proposal for *Kissing: Everything You Ever Wanted to Know*. A major New York publisher bought the book in 1990 and offered her an advance of $7,500. Several more months passed until the book was completed and the advance money was in hand. She then invested $5,000 in an injection mold for the TopsyTail. And suddenly she was in business! She also became a best-selling author and went on to write two additional books on the subject of kissing.

By early 1991 the TopsyTail was in production and Tomima set up her business in a second bedroom of her house. "I still didn't have much money," she says, "so I could only market the TopsyTail by mail order. I also didn't have much time. I was employed by IBM so I only had evenings and weekends to work on my own business." By April 15, 1991, her birthday, she received her first two product orders. "I knew then that it was going to be successful," she says. She rented a post office box to collect orders and every evening after work she went to the post office to pick up her mail. She took the orders home, entered the customer information in a database, and then fulfilled the orders during the weekend. Every Monday she carried a load of packages to the post office during her lunch break.

For about a year Tomima continued to sell TopsyTail by mail order and most months her efforts generated $2,000 to $3,000. For someone who was "out of gas," as she says, "that was good money. It was the equivalent of being promoted two or three times at IBM and I was earning it with a lot less stress because I was still a marketing rep, and I didn't have the responsibility of someone who would have been promoted a couple of times. Plus, I was in control."

Tomima says she would have been content to continue working for IBM and selling her product on the side, but two events in early 1992 helped change her mind. First, IBM decided to downsize its workforce. Second, *Glamour* magazine published an article that promoted the TopsyTail.

IBM offered money—big money—to employees who voluntarily resigned. By accepting the offer, Tomima would collect a cool $25,000. She decided to go for it, especially when the article in *Glamour* landed $100,000 of orders in her post office box within three weeks.

With the savvy of a marketing rep, Tomima wasn't fooled by the flood of orders created by the magazine. "It was wonderful," she says, "but I knew it was fleeting. I couldn't keep up that level of excitement." Now, fortunately, she had some money to invest in her business. So she relied on another idea to catapult her business to the next level of success.

By this time, she had already placed the TopsyTail in the "mall of malls, the Galleria in North Dallas." One day in the mall she had discovered a kiosk that sold hair bows and other accessories and she convinced the owner to carry her product on consignment. But it didn't move. "Sitting there on a shelf, the TopsyTail wouldn't sell," explains Tomima. "It's a product that has to be demonstrated."

Her solution was to produce a video to show women how to use the TopsyTail to fashion fifteen different hairstyles. "I produced the video and took it to the kiosk with a video player and monitor and asked them to air it continuously during the weekend. Later that day, I got a call from the kiosk. The video caused a traffic jam in the mall! They needed all the inventory I could deliver immediately."

Within the next couple of weeks, Tomima began to realize the value of her idea. "The Galleria is an incredible mall. I wasn't aware of the kind of traffic it pulls. People come from all around the world. I started getting calls from Japan, Sweden, Germany—everywhere. They had all seen my video in the mall and they wanted to buy the TopsyTail and sell it in their countries."

The mall also opened the doors to a now defunct chain called Accessory Lady. "I had been trying to get their attention," explains Tomima, "but they weren't interested. They had 200 stores across the country and I wanted to be in them. When someone from Accessory Lady saw the video at the kiosk, they called me. I met with the president of the company and told her that the video made the difference. She decided to put a video in all 200 stores and the results were incredible. They put the video in the front windows and it stopped traffic. I eventually gave them a short-term exclusive license to sell TopsyTails in the USA."

The TopsyTail Corporation was now on a roll. "It was incredible," beams Tomima. "I started with no money and one day I was selling millions of units of my product . . . But it wasn't an overnight thing. People want immediate success in our society. We all want instant gratification. But success in business requires a game plan. I realized it would take more than a year or two to make my idea successful. I stuck to my game plan. I moved slow and steady, like a turtle."

By the mid-1990s, she was no longer moving slow, but progress was steady. Her video created an opportunity to feature TopsyTail in an infomercial. In its first three months airing on television, the TopsyTail infomercial sold 3.5 million units! The infomercial continued to air for about a year, but then knockoffs of the product started appearing and slowed sales.

"There's a cycle in this business," explains Tomima. "You get on television, you get into the department stores, then into the mass merchandisers, and finally you end up in the drugstore chains, where the product is deeply discounted. We used to sell the TopsyTail for $15, but you can buy it now for $5. We've run the full gamut with this idea."

A full gamut that, by the late 1990s, had resulted in more than 7 million units sold and substantial profit!

Since inventing the TopsyTail, Tomima has developed several new ideas, including a shield to protect celebrities from paparazzi. She also has invented a collapsible hat called the Halo. "I got the idea while I was on a cruise with my husband. I'm light-skinned, so I don't tan easily, I burn. I always want protection from the sun and it's frustrating because you can't travel with a big hat. They wreck your hair and you can't fit them into the overheads on airplanes. So while we were strolling on a pier in the Seychelles Islands, I said to my husband, 'Wouldn't it be great to have a hat that you can pack and carry and flip it open when you need it?' He thought it was a great idea, so when we got back to our stateroom I started working on it. I call it Heavenly Headware."

Once again, Tomima proves that frustrations lead to ideas. And her ideas tend to start small and finish big.

CHAPTER SEVEN

THINK LIKE
A VISIONARY

A "Big Picture" attitude helped Jim Cavanaugh start small in commercial cleaning and finish big with the world's largest company of its kind, Jani-King.

"We need to think beyond the first store. Let's set a long-term goal," Pete Buck said within an hour of my agreement to get into the submarine sandwich business with him.

It seemed to me like an unusual idea, setting a long-term goal when we hadn't even begun, but I later realized it was one of the best decisions we made. Setting a long-term goal moved our focus from the immediate goal of opening a store to the larger idea of what we might be able to achieve as entrepreneurs. It's been my experience that when people decide to start a business they don't always think about the "Big Picture." Usually they focus on getting started and accomplishing their immediate goals, and while that's a practical approach, the best entrepreneurs don't think like that. They are visionaries who benefit by their ability to see the Big Picture.

Of course, I really didn't understand this on that Sunday afternoon in Pete's backyard, but Pete did. Up until then, Pete hadn't been an entrepreneur, nor had he owned a business of any type, but he intuitively understood the importance of setting a long-term goal. Ultimately, setting a long-term goal proved to be critical in the development of our business.

Why is a long-term goal so important? Because it provides an ultimate destination that helps keep you focused. When you're challenged by problems and you think you've encountered a roadblock, you can focus your energy and make course corrections to keep your business moving toward the Big Picture. Day to day, the long-term goal may not seem relevant, but if you can't see the Big Picture you're probably going to lose your way and end up somewhere else.

Often just thinking about setting a long-term goal makes people uncomfortable. There's a lot of talent in corporate America consisting of people who want to do the best job they can for their company, and while they focus on the day-to-day work, they often fail to identify long-term goals. As a result, they don't always accomplish as much as they're capable of doing. There are articles, books, and seminars that teach people to think "outside the box" to set long-term goals, and while this may sound like a complicated subject requiring elaborate charts and graphs to extrapolate information, it's really much simpler than that. Anyone can set a long-term goal rather quickly, just as Pete and I did. In fact, it only took us a matter of minutes, and I'll tell you exactly how we approached it.

We followed Michael Davis's lead. The newspaper article about Mike's Submarine Sandwiches said he had opened thirty-two stores in ten years. The newspaper said that Mike Davis started out small, without a lot of money. He slept in the back room of his first store to be able to pay his bills. We didn't know any more about Mike's struggles than what we read in the newspaper, but if Mike opened thirty-two stores in ten years, that proved it could be done. That meant it could be done again. It was a goal worth working toward. It was a goal we believed we could accomplish. How we were going to accomplish it we didn't know, but at least we saw the Big Picture.

Through the years, we've set other Big Picture goals at

Subway. In the early 1980s, with only 200 stores in operation, we set a goal to reach 5,000 stores by 1994. Why 5,000 stores? That's the number I came up with after doing a quick market study of the leading fast food chains in America. I studied their store density, their rates of growth, their areas of heaviest distribution. Then I looked at their highest-density markets to gauge how well their stores were performing and I compared Subway's results in the same high-density markets. Based on industry trends, I concluded that if we focused on our development, there was a good possibility we could open 5,000 stores by 1994. So that's how I set the goal. It was more than an intelligent guess. It was more than desire. However, it wasn't a long, drawn-out process, either.

You don't need to agonize about setting a long-term goal. It's merely a matter of deciding what you want and setting your mark. More important than the long-term goal itself is the effort that's required to hit the mark. Both the goal and the time period allotted to accomplish the goal must be ambitious. But it shouldn't be a pipe dream. If you're really going to focus on the Big Picture that your goal represents, you need to believe that it can be done and that you can get it done.

Once you get started toward accomplishing a goal, stay focused, but don't be disappointed if you fall behind schedule. We missed our ten-year goal by one year by opening our thirty-second store in our eleventh year of business. On the other hand, we surpassed the 5,000th store several years ahead of schedule. By 1994, we had opened 8,000 stores, 3,000 more than our goal of 5,000 stores by that year!

Your goal is simply your objective. Figure out what you need to do to reach the goal, and then focus on making progress. It's the day-to-day progress that produces results—as well as excitement—and eventually helps you achieve the Big Picture. When you start, you don't know if you can accomplish the goal, but because you have a goal you're able to work toward it. At times you'll move ahead of schedule and occasionally you'll fall behind schedule. The important point is that you stay focused on your goal and continue to work toward it.

And if you miss the goal? You miss the goal. It's not the end of your business. Don't beat yourself up over it. Nothing bad is going to happen. It simply means the Big Picture you imagined for your business is further off in the distance. When we missed our ten-year goal we never for a moment doubted our abilities. We didn't have a memorial service, and we didn't obsess about it. We were still reaching milestones, so there was no reason to despair or give up. Based on our progress, we knew that our thirty-second store was within reach. It just took a little longer than planned to open it.

By the way, the Big Picture is different for everyone in business. Some people plan to own just one store, or operate one business from home, or from a van. Others plan to own several units of the same business, or perhaps several different businesses. Some people think nationally and others think globally. I want to emphasize that what matters most is that you think like a visionary and you determine your personal Big Picture, whatever it may mean to you.

Jim Cavanaugh started out as a microentrepreneur with a Big Picture attitude. He has built the world's largest commercial cleaning company, Jani-King, Inc., with sales in excess of $300 million. When he started the business in 1969, everyone he knew told him it was a bad idea and that he ought to remain in college, get a degree, and get a job. But Jim borrowed $3,000 and mentally set a goal to build a nationwide enterprise. He didn't tie his goal to a date, or to specific numbers, but he committed himself to continual progress in spite of adversity and frustrations. Today he oversees a company with 100 regional offices in a dozen countries. He'll tell you he accomplished it all because he remained committed to fulfilling his business vision. Here's his story.

Anyone who knew Jim Cavanaugh as a kid growing up in Norman, Oklahoma, might have guessed that he'd become a successful businessman even though he came from modest surroundings. He always had a job, and he almost always recruited friends to work with him, especially if they could help him get the job done faster, or if they could handle some aspect of the job that he didn't like. As an example, he built one of the largest paper routes in Norman, and probably all of Oklahoma. But he hired other kids to collect the money from his customers because that wasn't something he liked to do. Instead, he spent the extra time mowing lawns or selling greeting cards.

He was also quick to figure out how to make money. Every summer the University of Oklahoma hosted a preseason professional football game in Norman. A ticket to the game cost $6 but with $50 worth of grocery receipts from the local market, a ticket could be purchased for $1. Jim stood outside the grocery store and asked shoppers for their receipts. As soon as he collected $100 worth of receipts, he purchased two tickets, shelling out only $2 of his own cash. The next day he showed up at the supermarket to collect more receipts, and also to sell tickets—at $5 apiece! Every ticket he sold netted Jim a $4 profit, minus commissions for any friends who helped him.

It was 1969 when Jim started thinking seriously about a business career. He had spent several years studying at the University of Oklahoma's business school, but he wasn't very interested in the academics. It wasn't unusual for him to begin a semester and drop out, distracted by a job or an opportunity in another city. "I remember my friends in college talking about who we could go to work for, who would offer us the most money, and where we could get the best jobs," Jim recalls. "But I wasn't going to college to get a job. Jobs were easy to get. I already had several of them. Finding a job never interested me. I was entrepreneurial and I wasn't thinking about going to work for anyone." That he didn't have the money to start a business, or the experience, didn't concern him. "I knew the right opportunity would show up sooner or later," he says. "All I had to do was be prepared for it when it arrived. I learned that growing up as the oldest of eight kids."

While attending the University of Oklahoma, Jim was employed as the night auditor at the local Holiday Inn, and that's where he started thinking seriously about opening his own business. The job at the Holiday Inn required balancing the day's journals, including receipts from the hotel's restaurant. "Some nights," he recalls, "I'd have to check in guests, especially if they arrived after midnight, but mostly I balanced the books. To speed up the process I used three or four calculators to track the different entries, including phone charges and room service tabs, and even though I worked until 7:00 A.M. I usually had the job under control by two or three in the morning. That gave me time to study, and to catch a few winks." It also gave him time to think about the Big Picture that he might pursue.

"I read a lot about business and businesspeople," he recalls. "We had a newsstand at the hotel and I would borrow magazines at night and read them. I read about Holiday Inns and McDonald's and many of the other franchise businesses that were growing by leaps and bounds at the time. Those magazines gave me a lot of ideas." He researched a college report about Holiday Inns and took special notice of the company's national expansion via franchising. "I liked the idea of franchising. I already understood that people could help me get things done faster. But I especially liked the idea of a national enterprise. I hadn't spent much time out of Oklahoma, but I wasn't interested in starting anything local or regional, or owning a business in Norman. The type of business I owned didn't matter, but my dream was to expand nationally."

Since he didn't have much money, he read about how to earn more of it. *Think and Grow Rich* and similar titles attracted his attention. He attended seminars and he checked out opportunities that promised a path to wealth. He looked into real estate and didn't like it. He answered newspaper advertisements that promoted "get rich quick" schemes and fortunately discovered they were fraudulent before committing himself to any of them. He talked to as many people as he could about business, types of businesses, and opportunities to start businesses. Curiosity led him to dream up business ideas of his own.

One of Jim's first ideas was to set up greenhouses across the country to grow hydroponic tomatoes. It was an expensive idea, however, and he quickly dismissed it. Next, he thought about opening a network of day care centers. "Everything I read said that more women would be going to college and working outside the home," Jim remembers. "That led me to believe day care would become important in the future. So I designed a concept for 200 children, to include a medical staff and nutritionist, and playgrounds that you wouldn't believe. I wanted to create a day care environment that would make any parent feel comfortable about leaving their child with us." His enthusiasm for this idea led him to write a business plan. But when he added up all the costs he realized he had created a financial monster. "I didn't think I could find the investors for such a large business. I tried to scale it down, but that didn't work either. I talked to a bank about it and they said it would be nearly impossible to get any money. I was only twenty at the time and I didn't have anyone who could help back me financially. So I put the project aside and thought that I might return to it eventually because it was a great idea."

Meanwhile, in 1968, he struck up a friendship with a man who was contracted to clean the lobby, the rest rooms, and the restaurant of the Holiday Inn. "Don McGuffin was a meticulous janitor," recalls Jim, "and I used to talk to him at the hotel. He arrived every evening with his wife, or someone else to help him, and they'd bring in their equipment and vacuum the floors and buff the lobby floor. They usually came in between midnight and 2:00 A.M., depending on their previous cleaning jobs, and they'd spend a couple of hours at the hotel, then move on to their next job. I knew Don was being paid $400 a month for the cleaning contract and that was good money. It was much better than my $2 an hour. He worked at his own pace, his hours were flexible, and he could take on as much work as he wanted. All of that appealed to me."

Jim decided to do some research at the library about the commercial cleaning industry. "Most people wouldn't think of janitorial work, and most people wouldn't give it much respect. But I found out that a major communications company owned a janitorial business and one year it was the only company that made them any money. That impressed me. I thought that was respectable." Suddenly, Jim was extremely interested in commercial cleaning and he started spending more time with McGuffin.

One night Jim asked the janitor how he attracted new customers. "That was a sore point with Don. He got most of his work through word of mouth, but he could have had more of it had he been willing to go after it. He had his son hand out business cards and that occasionally generated some new business, but Don hated anything that had to do with marketing and sales. I said to him, 'Don, you own the business and you do such great work. You could have a very profitable business if you did more marketing. Why don't you create a brochure and pass it out to prospective customers?' He told me he wasn't interested. So I offered to make a brochure for him. 'If I get you some additional work, will you pay me a commission?' He said he'd be happy to."

If there was an area of expertise that Jim Cavanaugh had developed by the time he was a teenager it was marketing and sales. He wasn't afraid to knock on a door and ask for an opportunity to make a sale. Selling greeting cards and newspapers was good training for him. To Jim, the finder's fee that McGuffin promised to pay was like money in the bank. He wasted no time distributing a flyer that promoted carpet cleaning, and later, full-service cleaning. People responded immediately. "I got a couple of one-time contracts at sorority houses," he remembers, "but then I landed a bank and a real estate office. They needed to be cleaned nightly." It wasn't long before McGuffin told him to stop selling. He couldn't handle any more work!

By this time Jim was hooked on the commercial cleaning

industry. He started working with McGuffin to get comfortable with the equipment and to learn cleaning skills. He wasn't interested in cleaning long-term, however. He just wanted to know what was required. "I liked this business," he said, "so I wanted to know everything about it."

What he particularly liked about commercial cleaning was that just about anyone could do it. "You didn't need much money to get started in this business. With a mop and a bucket, a vacuum cleaner, a buffer, feather dusters and rags, a man or a woman could make a good living working from the back of their car or truck. There was no pressure. You could clean part-time or full-time and keep a daytime job if you wanted to. Even though people would make fun of being a janitor, this was a tremendous opportunity for the right people. I liked the idea that I could be the person who would help people get into their own business, fulfilling their own dreams."

It seemed to Jim that those tremendous opportunities were awaiting someone like him to come along and deliver continuity and professionalism to the commercial cleaning industry. Most cleaning was handled by mom-and-pop operators like the McGuffins. Most of them were capable of doing the work, but they didn't stay in the business very long. For one thing, they didn't know how to generate new accounts, so it was difficult to maintain a profit year after year. But also, they didn't know how to run a business. They could do the cleaning, but they weren't comfortable hiring and training employees, or handling customer complaints. They wanted to clean and they didn't want to run a business. That's where Jim Cavanaugh saw himself entering the scene, building a national enterprise.

Having read about franchising in *Forbes* and *Fortune* magazines, Jim understood the concept of making money by using other people's money. Soon he created a franchise program for janitors and he thought about selling it nationwide, even though the concept existed only in his mind and on paper. He never owned a franchise himself, and he never would, but he learned every aspect of the business.

111

"I believed I could help people in the cleaning industry and charge them for my services," he explains. "I could get them new work and also provide an office for them, making them appear all the more professional. All of their phone calls could be directed to my office, where I would take care of customer service for them. I would even do their billing and collect their money. Whatever needed to be done to operate their business, I would do it for them, or get it done for them, better than they could do it themselves. All they had to do was show up and clean, or supervise a staff of people who would do the cleaning for them. I figured this was an opportunity that I could roll out nationally."

McGuffin and other naysayers didn't think so, however. McGuffin told him his plan would never work and he advised him to get his college degree and look elsewhere for an opportunity. Several of Jim's family and friends agreed. He was a young man, so what could he possibly know? What he proposed to do—franchise the commercial cleaning industry—had never been done before. It was too risky, and it wouldn't work, they said. But Jim refused to yield to these objections. Obviously his family and friends didn't see the same Big Picture. They also underestimated his determination.

In 1969, Jim was still attending college, but not with any regularity. "I'd start a new semester but I'd quickly fall behind in my schoolwork because I was busy doing other work. To protect my grade point average I'd drop my classes, and after a while I really didn't have much interest in getting a degree. I only went to college because I lived in Norman. With the university in town everyone went to college." But after several years of on-again, off-again attendance, he decided to give up college and devote himself to building a business. He never did earn a college degree.

Eager to test his concept, which he had already named Jani-King, he borrowed $3,000 from a college friend in 1969 and launched his own commercial cleaning operation. For the next several years he operated the business so that he knew every detail of how to make it work. During this time he made a couple of attempts at selling a franchise, but he didn't get serious about franchising until 1974. That's when he advertised for franchisees in the Oklahoma City newspaper. For $2,500, and a small ongoing royalty, the Jani-King franchise opportunity included the basic cleaning equipment and supplies, and the promise that Jim would generate cleaning contracts. He even offered to finance a portion of the fee, requiring only a small down payment to get started.

"I knew people would be hesitant to pay me any money. I was a young guy and a stranger to Oklahoma City. Besides, franchising didn't have a very good reputation at the time. Prior to the laws that have since regulated franchising, there were many fly-by-night concepts that gave franchising a bad name. So I made it as easy for people to invest as possible. The equipment that I provided was worth every bit of the down payment, so my prospects could see that I wasn't going to pull a fast one. I told people that the only way I could make any money was to go out and sell cleaning contracts for them. I was banking on their future."

His sales pitch worked. Within ninety days he sold five franchises in Oklahoma City and he opened a local office with a receptionist to provide support. In much less time he sold enough cleaning contracts to keep all of his franchisees busy. In fact, his productivity quickly became problematic. He generated more work than his franchisees wanted—and that was a challenge he had not anticipated. He was honor-bound not to sell any more franchises in the city because that was part of his original sales presentation. There would only be five franchises in Oklahoma City, he had told his prospects. He would never have guessed that he could generate more work than the five franchisees would desire. That being the case, however, he decided to expand his network to another city sooner than planned. "After selling contracts that I couldn't place, I told the franchisees that I couldn't earn enough money working with them. They would continue paying me a royalty, and I would return to generate new contracts for them, as needed, but I had to move on. They didn't have a problem with that. They were happy." So Jim moved to Tulsa and started the process all over again.

This time, however, he didn't promise to limit the number of franchises. That way, as he sold cleaning contracts he could continue selling franchises. He made some other adjustments to his program and he quickly established his second Jani-King market. There was little doubt now in Jim's mind that he had something of value to offer the commercial cleaning industry. What he didn't know for sure, however, was whether or not he could make any money at it. "I quickly learned that I didn't know the numbers well enough," Jim explains. "In the early days I made some critical mistakes that I had to correct along the way."

For one thing he didn't charge a high enough royalty. For another, he didn't charge the franchisees a finder's fee when he sold cleaning contracts for them. Consequently, the franchises didn't generate enough revenue for Jim to cover the costs of supporting them through local offices. Even worse, there was no money left over to pay his salary. He didn't let the franchisees know it, but he was personally broke. In fact, he was evicted from his apartment in Oklahoma City and forced to live at the office. Before things got better, his car was repossessed in Tulsa. He was living from day to day, but he never missed a beat. Even while he was being clobbered with problems, he never lost sight of the Big Picture that he envisioned for Jani-King. Instead of getting discouraged and possibly quitting, Jim remained persistent and obstinate. He clung to his commitment to build a national enterprise.

"I believed in what I was doing," he remembers. "I never expected to get rich quick. I had developed a unique concept and I had the confidence that eventually it would work out for everyone, including me. I made some mistakes in the beginning, but there was no playbook. No one could show me the right way to do it because no one had done it before. There were other companies in the industry that I could study, including another franchise company, but they weren't doing things my way. I was a pioneer." And he wasn't giving up.

From Tulsa he moved south to Dallas. He borrowed a station wagon from his father and lived out of it until he could afford to rent an efficiency apartment. For the next several years he devoted his time to the franchise networks in Dallas, Tulsa, and Oklahoma City. As he improved the franchise opportunity he stabilized the business until he was ready to begin expanding again. He opened Fort Worth in 1979, and he began a business blitz in the 1980s that continued well into the 1990s. He opened Houston, Atlanta, St. Louis, New Orleans, Kansas City, Detroit, and as many additional cities as his money would allow. By the early 1990s Jani-King also entered international territories.

"Our growth was slow," explains Jim, "because I didn't have the money to expand any faster. I'd open a city, wait for it to become profitable, and then move on to the next city. I didn't want to sell off parts of my company for additional capital, so I made the choice to invest in my business rather than in my lifestyle. Instead of buying a new car, or taking a great vacation, I plowed the money back into the business." His personal life was practically nonexistent, but he considered the loss part of the price he had to pay to fulfill his vision.

In some cities he hired managers; in others he licensed the franchise rights to entrepreneurs. For years he was constantly on the road, or in the air, opening a new city, or backtracking to lend support in another city. Even though he was based in Dallas, he kept his office in his briefcase. During weekdays he sold cleaning contracts and franchises, bought and tested equipment, trained managers, master licensees, and franchisees. Most nights someone wouldn't report to work with a cleaning crew so he'd pitch in to help. On weekends he sold franchises and worked on his business plan. It was a pace that he maintained for many years.

As is true of most entrepreneurs, Jim Cavanaugh's energy was boundless. So was his desire for perfection. "Whatever

Jani-King did," he explains, "it had to be first-class, and that's the way it always will be. I want everything perfect. Our letterhead, brochures, our franchise program, the cleaning we do, it has to be done right or I'm not happy about it."

Many days there was plenty not to be happy about. "Building my business, building any business, is 99 percent perspiration and 1 percent inspiration," he says. "A lot of people can find the 1 percent, but it's the 99 percent that's difficult to sustain. There were lots of days when things went wrong and I'd want to ask myself, 'Why am I doing this?' Most of the time it was impossible for me to plan to do anything outside of work. I never knew when we were going to start a new cleaning job that might require my help. I worked Christmas, the Fourth of July, weekends, holidays—but it didn't matter. I was dedicated to building a national brand and I never expected it to be easy. On those days when I thought about being discouraged, I just took a look around me. In every city there were people who had jobs who weren't happy. I wasn't going to be one of those people. I wouldn't let discouragement creep into my life. I would talk to myself, remind myself that the future for Jani-King was sound. If I needed to make some changes, I'd make them and we'd move on. I was focused. But I had to be if Jani-King was going to be successful."

Actually, Jani-King's success was pretty much a given the moment Jim Cavanaugh decided not to listen to his detractors in 1969. His commitment to his goal made all the difference. However, there was a lapse of many years before anyone but Jim recognized the company's success. And then, the public discovered Jani-King, and Jim became a hero within an industry that he had created. In 1985, *Venture* magazine listed Jani-King among the top franchises for return on investment. That same year, *Entrepreneur* magazine ranked Jani-King among the top janitorial and maid service franchises. Two years later, *Entrepreneur* created a new category solely for commercial cleaning franchises and ranked Jani-King number one. The company held that honor through the late 1990s when Jani-

King's network included more than 6,000 franchises and the company was selling a franchise every hour of the business day.

Among franchise companies worldwide, few success stories compare to Jani-King's. And few microentrepreneurs have reached the success of Jim Cavanaugh. From the profits of his business Jim has been able to make many investments, including several that coincide with his personal interests. Aircraft always fascinated him, for example, and so he developed the Cavanaugh Flight Museum, which preserves and protects many of America's most famous warbirds. Housed at the Addison Airport near Dallas, Texas, the museum chronicles the heroes, battles, and technological advances of seven decades of flight. More than thirty aircraft occupy several hangars that span 50,000 square feet. The museum is a magnificent treasure that Jim has opened to the public.

He also has invested in his own aircraft for business and personal adventures. He owns a couple of yachts, he publishes a magazine devoted to the subject of franchising, and he has invested wisely in real estate.

"I like to tell people that the nice thing about not growing up with anything is that I didn't think I was missing anything when I remained devoted to building my business year after year. I was also fortunate that I didn't graduate from college and go to work for a company and get comfortable. I wasn't afraid to keep my focus on the vision that I held for Jani-King. The road to success was more difficult and time consuming than I had imagined, but as a result of sticking to the plan, I have helped thousands of people own their own businesses and create rewarding lives for themselves. At the same time, I created a life for myself that probably would not have been possible working for someone else."

Jim Cavanaugh's success is summed up in this single lesson: *Think like a visionary. Always look for the Big Picture.*

CHAPTER EIGHT

KEEP THE FAITH

Even an F from his college professor didn't stop Ian Leopold from starting his publishing business. That's because he believed in what he was about to do. Today, he's the mastermind of a $10 million company.

When you tell your relatives, friends, and neighbors that you plan to start your own business, some of them will go out of their way to convince you that you can't do what you plan to do. They may say your idea will never work, or they may tell you to keep your job and play it safe. They might tell you it's too risky, or you don't have the background, the money, the knowledge, or the drive to succeed in business.

Certainly you should consider what they say because it's important to evaluate the upside and the downside of any business venture. There may be kernels of wisdom in their negative comments, but regardless of who the naysayers are, it doesn't mean they're right. While you should consider their opinions, and weigh them as you make your plans to start a business, don't allow others to throw cold water on your plans. If it's going to be your business, you need to make decisions for yourself. And as you do, you have to continue to believe in yourself and your business.

Few people, it seems to me, start a business with as much support as I received. I suspect people realized that since I was young, if I made a mistake, I could rebound. Plus, there wasn't much at risk for me, and for Pete there was only a small investment.

In spite of the support, I didn't have a grand plan for my life. I was enrolled in college and I was building a business, but I never actually thought of the business as my long-term future, or as a career. That changed, however, when the Vietnam War was heating up. I had decided to join the Army Reserve before my draft board intervened in my life, and that's how I arrived at Fort Polk, Louisiana, with other college guys from around the country.

One night in the barracks I sat in a corner with several other guys who were talking about their future. Some of the guys took turns explaining what they planned to do after graduation. I was impressed. Some would become doctors and lawyers. One shared his political aspirations. Another planned to work overseas. Others looked forward to starting their own businesses, or joining family businesses. They were planning some exciting things.

Sitting there, I started thinking about my future. Where was I headed? What great plans had I made? What was I going to do? I was only a few months away from graduation. So what were my career plans? Like the fellows around me, I was capable. I could achieve success. There probably wasn't another guy in the barracks who had already started and operated a successful business, humble though Subway was at the time. But what *was* I going to do?

That's when it occurred to me.

I was already doing something meaningful; something that was way ahead of the other guys. Subway was a tangible business, and it had more substance than any idea these fellows were talking about.

In the barracks that evening, I realized that the work I had done to date really created a foundation for something bigger and better. Until then I had not thought of Subway as a career; had not thought of myself as a business leader. But then I realized that these fellows in the barracks were still preparing to take their first steps, while I already had a great start. By struggling to establish a business, I had already developed skills, learned a lot, and was now ready to accomplish something bigger.

Not long thereafter, I left Fort Polk a better man: physically stronger, and mentally committed to building a successful business. Regardless of the challenges that came my way, I was going to keep the faith. And, while I wouldn't have said it quite this way at the time, I was going to finish big; bigger than I had ever imagined.

I've often wondered if this epiphany would have occurred had I not already enjoyed at least a little bit of success in my business. Would Subway exist today had people discouraged me along the way? I'll never know because that wasn't my experience.

It *was*, however, the experience of a microentrepreneur in Baltimore, Maryland. Even before Ian Leopold started his business, he had to learn to keep the faith. A dozen successful years later, people still try to discourage him. "I don't think that ever stops," says Ian. "But after a while, you don't even hear them."

———————

Everyone told Ian Leopold that his idea for Campus Concepts wouldn't work. It was a crazy idea, they said. In fact, when he wrote a business plan and submitted it to his economics professor at Hobart College during his senior year, he got an F! You'd think a failing grade from an authority figure like an economics professor would have put Ian in his place and convinced him to come up with a new idea. But it didn't happen.

"If you want to survive in business," says Ian, "you've got to dig deep." In other words, you've got to believe in yourself and your business.

While growing up in Connecticut, Ian began thinking of himself as a businessman while he was a teenager. "I think I've always been an entrepreneur," he explains. "When I was fifteen I started Little League Photo. It didn't cost me anything to get started. I played baseball and I knew how to use a camera. So I would snap team photos, and then offer to sell the photos to parents. Then, I underbid the other photographers in town and became the official team photographer—my first coup! I wasn't old enough to drive at the time, so my mom drove me around to deliver the photographs."

Several years later, Ian entered Hobart College in Geneva, New York, where he was attracted by the small liberal arts environment and the opportunity to play soccer with the Hobart Statesmen. During his junior year, at age nineteen, he conceived the idea to start the Statesman Lobster Company and sponsor an annual Lobster Bash for the local college crowd. "I wasn't as interested in making money as I was in the experience of operating the business," he says. "The idea was to throw a big bash with steamed lobsters, beer, and live music, and donate the profits to the United Way. I worked out a schedule to call the docks in New Hampshire the morning of the bash. I'd buy the lobsters with my credit card, and get them picked up and flown to campus by that afternoon. I thought it was a great idea."

So did a thousand other people who showed up for the first Lobster Bash. With only 1,800 students at Hobart, 1,000 people was a huge turnout.

But even so, Ian lost $3,000!

"I was stupid," he says. "I hired all my college friends to help me. The guys who were supposed to collect tickets that had been sold in advance, and sell tickets at the door, decided to let everyone in, with or without a ticket. After it was all over, and I was back at my dorm trying to figure out where things had gone wrong, I ran into a teammate from soccer. He was happily drunk, and he told me that he had just come from the Lobster Bash where he drank and ate all night and didn't have to pay. He couldn't believe it. 'No one had to pay!' he gushed.

"I couldn't believe it, either. But that's what happened. After that, I learned the importance of control points in business."

For the next three years, Ian organized an annual Lobster Bash in Geneva, and beginning the second year, he made certain no one was admitted without a ticket. The events never produced much money for him, but his payoff came later when he was accepted at Northwestern University's Kellogg Graduate School of Management, at the time, the top graduate business school in the country. Many newspapers, including the *New York Daily News*, wrote about the Lobster Bash and featured the young entrepreneur who conceived the idea. "When I interviewed for admission to graduate schools, the articles that had been written about me carried a lot of weight," notes Ian. "Everyone saw that I was entrepreneurial. They saw that I made things happen, and ultimately, that's what won my admission to Kellogg."

Between his junior and senior years at Hobart, Ian moved home with his parents, who had relocated to Michigan. To earn some money that summer, and to maintain ties with his contacts on the docks in New Hampshire, he decided to open the LobsterShack restaurant. "The docks in Saugatuck, Michigan, were close to my parents' home," he explains, "so I went down there one day and found an old shack that I thought I could rent. I told the owner of the shack what I planned to do. I had this idea for a down-and-dirty Red Lobster type of establishment, and I thought I might open shacks around the country and build a $200 million business. The owner of the shack looked at me and said, 'Okay, I'll be your partner.'

"I wasn't looking for a partner, and I told him so. He then said, 'You see those four restaurants that surround my shack? I own those restaurants. If someone is going to eat at your shack and not eat at one of my restaurants, and all I'm getting is your rent, we're going to be partners. Or you can read about the great idea you just gave me. I'll do it without you.'

"I extended my hand and said, 'Hello, partner!' And all that summer I worked my butt off and didn't make a dime."

The summer wasn't a total loss, however. Ian explains that "two good things" came from his experience with the Lobster-

Shack. First, he learned that he didn't want to own a restaurant, or for that matter, any retail business. "You don't own those kinds of businesses," he says, "they own you. You always have to be there." And that was too confining for him.

Second, all summer he was approached by people who wanted to sell him advertising. Business owners generally frown upon unsolicited sales calls from advertising representatives. Ian was no exception. He didn't want to buy advertising. He wanted to make money. However, the constant flow of salespeople to his shack that summer inspired the genesis for his next business brainstorm.

"When I went back to Hobart that fall for my senior year, I noticed a variety of publications that were targeted to capture the interests of the college student population. *Campus Voice, Newsweek on Campus*, and *Business Week Careers* were three of the more recognized titles," Ian recalls. Big media companies, including Time Warner, McGraw-Hill, and Whittle Communications, had published these magazines for several years and distributed them on campuses around the country. "The subject matter of the magazines was pretty much the same: How to write a résumé, What to do on spring break, and similar routine topics. Of course, the magazines were loaded with national advertising.

"From what I could tell," Ian continued, "distribution was a problem. The media companies shipped stacks of shrink-wrapped magazines to our campus and somehow someone was supposed to unwrap the bundles and conspicuously place the magazines in locations where students would pick them up and read them. But when you went into the Student Union at Hobart, kids were sitting on stacks of these magazines, or standing on them, or the magazines were strewn on the floor. I don't know that anyone ever read them.

"While I saw this happening, the memory of all those people who tried to sell me advertising in Michigan was still fresh in my mind. I liked the freedom of an ad rep's life. They weren't confined by the walls of their business. They could go out and make business happen. At the same time, I thought these big media companies had a good idea. They simply weren't executing it effectively. The college student market is huge and lucrative, and there had to be a better way to tap into it."

Ian intended to develop that "better way." After thinking about the opportunity for a few weeks, he concluded that the problem wasn't really distribution, it was the generic content of the magazines. "How many times do you want to read about the best way to write a résumé?" The content was bland, and college students weren't interested in reading it, at least not more than occasionally. "What students needed," Ian explains, "was a book about students, by students, and about the student community. Local advertisers would support that kind of publication. With relevant content, including schedules, campus phone numbers, and a variety of information, I imagined every student would use this book regularly."

Ian shared his idea with a friend, and almost overnight the two of them created Campus Concepts, the business entity that would publish the *UnOfficial Student Guide*, the title they selected for their book. "Giving ourselves a few weeks to sell the advertising to support the book," Ian recalls, "we scheduled the premiere issue for January 1988." Total start-up costs for this venture were $96, which the partners split evenly. "We used some of the money to buy business cards," says Ian, "and the balance to pay for an answering machine, although we argued about whether or not we needed it. That was it. That's how we got started."

Right on schedule, the partners sold $2,000 of advertising space to local retailers, gathered the content of the book, designed the book, and found a printer.

Before going to press, however, they decided to insert their own ad in the book to sell college sweatshirts. "The bookstore manager at Hobart had a disagreement with Champion, who supplied heavyweight college sweatshirts, so you couldn't buy a Hobart sweatshirt. I was a soccer player and I wanted a sweatshirt with a big purple H on the front. Many other students did, too. So we saw the opportunity to contact Champion, sell sweatshirts, and create a second profit center for our business."

In January, copies of the *UnOfficial Student Guide* were delivered to the Hobart campus and students grabbed them upon sight. "The book was immediately popular," explains Ian, "because it was relevant. The content provided useful information as well as coupons that the students could use locally."

More importantly, the guide was a financial success. Producing the books cost $1,000, leaving $1,000 of ad sale money for the partners to split.

"In addition, we made a good profit from sweatshirt sales," Ian recalls. "We sold at least one sweatshirt for every student enrolled. Many students ordered two and three." However, this profit center would quickly disappear. "We sold so many sweatshirts that Hobart wrote a letter to Champion and claimed possession of the block-styled H. Rather than get into a tiff with the university, Champion decided not to sell sweatshirts to us in the future."

Nonetheless, Ian relished the success of the *UnOfficial Student Guide*. "Our advertisers loved the guide as much as the students did," he says. "Some of them bought me lunch to thank me for the exposure. The book really worked for them, and that made me feel good. Many of the advertisers encouraged me: 'Looks like you've got something here,' they said."

The added encouragement helped Ian envision a future for the publication. "I started thinking about producing these books on college campuses across the country. My partner liked the idea, too. By hiring students on other campuses, and teaching them how to produce a book for their campus, we could create a critical mass circulation for advertisers. Then we could compete with the big media companies."

The idea was so compelling that Ian decided to write a business plan and submit it for credit in an independent study course. He needed a passing grade to graduate that spring.

Grades, however, didn't interest him, especially since he had already been accepted by Kellogg, where his transcript proved less important than his entrepreneurial drive. Ian describes himself as a "crappy, inconsistent student." Up to this point, he hadn't earned an A in his life, although he maintained a B-minus average. Unfortunately, his average didn't hold up that spring. His business plan was returned with an F.

"Even though I had already proven that my concept worked, the professor failed me," explains Ian. "He criticized my economic models, and my analyses, but mostly he said my work was 'sloppy.' He said he either gave an A or an F for an independent study, and nothing in between. Since I hadn't turned in A-quality work, I got an F." Ian admits the business plan was rough, and while it didn't deserve an A, it didn't deserve an F. "I had asked another professor to read the business plan and he agreed that it was good enough for a passing grade. But my economics professor had the final word. I said to him, 'Maybe in ten years I'll understand why you failed me.' He said, 'No, you probably won't.' And that's how we left it."

The F was a serious blow not only to the future of Campus Concepts, but to Ian's immediate plans for graduation and graduate school. "It was a devastating moment," Ian remembers, still troubled by the experience. "Here I was, twenty-two years old, and I'm on my way to earn an MBA at Kellogg. I'm feeling great about my business, my future, and myself. And suddenly I can't graduate with my class.

"As I left the professor's office I was shocked. I'm thinking, I've got to call my parents and tell them the bad news. They'll have to postpone their plans for my graduation. I'm not getting a degree. I'll have to spend another semester at Hobart. Just when I thought things couldn't get any worse, I walked out of the building and a bird dropped a load on my head! That brought me back to reality real fast, and I started laughing hysterically."

But nothing changed the fact that he wouldn't graduate that spring. The president of the university came to his aid, and asked the economics professor to reconsider the grade, but to no avail. "I was stuck in Geneva for the summer," Ian says, "and there was no way around it. I signed up for another independent study course, this time with the chairman of my department, and that's how I finally got my degree."

Meanwhile, in spite of his economic professor's evaluation of his business plan, he decided to continue Campus Concepts that summer in Geneva. His partner had already graduated, had fallen in love, and left for Europe, only to return a year later to attend graduate school at Columbia University. "He lost interest in the business," explains Ian. "I decided to keep the business going myself."

During five weeks of summer, while he completed his independent study, he more than doubled the advertising revenue in the *UnOfficial Student Guide*. "Ad sales hit $5,000 for that second issue, and the additional money made up for the loss of sweatshirt sales. It wasn't a bad return for five weeks of work."

That fall, Ian arrived in Chicago and registered at Kellogg where he would concentrate on brand management. "Even though I saw an opportunity with the *UnOfficial Student Guide*, and I had proven its value twice, I wasn't totally convinced that I was in the business for the long term. It was a great way to make some money while I was in school. I wanted to own my own business someday, but I also had dreams about working in a large corporate environment. Kellogg was a great place to position myself for a corporate job that might eventually lead me to an entrepreneurial career."

Even so, he didn't intend to surrender Campus Concepts. He hired a student at Hobart to produce the guide during the next year. The guide's first-year popularity helped increase ad revenue to $10,000 that fall.

Meanwhile, at the end of his first academic year at Kellogg, Ian was awarded an internship at Frito-Lay for several weeks, and then a one-week internship at the Leo Burnett Advertising Agency. At the time, it was exactly what he wanted. Or so he thought.

"Frito-Lay is a multibillion-dollar company and of all the marketing internships to be had, this was the one everyone wanted," explains Ian. "I expected it to be an exciting opportunity that might lead to permanent work." He was disappointed when the internship failed to live up to his expectations. "It just wasn't fun," he says. "They were into corporate structure, which is okay, but the work was dull. It was pretty much an exercise in minutiae. I did drills of various types, and spreadsheet analyses, but no one asked for my opinions or interpretations, or even offered an explanation of why I was doing what they assigned me to do. I had no idea if my work had any relevance to the company, and no one was going to tell me. It was basically 'Do this and get it back to me.' It wasn't creative, and even though it was only an internship, I suddenly began losing interest in a big corporation. I expected something greater than what I discovered."

That fall, when he returned to Kellogg, he still intended to work for someone other than himself after he graduated, and during the academic year he interviewed for several jobs with Fortune 500 companies. By October, Progressive Insurance in Cleveland, Ohio, offered him a position to start the next September. Simultaneously, he developed a plan to expand Campus Concepts in New York state as soon as possible. After he graduated, Ian moved back to familiar upstate New York and executed a plan that launched the *UnOfficial Student Guide* on college campuses in Syracuse, Rochester, and Ithaca, all within proximity of his flagship book in Geneva.

"I was going to have a great summer before I went to a real job," he says. "I was out of money by this time, but selling was always easy for me. During the nine weeks before I had to report to my job, I was going to establish the new books, and make a lot of money. I wasn't going to do it all on my own. I hired several college students to help me. I paid them commissions on their sales. At the end of the summer, I intended to turn the guides over to them to manage for me."

While it all sounded good, by now Ian should have known

that even a sure thing isn't a sure thing in business. What do they say about the best-laid plans? Of course, with the exception of that first Lobster Bash, Ian had never lost money in business, and he wasn't going to that summer, either. However, he also wasn't going to make as much money as he had intended.

"I learned a lot that summer," he recalls. "First, I learned that you have to hire smart people when you have your own business. Then, you have to train them, and continue training them, motivate them and listen to them. Unfortunately, I made some mistakes hiring people and I lost a lot of money.

"I also made a mistake when I selected Ithaca. It was close to the other cities, and it seemed to make sense to start a book there, but the guy I hired couldn't make enough sales. So I moved to Ithaca to try to salvage the book. That was painful. I didn't have any money, so I rented a room at a fraternity house for $25 a week. I had a little refrigerator, but all I had to eat were bagels and cranberry juice. I didn't have a phone, and I didn't have a calling card, so I carried rolls of quarters with me and used pay phones to make my calls. In the end, it didn't work. The retail community was too small to support a book, and I just didn't realize it."

There was at least one other mistake made that summer. Ian hired a friend to start the *UnOfficial Student Guide* at the University of Colorado in Boulder. "That made no sense geographically," he says retrospectively. "I couldn't manage Boulder from Ithaca, and my friend needed more help than I thought. Along with Ithaca, it was another loss."

Even so, by summer's end, after all the advertising revenue was collected, and commissions and printing bills were paid, Ian netted a little less than $30,000. "For the time I invested I think I should have made a lot more," he says with disgust. "But for nine weeks of work, it wasn't a bad return."

In September 1989, after hiring a full-time manager to continue Campus Concepts, twenty-four-year-old Ian reported to work in Cleveland and won the respect of his superiors in short order. "Progressive assigned me to their credit life business, which was losing half a million dollars a year. My job was to turn it around. So I brought in new accounts, canceled bad accounts, and within five months the division was profitable. The company then assigned me to a start-up business selling annuities, and not long after that I was promoted to director of sales for another unit of the company. Within eighteen months I was promoted three times, and they were paying me $100,000 a year, including salary and bonus. Meanwhile, Campus Concepts generated revenues of $75,000, and out of that paid me another $25,000." For a guy who lived off bagels and juice just eighteen months earlier, it was a ton of money.

But he wasn't particularly happy. More than ever, he realized that his future wasn't in corporate America, and he began plotting his return to upstate New York and his own business. It wasn't until his mentor left Progressive, however, that he found a graceful way to tender his own resignation.

In 1990, he moved into an apartment in Rochester, New York, assumed his role as president of Campus Concepts, and announced to family and friends that he intended to build the greatest college marketing company in America.

"Are you sure that's the best use of your time and talent?" some wanted to know. "Do you think you did the right thing giving up the prestige and security of a job with a Fortune 500 company?" others wanted to know. For Ian, there was no turning back.

"Before I take my greatest risks," he explains, "I tend to share the news and maybe boast about it. That sort of forces me to jump off the cliff and succeed."

With Ian at the helm full-time, Campus Concepts generated sales of $250,000, and with continued expansion on the East Coast, the business topped $500,000, and then $1 million by 1991. That year, Ian relocated the company to Baltimore. "It looked like a good city for a corporate office, and we could easily continue our expansion from there," he explains.

He was as much right as he was wrong. Baltimore proved to be the right place for a young, enterprising businessman, but it was the wrong time to expand the business. "The downturn of the economy in 1992 cut right into the heart of local advertising sales, and for the first time ever we lost money. I didn't see it coming, either. Here I was, an MBA, a graduate of Kellogg, and up to this time, except for that F, things had pretty much gone my way. I was a young guy with a big ego. Made $100,000 income right out of graduate school. Built a million-dollar business with a $48 investment. Told people that I was going to build this great marketing company. And all of a sudden I took a big whack. I lost $350,000!"

It was bad, but it wasn't bad enough to shake Ian's belief in his business. "No, I wasn't giving up," he says. "I felt defeated, things were out of control, and I thought the situation stunk. I could have filed for bankruptcy, but I had too much pride to do that. I was still passionate about Campus Concepts. I may have failed that year, but I didn't see myself as a failure. I still had a lot to learn, but one thing I instinctively knew was that I had to believe in my business and myself. Give up on either one, and your business is dead."

To climb out of that 1992 debacle, Ian reevaluated Campus Concepts. "First thing I did was call two of my roommates from graduate school and I sold a third of the company. This business was far from being dead. We were approaching a circulation of a million students, and our advertisers continued to be excited about our product. In spite of the loss, Campus Concepts was a valuable asset, and my friends eagerly bought into the company. When I said I was going to build America's greatest college marketing company, they believed me."

He also developed a new marketing strategy. "I kept thinking there had to be something other than local advertising to drive revenue into these books. Obviously there was national advertising, but we needed a stronger presence to get the attention of national accounts, and their savvy ad agencies. Then one day it hit me. The number one extracurricular activity on college campuses is intramural/recreational sports. A dozen guys play basketball for the University of North Carolina, but thousands play intramural basketball on that campus. So I contacted the National Intramural Recreational Sports Association, and after a series of meetings we formed an alliance to promote participatory sports nationwide." Eventually, this partnership began producing national intramural sports championships with top brands contributing the money. Nike, for example, sponsored a national Flag Football Championship, which included 100 college intramural programs. Pepsi sponsored a basketball tournament that attracted 100,000 students. Diet Pepsi, Aquafina, and Nike backed a training and fitness program with 500,000 student participants.

"After a few years of fiddling with the same idea," says Ian, "we changed the paradigm, broke the mold, and created a greater opportunity."

And he wasn't finished yet. By 1997, he stopped selling local advertising and started pursuing national accounts. "Local ad sales were labor intensive," he explains. "Our average sale was $500, with 3,000 transactions a year, and we only had about nine weeks to hit our revenue goals before we had to prepare a book for publication. That required a huge sales force of college students. Managing the people, and dealing with the problems at the local level used up a lot of my brainpower. So I decided to give the local retailers free advertising on a selective basis. We chose the most popular retailers and then, if they agreed to give our readers at least a 25 percent discount, we gave them a free coupon in the guide."

By transitioning from local to national accounts, Campus Concepts saved overhead and time. "We no longer needed a big sales department, just five people," continues Ian. "Our client base dropped to fifty companies, cutting our transactions in half. However, our minimum sale immediately jumped to $40,000, and our average sale to $200,000-plus. Dealing with larger accounts, rather than many small accounts, we have more time to give our clients better service. We've also been able to make improvements to the books and that has encouraged more readership. On average, students use our books 3.5 times a month. National advertisers love what we've done. The guides are utilitarian and unique to each campus. Even in the Washington, D.C., market, Howard University, American University, and Georgetown each get a different book. They're not sexy, but they're efficient and very well targeted."

By the late 1990s, Campus Concepts had hit its stride. The company was publishing the *UnOfficial Student Guide* on 100 campuses nationwide. By 1999, annual revenue from ad sales exceeded $10 million.

All this from an idea that failed!

Not that Ian would have you believe he's a success. He'll tell you he remains a work in progress. "I compare Campus Concepts to Disney and GE," he says. "I want people to feel the magic of Disney when they experience my company. And I want my shareholders to get the return of an investment in GE. When those two things happen, then I'll be ready to say I'm a success."

Meanwhile, Ian emphasizes keeping the faith. "For an entrepreneur, that's a never-ending issue," he says. "It used to be people would tell me that my idea wasn't any good. Even now, with $10 million in sales, I get banged up by people who want to get in my way, or they want to discourage me. But I can handle the naysayers because I believe in the fundamental vision of this business, and I'm passionate about achieving our goals. At the end of the day, I believe in myself. I believe that I have the innate ability to make it happen. I believe in what I'm doing, and I'm convinced that I'm the best guy to do it."

As long as he keeps the faith, it's a good bet that Ian Leopold will find the people who believe in him, and his business.

CHAPTER NINE

READY, FIRE, AIM!

Tom Morales wasn't quite ready to give up his job, but today he's happy that circumstances forced him to launch a catering business for the movie industry. Now he's serving Sharon Stone, Steve Martin, Jodie Foster, Tom Hanks, and a host of other movie stars.

Let's assume you've decided you want to start your own business. What must you consider and what must you do to get started?

Must you consider your idea, your experience, the knowledge that you bring to the business and your ability to carry it out?

Do you have to write a business plan? Find some start-up money? Contact a banker? Hire an accountant and a lawyer?

Do you think about further planning before getting ready to start? Do you consider the risks and how you'll feed your family? Shouldn't you consider what others will think about your business idea and the advice they may offer?

One of the reasons more people don't start businesses is because they think there are too many things to think about! As you read books about how to start a business, or you enroll in seminars, or as you seek the advice of experts, or even friends, you may come away with an insurmountable list of worries.

I'm not suggesting that planning is bad. If you're giving up everything to start a business, or you're taking a big chance on your future, it's probably a good idea to feel fairly comfortable before you begin. However, if you have to feel absolutely confident before doing anything, you'll probably never get started.

Business isn't a science. It's not like mixing this chemical with that chemical to get a predictable outcome. You can make a plan and set a goal and even be reasonably sure that you'll reach that goal, but until you do, you won't know if you will. There's not much comfort in the unknown and there's not much comfort in the elusive art of business. Consequently, many people who say they want to start a business never move beyond thinking about it. They get stuck worrying about the "what ifs." They spend their time getting ready, and aiming, but never firing.

Think about what the ancient Chinese philosophers had to say, "A journey of a thousand miles begins with a single step." This applies to starting your business. If you want to get started you must take the first step. Neither a big step nor a small step. Neither a right step nor a wrong step. Just a step. No matter what business you're thinking of, you must get started at some point. Thinking about it, discussing it, and even writing a business plan for the business are all good things to do, but until you do something concrete you haven't really started.

When I left Pete Buck's home that Sunday evening with a thousand dollars of start-up capital in my pocket there were a lot of things to think about. Riding home in my parents' car I might have reevaluated the idea and decided that it was silly to think that a teenager with no business experience could start a business. What did I know about submarine sandwiches? How was I going to find a store to lease? How would I get it built? Where would I buy supplies? Who would take me seriously? Would anyone buy my sandwiches?

My parents could easily have added to this litany of concerns: How will you find the time to start a business and go to college? What kind of a career will this lead to? What does a sub shop have to do with studying medicine? What will you do when you run out of money and how will you pay for college then?

Fortunately, those thoughts and questions were never spoken. I'm sure my parents had some concerns, but they thought Pete's idea was worth pursuing, and they intended to help in any way they could. As for me, I was focused on the short-term objective of getting a store open, and not the long-term goal of thirty-two stores in ten years. I needed money to pay my way through college, and the opportunity to start a business was a way to get there. I didn't think it was going to be easy, but I also didn't think it was going to be impossible. I simply thought there was a business to start, there were things to be done, and that I would have to get going immediately.

The alternative was to microscopically analyze the opportunity. That approach might have resulted in me doing nothing at all. Had I responded to Pete's offer by suggesting that we write a business plan, or we talk to an accountant and a lawyer, or that we do more research, or had I delayed in any other way, I might not have taken the first step that was required to begin the journey.

That's why I prefer the philosophy of: Ready, Fire, Aim . . . especially when you're starting small. If you make a mistake, if you guess wrong, if your aim is off, you can fix it, and fire again, and adjust again, and again as needed.

We used the Ready, Fire, Aim philosophy to start and grow Subway. When you're just getting started it's sometimes necessary to make a quick decision, take a shot, and then make course corrections as necessary. If you're willing to fire before you aim perfectly, you probably won't hit your target precisely, but you'll have taken that first step in the journey of a thousand miles.

———

Tom Morales is a ready, fire, aim kind of microentrepreneur who graduated from college with a degree in psychology and decided to give up pursuing that profession for a career in the food industry. Sounds familiar!

In fact, Morales gave up a promising job with a national restaurant chain for the opportunity to become his own boss. But not without people telling him he was making a big mistake. "One thing I've learned through life is that you have to battle through people telling you that you're crazy or stupid," says Morales. "People told me that I was too slow and too skinny to play football, but I played through college. People told me I was crazy to give up my job to start a catering business, but I was determined not to let them discourage me. Every naysayer has served as a motivator for me. The way I see it, if I had listened to everyone who told me not to quit my job, I'd be an eight-to-five guy baby-sitting 120 people today. Some would argue I'm doing that now, but at least I'm the owner!"

Morales owns TomKats, Inc., a catering business that serves the music and film industries. He borrowed $2,000 from his brother-in-law in 1986 to start the business in Nashville, Tennessee. By 1999, TomKats was grossing nearly $5 million annually. The business employs nearly forty people full-time (up to 200 more part-time in the summer), and operates from a 12,000-square-foot headquarters. "We've catered 200 feature films since we started," Morales says proudly, "and we've become one of the top three caterers in the movie industry." It's an accomplishment that Morales can easily credit to his consistent ready, fire, aim personality.

He began practicing the ready, fire, aim philosophy as a youngster, the fourth of ten children. "With ten kids in the family," he explains, "my mother was like a short order cook. So on weekends, dad made us kids do the cooking. 'Go out to the grill and cook something,' he'd say. I didn't know how to cook. None of us did. But we did what we were told. We went out to the grill and cooked *something*, and along the way we learned from each other *and* from our mistakes."

The experience made a lasting impression. As soon as Morales graduated from Auburn University in 1976, he accepted a job as a manufacturer's representative selling hardware and industrial supplies. However, he also decided to start a barbecue restaurant near a state park in Prosperity, South Carolina. It didn't matter that he wasn't trained to run a restaurant. He wasn't trained to be a manufacturer's rep, either. "We did so much barbecuing in our family," he quips, "that it seemed like someone should get into the business."

There was, however, the issue of money. As a recent college graduate, he didn't have any, even though he had a good paying job. So he visited a local bank and requested a loan. "They said they didn't loan money for barbecue restaurants," Morales recalls. "But I wasn't going to let the bank make a decision for me. One thing everyone has when they graduate from college is plenty of offers from credit card companies. And that's how I got the money." Over a period of time, Morales used the cards to borrow about $6,000. Of course, that wasn't enough money to build a restaurant. "I had to settle for something less than I had originally envisioned," he explains. "All I could afford was a little shack with a couple of barbecue pits. I called it Uncle Tom's Barbeque." It was a seasonal business, open only in the spring and summer. "My future wife and I started cooking on Thursdays for the people who arrived at the park for the weekends. We cooked chicken, pigs, and even whole hogs. Before the first season was over, we had developed a tremendous following."

Nonetheless, the business required "a lot of work for very little return." Morales says that people expected barbecued food to be cheap, especially on the outskirts of a state park. "In addition to that, when we cooked pork, we ended up with a third of what we started out with. We cooked it, then we shredded it. And if by mistake we put an extra toothpick into a pork sandwich, we lost money! The margins were very slim." At the end of three years, Morales decided to give up the business. "Actually," he explains, "the guy who leased us the property saw how much business we were doing and he decided to take over without renewing our lease." It was just as well.

That left Morales with his full-time job that paid well—in the range of $50,000 a year. But by now his dream was to work in the restaurant industry and eventually own a restaurant. In 1980, intuition led him to the rapidly expanding Florida panhandle where he accepted a job in Destin managing a restaurant for half of his earnings as a manufacturer's rep. "There's a point in time when you can't let money be an obstacle," says Morales. "I was bitten by the food business, so the lower income didn't matter to me. Managing a restaurant is what I wanted to do."

During the next five years, Morales accepted several jobs managing restaurants in Destin. "I was the lead guy in numerous start-ups," he explains. "I would get into the restaurant before anyone else got involved. My job was to open it, then manage it. Sometimes that meant I painted the floors. Other times I developed the menu and placed the food orders. I learned the business just like an entrepreneur. At this point, though, I wasn't in a position of risk, except for my reputation."

As it turned out, his reputation fared well enough to attract the attention of one of America's most successful restaurateurs. Ray Danner, another microentrepreneur who became chairman of the Shoney's restaurant empire, headquartered in Nashville, visited Destin in 1985. He stopped for a meal in a Morales-managed restaurant, but he didn't stop by chance. He later told Morales that when he asked around town for a good place to eat, *everyone* recommended Morales's location.

Morales recognized Danner as soon as he entered the restaurant. He had worked for Danner in Nashville. His first job as a kid was washing dishes at a Shoney's. "I would never have guessed that twenty years later Ray Danner would be eating in *my* restaurant. But there he was."

He was all the more surprised when Danner finished his meal and asked to speak to the manager. Danner didn't summon him to complain, however, but to make him an offer. "I'm wondering if you'd come to Nashville and manage a restaurant for me?" Three weeks later Morales returned to his hometown.

By this time he had married, so he was accompanied by his wife, Kathie, and their young child.

Suddenly, Morales was right where he wanted to be, not only geographically, but also career-wise. He had been "discovered" by a chairman of the board of a national restaurant chain. Even though his first assignment was to turn around one of Shoney's struggling locations, he anticipated climbing the corporate ladder faster than anyone before him. If anyone had told Morales that within six months he'd be off the ladder and out of Shoney's altogether, he wouldn't have believed it. But that's exactly what happened.

"From day one," Morales explains, "I was targeted as Danner's boy. By hiring me himself, rather than going through the normal channels, he put me in direct conflict with my immediate boss. I tried to prove myself by concentrating on my job. Within a few weeks I cut food costs by ten points, and within a few months the restaurant was earning a net profit in excess of 12 percent, which meant that I was entitled to a hefty bonus. What I accomplished wasn't the work of a genius. Mostly I took advantage of my previous experiences. But the turnaround only made my boss angrier because he had managed this particular restaurant for two years and struggled with it. Now, instead of praising me, he started hassling me. He required frequent inventory audits, and then safe audits. When he started calling me in on my days off, I got annoyed. One day I was home, it was my day off, and I told Kathie, 'If he calls me in today, I'm going to resign.' Five minutes later he called. And I quit."

Voluntary unemployment isn't necessarily a ready, fire, aim tactic. People said Morales was foolish for giving up his job. After all, he was the sole breadwinner for a family that included a toddler and a wife who was now expecting a second child. A job at Shoney's might have led to an executive position, or possibly the ownership of a restaurant or two. But Morales was disgusted by the corporate world and never regretted resigning.

"Suddenly, the dream to be in business for myself became a bit more urgent," he recalls. "The only problem was, I still had no money. That's when I decided to become a consultant. Experience is what you get when you don't get what you want." He formed a company in 1986 and called it TomKats, named after himself and Kathie, who became his partner. "Kathie is the opposite of me," says Morales. "I'm a type A personality. I love to go out and shake hands and meet people. Kathie is good at managing behind the front lines. Once we got into the catering side of our business, Kathie developed all of the systems that we needed to use."

For the next several months Morales promoted himself to the local restaurant industry. "I went out and shopped my wares as someone who knew computer systems, food systems, and everything else that was involved in running a business. I got out there and found restaurants that were losing $25,000 and $30,000 a month. But unfortunately none of them wanted to pay me to solve their problems."

Money continued to be a problem personally. Morales was forced to give up his home and move his family into an apartment, and then into his parents' home, where the rent was free. "We cut every corner that we could," he says, "and I gave up a lot of pride." Kathie went to work at Opryland as a banquet waitress to help support the family. "These were tough times," Morales continues. "I frequently had to take our oldest child to work with me. She didn't have a normal childhood. Getting the business started was thrilling, but it was difficult for my family."

Nonetheless, he and his wife never doubted TomKats's future.

One day TomKats got a call from an outdoor amphitheater in Nashville. "The managers of the Starwood Amphitheater had been using an outside caterer to feed the stars and crews who performed each week during the summer. Their goal was to take this business in-house. They had a small kitchen and they wanted me to show them how to set it up. I did," says Morales, "and then they asked me to run it."

Summer touring troupes aren't necessarily accustomed to quality meal service on the road, but in the summer of 1986, TomKats raised the standards in Nashville. "Everyone loved our food," Morales recalls. "In Destin I had learned how to prepare fresh seafood, and I was also particularly good with Cajun cooking. So I was ahead of the curve in terms of the health kick. My skills just happened to coincide with a period of time when the stars were giving up drugs and they were more interested in eating healthy foods. I was in the right place at the right time, and we developed a great following. By summer's end, we were getting more calls for catering than we were for consulting."

But when the summer ended, so did Morales's steady job. "I had no work scheduled, and no real income. I had no money." He had, however, one valuable asset: a Director's Award. The Starwood Amphitheater presented the award to Morales for contributing to a successful season. The certificate didn't seem like much until Morales decided to use it in a direct mail piece. There were plenty of other companies in Nashville's vast music industry that could use a caterer. Perhaps, he reasoned, a few of those companies would be impressed by his award and hire him.

With a loan of $2,000 from his brother-in-law, he paid off several debts, bought catering equipment, some dishes, and mailed sixty letters, including a copy of his Director's Award, to production video companies in the Nashville area. "From that mailing, we got three jobs, and we went out and became the best-known caterer in the country music and music video production industries. Of course, I still didn't know what I was doing. I had no direction. I didn't have a plan for my business. We were just happy to book the jobs, and we were willing to take whatever came along."

The next summer, TomKats returned to the Starwood to serve the likes of Elton John and other stars. "One night my sister helped me serve the food," Morales recalls. "She was home for a month from Los Angeles where she was a set decorator in the feature film industry. At the end of the evening, after hearing everyone rave about our food, she asked me what I was doing at the amphitheater. 'You don't get any repeat business,' she said. 'You won't see these people for another year.' That's when the reality of my business hit me. In a restaurant, you build up loyalty. But here I was, kissing butts and serving food that blew people away, and while they loved us, they weren't coming back for a year, or more. Without repeat customers, there was no payoff. My sister said, 'You ought to try the movie industry. At least you could serve the same people for ten to twelve weeks at a time.' "

Morales knew nothing about the movie industry, but that was a minor detail for a ready, fire, aim personality. The next week he read about a movie that would be filmed in middle Tennessee. He called the production company, asked for an interview to provide catering services, and unknowingly set himself up for the biggest risk of his life.

The interview was smooth going for the affable Morales until the last two questions: "They asked me if I had a mobile kitchen," he recalls, "and without hesitating I answered yes." The truth was, he didn't even know what a mobile kitchen looked like. "Then they asked me if they could see it, and I told them it was out in California working." Two answers, two lies.

"I didn't think about the lies, but it's not something that I boast about," says Morales. "I felt I was in a catch-22. If they disqualified me because I didn't have a mobile kitchen, how would I ever get the money to buy one? I knew that if they gave me the opportunity, I would deliver. I didn't know what a mobile kitchen was or where to find one, but if they offered me the job, I'd get one. And if I couldn't get one, I would still have time to turn down the job."

The interview ended with a "we'll call you if we're interested," and Morales rushed home to phone his sister in Los Angeles. "What's a mobile kitchen?" he asked her. She told him to picture a Winnebago with a full-size kitchen on board and two serving windows on one side of the vehicle. Instead of bunks and a bath and a kitchenette inside, a mobile kitchen includes ovens, grills, refrigerators, pots and pans, glassware, dishes, and all the utensils. In other words, it's a moving kitchen, equipped to feed an army, or at least a movie crew. "Where do you buy one?" he wanted to know. His sister suggested that he look in the classified section of the *Los Angeles Times*.

"For the next three days," Morales relates, "my sister sends me the classifieds by overnight mail and I search them for used mobile kitchens. I found one in Phoenix. At the same time, the production company calls me and says I've got the job. The guy in Phoenix says he wants $40,000 for his mobile kitchen. I don't have that kind of money, but I offer him $36,000 and he says okay. So now I go to the bank and ask to borrow the money. When I told them I wanted to buy a mobile kitchen, they had no idea what it was and they laughed. I mean they *belly-laughed*. 'You want to buy a *what?*' they roared. Once I explained my business, the bank agreed to give me a loan, but only if I contributed $12,000, a third of the deal."

Coming up with his share of the money was less difficult than he imagined. His brother-in-law loaned him $2,000. And then he went to the production company and asked for a $10,000 deposit. "I thought they'd laugh at me," says Morales. "But I explained to them that if I had to block out several months to provide food service for their cast and crew, I'd need some money up front. They said fine, and they handed me a check."

Morales was on the next flight to Phoenix. "When I get off the plane," he continues, "I was met by a Mexican who led me to the mobile kitchen. As soon as I saw it, my stomach turned sour. The outside of the vehicle read Ricky Ricardo's Chili Express. It was a mobile kitchen, but it wasn't the glamorous vehicle that I had in mind." Nonetheless, he paid the man, hopped in the vehicle, and started driving toward Nashville. "For three days I was sick to my stomach," he says. "I had just spent $36,000 for a chili wagon. It looked like something that you'd see on a construction site. But given the circumstances it was the best I could do. So while I drove home, I thought about how I could fix it up."

Back in Nashville, he went to a hardware store and bought several gallons of white paint. "It took eight coats of paint to cover up Ricky Ricardo's Chili Express!" He then added the TomKats logo to the side of the vehicle, along with *Mobile Kitchen #3*. "I had read that when Fred Smith started Federal Express he didn't even have an airplane," says Morales, "but he gave everyone the impression that he had a big company. *Mobile Kitchen #3* made us look bigger." Inside the vehicle, he ripped out the steam tables, cleaned the equipment, loaded it with supplies, and prepared to serve his first movie crew.

"I was scared," Morales admits. "I was confident that we could take care of the people, because that's my personality, but I didn't know if we could meet their expectations. We were good at talking to customers and listening to them, but I didn't know what they would expect because I had never done this before. Not only that, I had never seen *how* it was done before! I had no idea if what we planned to do was right or wrong."

He didn't know, for example, that he planned to serve a larger variety of food, and a better quality of food, than any cast and crew had ever enjoyed previously on a movie set. He didn't know that the industry was accustomed to fried and sautéed foods, much of it cooked and placed in holding boxes for ninety minutes before it was served. His menus would consist of salads—not just one, but four or five. Fresh seafood, including tuna and even sushi. Prime rib, cooked for hours on a grill, and, of course, barbecue. Pastas, including seafood and vegetarian lasagnas baked from scratch by his own mother. TomKats was prepared to serve this cast and crew for ninety days without repeating a meal! "Even the finicky people were thrilled about our food," says Morales.

He also planned to serve the food in a novel way. Up to this time, movie crews were served food from the side of the mo-

145

bile kitchen. "They would come up to the first window and order their meal, then move to the second window where it would be served to them," explains Morales. "But I didn't like that idea. It was impersonal, and it didn't offer the customer the opportunity to see the food and then decide what they wanted to eat. So we decided to set up a buffet line and be present to explain the food. Double-sided, go down either side of the line, get as much or as little as you want. To me, this seemed like the only way to feed a movie crew, but it had never been done before, and everyone loved it."

Not to suggest that everything was perfect about that first movie. "We went out and made all the typical mistakes," Morales remembers. "The tables that we bought for the buffet were very heavy, and we didn't realize that we'd have to set them up, tear them down, and lug them around two and three times a day. We had to serve three meals a day, so the learning curve was very steep. There were several demanding people in the cast who insisted on drinking only Evian water, even though we were in the middle of nowhere. The first day I sent my crew out and they bought every bottle of Evian in the county. We had to drive to Nashville to buy a large enough supply. We were getting only two to four hours of sleep a night, but just about everything we had to learn, we learned on that first movie."

It was a good thing, too, because TomKats's reputation spread faster than gossip through the movie industry. One movie led to another, and it wasn't long before *Mobile Kitchen #3* was more a reality than an exaggeration. From gross annual sales of $60,000 when TomKats was mostly a local, Nashville caterer, the company grew to $264,000 its second year, when Morales discovered the movie industry, and $1.5 million at the end of year three. While Morales concentrated on feature films, Kathie managed their local catering business in Nashville.

By 1999, with gross sales approaching $5 million, TomKats's list of credits included: *A League of Their Own, Die*

Hard 3, Mrs. Doubtfire, The Prince of Tides, Random Hearts, Flawless, Simpatico, White River Kid, The Green Mile, Gloria, Practical Magic, and *Beloved,* to name just a few. Among movie caterers, most of whom were located in Los Angeles, TomKats became a star, in demand by producers, actors, and actresses.

Actress Sharon Stone eventually wrote TomKats into her contract. "When Sharon works, we work," Morales says with a smile. "And there are many other stars who have become regular customers, including Steve Martin, Jodie Foster, Jeff Bridges, Tom Hanks, Sandra Bullock, Danny Glover, and Penny Marshall. We know their likes and dislikes. We know their diets. Some of them are curious about how we prepare the food and they'll occasionally join us in the kitchen or at the grill. Harrison Ford and Dustin Hoffman have been known to do that. Like most of the stars, they appreciate good food."

Producers appreciate TomKats for economic value, as much as the good food. "We save them money," Morales explains. For one thing, TomKats's crew doesn't have to travel from Los Angeles to a movie set in the central or southern states. Producers are happy to find a caterer based in Nashville. The bigger advantage, however, is TomKats's trademark buffet line. "I didn't know it for a couple of years, but when we were on the set of *A League of Their Own,* a producer told me that by feeding 250 people in fifteen minutes we saved twenty minutes of production time a day. That was worth about $5,000 a day! Economically, it's easy to see why we're a favorite among producers."

Lending to that popularity is the fact that TomKats appears to be a star without an ego. "Our purpose is to serve," explains Morales. "We're the lowest man on the totem pole in terms of being subservient to everyone else. We're not into the ego world. We are driven by food, service, and cleanliness. And there's no substitute for someone who makes food from scratch, who is friendly, who doesn't have an attitude, and who runs a clean, efficient operation. Basically, that addresses the real needs of the movie industry, and the real needs of our company."

For a man who a few years earlier didn't understand what he was doing, and who had no plan for where he was headed, Morales caught on fast.

Or did he?

"We're more than ten years into this business," he says, "and some days it seems like we're starting all over again. We're constantly reinventing ourselves, learning as we go. The movie industry has become much more spoiled and we've seen tastes and demands grow exponentially over the years. Meeting some of the expectations has become more complex. We're the NFL of the culinary world. We face some horrible environments: snowstorms, desert air, forty-mile-per-hour winds. Sometimes the weather forces us to feed two hours early, or two hours late. And even if we're in the middle of a desert, some people expect a four-star French menu. It's a complicated business, but it's full of opportunity."

To Morales, the key word is opportunity. That's what keeps him committed to his business. "It's the opportunity that teaches you the power of positive thinking," he remarks. "If you golf, you can't make a putt if you think you're going to miss it. You can't do anything if you think you can't. I know this sounds trivial, and there's probably a guy in the ghetto who will say this is bunk, but I think there has to be opportunity. I'm the seeker of opportunity, and I love providing opportunity. That speaks to the core of my business."

In a word, it's opportunity that attracts a ready, fire, aim personality.

CHAPTER TEN

PROFIT OR PERISH

The day Everett Harlow figured out how to increase sales while decreasing costs was the day his graphic arts business began to flourish.

One day, several years after we started Subway, I was driving through Bridgeport looking at potential store locations when I noticed a sign that said the W. T. Grant department store was going out of business. I was astounded because W. T. Grant was a giant chain with big stores and lots of customers. They had stores across the U.S. and it had never occurred to me that a company so big, with billions of dollars in sales, could go out of business. How was that possible?

I had no answers at the time since I was just a kid working my way through college. But ever since that day I've realized that the size of the business doesn't matter. To stay in business you must earn a profit.

Everyone who starts a business wants to earn a profit, but *how to make a profit isn't as easy to grasp. In our ten-day train-*ing class, for example, Subway franchisees are taught to run their businesses. We teach hundreds of details related to the operation of a successful store and every detail is important, but some elements of business are more important than others. Without understanding the priorities, someone could graduate from training with the belief that all of the details were equally important, and wind up emphasizing the wrong things.

Also, some people get so focused on the details that they never understand what skills have to be developed to maximize profitability. One day, when I was planning to speak to one of our training classes, I decided to give them more of a Big Picture view of business. The idea was to show them how to look at the business from 30,000 feet. To aid my presentation, I built a flow chart that highlighted the various details of operating a Subway store and that's when it struck me that anyone in Subway, in fact, anyone in any business, only needed to develop two major skills. If a businessperson could become skillful at both increasing sales while decreasing costs then profits go up, and up, and up.

Of course, depending on the business, there are many ways to increase sales—effective advertising campaigns, better customer service, quality products, and so on—and many ways to decrease costs—better buying, greater labor productivity, cost controls, lower employee turnover, among others.

While I had never verbalized this message before, I had learned about increasing sales and decreasing costs in some surprising ways!

One bright summer morning in 1967, when I was nineteen years old, I was traveling between Subway locations—there were four at the time—when my car just died on a busy street in Bridgeport. My 1960 beige Rambler, a hand-me-down from my father, needed a generator, but I didn't have the money to buy a new part and pay for the repair job. So I decided to hitchhike to Milford, about ten miles up the road, where there was a junkyard. I figured I could purchase a used generator and then convince a friend to replace the parts for a few dollars.

A kid about my age picked me up on Boston Avenue in Bridgeport and he was headed toward the junkyard. As we passed through Stratford, talking about nothing in particular, this guy suddenly pointed to the Subway location on Barnum Avenue and said, "That's a great place to eat." Other than my first name, this fellow didn't know anything about me, so I was impressed that of all the restaurants we had passed, he pointed to mine.

"Why do you say it's so great?" I asked, trying to hide my personal pride in our third location.

"Well," he said, "they make terrific sandwiches. And all the soda you want is free."

"How does that work?" I asked, suddenly not feeling so proud.

"You go in with a friend," the driver continued, "and order your sandwiches. Then, when the guy behind the counter turns his back to make the sandwiches, your buddy opens the cooler, takes a case of soda and sneaks out with it. Nothing to it."

So that's *the problem,* I thought to myself, now too embarrassed to explain anything to my companion. *That's why we spend so much money on soda!* For the next several minutes I remained deep in my own thoughts. I remembered being so impressed with the amount of soda we purchased for the stores. I saw a vision of the soda deliveryman using his hand truck to pull cases of Pepsi Cola up three steps and into our Barnum Avenue store. Suddenly a light bulb flashed on in my mind. *It's not how much soda we're buying that counts. It's how much soda we're* selling *that matters. That's why we're not making the profit we should. The money is walking out the door. My God, it's so obvious. But now, how do I fix it?*

At the time our stores carried canned soda, and we sold it from a self-service cooler, the way you buy soda today in convenience stores. Also, we designed our food counters to run along the back wall of the stores, which meant that we had to turn our backs on the customer to make the sandwiches. Right then I decided to do something that we should have been doing all along, but had never before considered. *Starting immediately,* I thought to myself, *we'll count the soda cans and balance sales with missing inventory.*

By the time I arrived at the junkyard I wasn't as interested in buying a used generator. I looked around for an old Rambler, but I soon gave up and hitchhiked back to Bridgeport. I hired a local garage to repair my car, and then got busy counting cans!

Making a profit had always been a challenge in our business. During our Monday meetings Pete and I often discussed the importance of increasing sales, but as I learned during my ride to the junkyard, increasing sales is only half of the profit equation. Decreasing costs—all the costs—is the equally important other half. Many business owners do a great job selling their products and services, but if they don't control costs their profit-barren businesses can perish.

We started counting cans—first counting weekly, then daily, and we discovered we were buying a lot more soda than we were selling in each of our stores. That revelation hammered home the importance of measuring everything in our control, but it didn't put a lid on the soda issue. After several months of counting cans we still couldn't balance soda inventory with sales as well as we wanted to. By winter we decided to take a different approach. We substituted the coolers with vending machines and we stored whole cases in the back of each store. Each day during my store visits I'd refill the machines and remove the coins. That solved the problem, at least until the now popular self-service dispensers came onto the scene.

In the process of measuring results at Subway, counting the soda cans was the spark that ignited the fire. Over the course of a few years we developed some terrific control systems as we continued to focus on management issues that significantly impacted profit. For us, food cost is an important measurement. "Factor" is a word we invented to measure the cents received per sandwiches sold. "Productivity" measured the number of sandwiches sold per employee hour. These key indicators helped us understand the business and enabled us to control costs much better.

In spite of my interest in decreasing costs, and in spite of the numerous control mechanisms that we had developed since starting the business in 1965, we overlooked one of the most important measuring devices: a financial statement. Prior to 1972, when I visited the bank for a loan, we never used financial statements. But when my banker said I needed one to borrow money, I hired an accountant. Shortly thereafter, I got the surprise of my life and this led to the development of still another very important Subway control mechanism.

About ninety days after the end of 1972 my accountant asked me to come in to discuss the financial statement and our results for the year. It was like a "good news, bad news" joke, but it was for real. The good news was that we had surpassed $1 million in annual sales for the first time ever. The bad news was that we had lost almost $100,000 that year!

I was in shock. I had worked really hard during the past year and was stunned to find that I had lost almost $300 every single day. *How did that happen? How could we do better?*

I asked the accountant what could be done to prevent a similar loss in the future. He suggested quarterly, possibly even monthly, financial statements for better control. Dazed by the loss, I left the accountant's office promising to think about his advice.

Directionally, I knew he was right. But the frequency bothered me. As I walked to my car I said to myself, *Quarterly statements make sense, but by the time I gather the paperwork and get the results, what good is quarterly? It's too late then. Monthly would be better, but considering the accountant's fees, monthly would be too expensive. Besides, what good is monthly if I have to wait until long after the end of the month to get the results from the accountant? It would still be too late.*

By the time I arrived at my car and drove the mile back to my office I knew what had to be done. *If monthly is better than quarterly,* I continued, *then weekly is better than monthly. I need to see the operating results for every store every week, and it would be best to see the details the day after the week closes, if possible.*

I spent the rest of that day developing a weekly report. Actually, we had already developed many of the necessary reports to get to the information, but we had never looked at these tools as an integrated system. Now I simply had to consolidate the various daily and weekly reports that we had developed, add a few new ones, and keep all the information on a single piece of paper. We called this new report the WISR—the Weekly Inventory and Sales Report, and we used it to measure five critical parts of our business: food, bread, labor, soft drinks, and cash.

The WISR proved to be the solution that we needed to avoid future financial disasters. Every Wednesday, even to this day, every Subway store calculates its WISR, measuring the store's activity from the previous Wednesday through Tuesday. A quick glance at the WISR provides a clear indication of a store's progress, or lack of progress, and from there it's easy to note where improvements are required.

Of course, not every business needs to measure food, or bread, or soft drinks. But every business needs cost controls. The sooner you determine how to do that for your business the more profitable your business will become.

And if you fail to put the proper controls into place your business may perish, just like W. T. Grant did.

It almost ended that way for Everett Harlow, a New England microentrepreneur. A graphic designer, Ev, as he's known to his friends, decided to start his own business once he grew restless in corporate America. Even though he worked hard, and his attitude was always positive, neither he nor his employer considered him an ideal employee. Ev thrived on variety, a changing pace, and projects that he cared about. Money wasn't an issue. His salary and benefits were generous, and there was an annual bonus that exceeded his expectations. But the challenge of working for himself, meeting his own deadlines, and pleasing his clients motivated him more than any job ever could. One day he took the plunge, but it nearly destroyed him. His story is a good example of how to turn a failing business upside down and make it profitable.

The most important day of Everett Harlow's business career may very well have been the day he calculated that he was working for $4 an hour. This clean-cut, strapping young man was devoting upward of fifty hours a week to his business, doing something that he loved, and there was plenty of work to keep him busy. But that's about all he was doing. Keeping busy. He wasn't making a profit. No, he wasn't breaking even. And what was worse, he didn't know it.

But how could he? Ev Harlow had no business background. He had spent eight years in the Air Force as a personnel manager. Prior to that, he was a theater major for a year at California Baptist, where he had won a scholarship. Unfortunately the college terminated the theater program and that's when Ev joined the Air Force. It wasn't all that unusual a decision, especially when you realize that Ev Harlow is a Renaissance Man. He was looking for a free education, an opportunity to get out on his own, and the chance to explore life from every angle. On all scores, the Air Force was a perfectly good choice.

Between 1979 and 1987, Uncle Sam moved Ev around the country, transferring him to a new base every eighteen months. He was responsible for assigning enlisted airmen in the aircraft maintenance division. It wasn't a job that he would have selected for himself, but it's what he was told to do. At least it introduced him to computers. After hours, he studied graphic arts, enrolling in different colleges as he moved about the country. Graphic design was his passion, one of many. Music, theater, and art competed equally for his time.

As long as Ev remained in the Air Force the government would pay 90 percent of his education. He hoped to earn a degree in graphic design, and he might well have, had it not been for the Graham-Rudman Act. He was stationed in St. Louis at the time, attending Forest Park College in the evenings, when the U.S. Congress legislated a massive downsizing of the armed services. Suddenly, all assignments were frozen for three years. That meant Ev Harlow was out of work.

At first he thought the Air Force might reassign him to a graphic arts or photography post, in which case he planned to remain in the service. But when no such offerings were extended, Ev returned to the life of a civilian and looked to the private sector for his future. Since he couldn't afford to pay college tuition on his own, he decided he didn't need a degree. He relied on freelance graphic assignments to sustain him while he carried his expanding portfolio to St. Louis ad agencies in search of full-time employment. The private sector wasn't receptive, however, and Ev settled for a job selling vacuum cleaners door-to-door. It was nearly a year until an agency hired him to design corporate logos, lay out catalogues, and develop marketing materials. Ev couldn't have been happier . . . until he visited New England during a vacation with his wife, Lisa, whom he married when he left the Air Force.

The first time they stepped foot onto Cape Ann, near Boston, Massachusetts, Ev and Lisa knew that one day they would return for good. The seaside fishing villages and artist colonies were more than they could resist. The quaint quality of life beckoned, and the couple frequently vacationed on Cape Ann. Ev even managed to pick up some freelance work from local fashion designer Sigrid Olsen, who specialized in women's better sportswear. As fate would have it, when Olsen invested in a computer-aided design system for her business, Segrets, Inc., she offered Ev the opportunity to operate it. In 1991, Ev and Lisa relocated to Rockport, Massachusetts, where they rented a home that included a barn with an artist's studio. Life couldn't have been sweeter.

Sigrid Olsen, a microentrepreneur herself, became famous for potato print crafts. By slicing a potato in half, then carving a design into the smooth side of each half, she dipped the potato into textile ink and hand-stamped designs on fabrics. On a really good day she could produce only five yards of finished goods. Olsen worked out of her home until a semiretired dress salesman discovered her craft and offered to help her expand. He raised $150,000 to fund Segrets, Inc. By the time Ev arrived on the scene, Olsen was well on her way to building a $60 million business. Eventually, Liz Claiborne would purchase a majority stake in the company.

Olsen had advanced from hand-stamping her designs with potato halves, and then erasers (potatoes rotted too easily), to silk-screening her designs onto fabrics. Ev was hired to use the computer to transform Olsen's artwork into functional working prints. He became the middleman between the artist and the manufacturers who produced Sigrid Olsen's line of clothing. Prior to the computer, if Olsen decided a print didn't look quite the way she had hoped, her only option was to start over again. But the high-tech advancement of computer-aided design changed all of that. Now if she didn't like the way a design appeared, she had Ev to manipulate it until it looked just perfect.

At first, Ev had to pinch himself just to make sure he wasn't living in a dream. He didn't have the experience to operate a computer-aided design shop, but Olsen selected him because he had ten years of computer experience, most of it thanks to Uncle Sam, and several years of computer graphics experience. In addition, none of the fashion schools at the time taught computer-aided design, or CAD, as it's known industrywide. The manufacturer who sold Olsen the CAD equipment suggested that she hire a computer graphics expert and train him in the fashion industry. While thinking of a likely candidate, Olsen selected her capable freelancer, Ev Harlow.

While Lisa started her own Cape Ann catering business, Ev buried himself in fashion design, sometimes working thirty-six hours without a break. There was much to learn, and Ev thrived on it, particularly because he was in the center of all the activity at Segrets. It helped that Olsen was a fabulous employer, and that she had surrounded herself with people who were creative and engaging. The money was good, too, and Ev and Lisa needed it because they had run up some debts. In St. Louis, they had a monthly mortgage payment of $450. But in Rockport their rent was $850. Plus, they had purchased two automobiles, and they didn't hesitate to use their credit cards. Their debt wasn't massive, and they never fell behind on payments, but everything they earned was already spent before they cashed their paychecks. Thus, they were all the more grateful to have paychecks, especially Ev's.

All of this explains why it took five years for Ev to become restless. He wasn't used to living in the same city or working in the same job for more than eighteen months. But time had passed quickly, until one day he realized something was wrong. It bothered him that no matter what he did, there was no way to advance at Segrets. The CAD division would always be a one- or two-person operation. So Ev decided he needed a change. By pushing the envelope he had accomplished more than he or Olsen had expected. But now, even though he loved the work, the job simply didn't provide the kind of satisfaction that he craved. Corporate America didn't generate the soul-satisfying emotion that Ev saw Lisa take away from her small catering business. So much satisfaction was contagious, and *that's* what Ev wanted. By 1996, he knew it was time to start his own business.

Back in Sacramento, California, Ev's hometown, everyone in his family, except for his mother, seemed surprised by his career choices. Ev's father was long employed in the air conditioning and refrigeration/energy management industry, where he earned a national reputation, and his two younger brothers, both successful and happy in corporate America, had followed their father into the same line of work. The three of them had assumed Ev would come home, too. But he had broken the mold two or three times. First, he joined the Air Force. Second, he moved away from home. And now he was talking about starting a business. "The one thing about being in business for yourself," Ev's father commented, "is that you wake up every morning unemployed!"

Ev was undaunted. He knew that his family meant well. His parents were creative people and hard workers. His father had worked in the same industry for more than forty years. His mother went back to college after her sons were grown and she majored in both political science and theater. She, perhaps more than any of them, understood what Ev was feeling.

However, the missing piece of the puzzle was entrepreneurship. No one in the family had a bent for it.

Except Ev.

"I came to the realization," he says thoughtfully, "that I wasn't cut out to be an employee. Even Sigrid noticed that I treated the CAD system like it was my business, not hers. And I treated her company like a client. It became apparent to both of us that going out on my own was the thing to do. I could then seek out the types of projects that interested me, and include as much variety as I wanted. I realized I would still have to work hard. I'd still have to meet deadlines. I'd have to please my clients. But at the end of the day, the effort would be for me, for my own sake. It wasn't a matter of wanting more money. It was simply the challenge to do something magical for myself, and to feel the satisfaction that comes from such a challenge."

After accepting Ev's resignation, which allowed ample time for him to train a replacement, Olsen offered to become Ev's first client. He set up a studio in his rented barn, hung out a shingle to announce Lucky Dog Design, his new company, leased some equipment, and began prospecting for additional clients. It wasn't long before he won a contract from Victoria's Secret, a subsidiary of The Limited, and another from the lingerie designer Bennett & Company. "Without necessarily intending to," Ev explains, "I developed other fashion CAD clients." The upside to that was that he, as well as anyone, knew how to service these clients. The downside was that each of these clients, and all future fashion clients, expected Ev to produce their color reproductions via IRIS graphics. Ev didn't own an IRIS machine, which he describes as "an incredible ink jet printer, about the size of a washer and dryer welded together with a huge drum inside to produce the finest color reproductions."

IRIS was the output device of choice.

Without an IRIS, Ev was forced to outsource this portion of his assignments to other printers, and that was costly. It meant paying out a significant percentage of his earnings to these vendors. If Ev wanted to be taken seriously by his clients, and perhaps more importantly, if he planned to earn a fair profit, his only choice was to invest in an IRIS. But even the smallest IRIS required a capital investment of $30,000, and that kind of money he simply didn't have.

In talking with just one of his clients, however, Ev learned that if he owned an IRIS he could double his workload. His contacts at Mast Industries, the company that coordinated the reproduction work for Victoria's Secret, as well as other businesses owned by The Limited, told Ev that they would make Lucky Dog Design their primary source for CAD *if* Ev owned an IRIS. Mast relied on CAD houses in New York City for the majority of their assignments and they were frequently disappointed by the service and delivery time of the work. They were ready to favor one vendor.

Bolstered by this news, Ev developed a business plan, walked it into his local bank, and promptly received a $25,000 loan to help him purchase the equipment. The balance of the money came from savings and Lisa's parents. If getting the loan sounds too easy, it almost was. Lucky Dog Design had been in business for less than a year, and its financial statement was nothing to boast about. However, even before he started his business, Ev had wisely joined a local microenterprise organization operated by Working Capital. Lisa had introduced him to the group. She had joined Working Capital when she launched her catering business. Later, she went to work for the organization as a part-time enterprise agent. Her job was to help train budding entrepreneurs, like her husband. "The business skills training offered by Working Capital is fantastic," says Ev. "The curriculum they've built is like the *Reader's Digest* of an MBA. The lessons are like Aesop's Fables for businesspeople. They're written in a simple style so that people without any business background can understand them. Working Capital's tutorial includes twenty lessons. It takes a year to go through the curriculum. They teach you about pricing, contracting, marketing, cash flow, inventory—everything you'd learn in business school. That was very helpful to me. I'm a natural entrepreneur, but I'm not a businessperson. It's taken a lot for me to learn how to run a business. I work hard, and I'm willing to take risks. But it takes more than that to build a successful business."

By the time Ev needed a loan, he had nearly completed Working Capital's tutorial, including a lesson that showed him how to write a business plan and a loan request. He also had borrowed $500 from the organization for computer equipment and paid it back, thus establishing a favorable credit rating for Lucky Dog Design. Neither Ev nor Lucky Dog Design carried any debt (he and Lisa had paid off their debts before he left Segrets), and Ev's personal credit rating was excellent. Those details—plus one more—helped Ev get his loan. The other detail was Working Capital's introduction to a banker who supported the organization's mission, and who was willing to consider loan requests from its members. Maybe it was easy for Ev to get a loan, but it was no fluke.

Mast's commitment to increase Ev's workload also impressed the bank. The Victoria's Secret account already contributed about $4,000 a month to Lucky Dog Design. The loan on the IRIS would cost Ev $850 a month, a payment that he could easily afford, especially as his gross income doubled. To Ev, and everyone who was in his corner, it all made sense.

Until the worst happened.

Ev didn't even have the opportunity to make his first loan payment before The Limited, parent company of Victoria's Secret, as well as Lane Bryant, Express, and Lerner New York, among others, announced that it had created a design division in New York City to decrease costs. Beginning immediately, all of The Limited's CAD work would be handled by this new division instead of by Mast, which subcontracted work to Ev.

"I was out of business," says Ev. "That one announcement

canceled 75 percent of my income. It just went away. It was a good decision for The Limited. But it left me holding the bag."

Ev had two choices. He could sell the new IRIS at a bargain price and cut his losses, or he could get out of his barn and hustle up some new business. As you might expect, he chose the latter. "This is where my Working Capital group really turned out to be the best thing that could have happened to me," he explains. "I told the members about my situation, and I started marketing my graphic design services to them. When a new member joined the organization, I offered them an hour of free design time for a logo or business cards. I created most of the logos for our members at that time. Instead of having the five big clients that I was used to, I eventually had forty small clients." Meanwhile, Lucky Dog Design attracted a couple of new fashion clients, and by attending networking events sponsored by Working Capital and the Chamber of Commerce, Ev continued to expand his business.

But he had by no means replaced the work he had lost. It would take more than a year to do so. For several months, Ev and Lisa survived mostly on her income from the catering business, and her part-time job with Working Capital. They sold their second car for extra cash. They entertained at home, dined at home, and they didn't spend money unless they could use cash. "Fortunately," says Ev, "when we paid off our debts and we knew that I wanted to start my own business, we started thinking differently about how to spend our money. Perceptions and values change when you no longer have a guaranteed paycheck, but to us, that was exciting. We stopped being consumers. And it was a good thing, because it prepared us to lose the majority of my business."

While Ev rebuilt the business, the assignments from his new clients rarely required time on his expensive IRIS equipment. But it wasn't long before Ev discovered a new market for the equipment. Or more precisely, the market found him.

Artists, many of whom needed reproduction work, proliferated in the Cape Ann community. Traditionally, a fine artist who wanted to produce a limited edition print had to invest $10,000 to $15,000 in the reproduction costs alone, and he had to buy at least a thousand prints to keep the costs as low as possible. That was before the IRIS, however. Lucky Dog Design could render the same reproduction services for less than $1,000!

"Doing it the old way, an artist would have to sell 150 units just to break even on a limited edition print," explains an enthusiastic Ev. "But if I handled the job, and produced just half a dozen prints, the artist only had to sell one or two units to turn a profit."

Once the area's artist colonies discovered the IRIS equipment at Lucky Dog Design, Ev could barely keep up with the demand. Even if he had held on to the Victoria's Secret account, the artist colonies produced more work. And the clients marveled about the service. Ev continues: "With our equipment, we can take the artist's original artwork, digitally photograph it, and then print it on canvas, watercolor, or any other medium that wraps around our printer drum. Because we can do short-run print jobs, the artists don't have to carry a large inventory of their prints. They're thrilled. We opened up an avenue of profit for them."

Starting in 1998, Ev experienced increasing demand for fine art reproduction, more so than graphic design, so he changed the name of his business to Art Reproduction Technologies, or ART. By 1999, fine art reproduction would amount to 95 percent of the workload at ART.

In spite of this newfound success, as Lucky Dog Design transitioned to ART, Ev continued to struggle financially. He didn't know why, either. He was busier than he had ever been in his life. He understood, of course, that he had increased his company's overhead. Once he began serving a clientele that visited him, as opposed to the other way around, he moved from his barn to a commercial office. He had to buy office furniture and additional equipment. But as he increased sales, he anticipated taking home more money, or at least *some* money. But it didn't happen. Friends teased him about owning

$70,000 worth of equipment while driving a car that on a good day was worth maybe $2,500!

"Finally," Ev relates, "with some encouragement and help from my group at Working Capital, I decided to take a look at what was going on financially. Two of the Working Capital tutorials discussed cash flow and pricing. They included simple formulas that helped students project income. At the time, I was charging graphics and CAD clients $35 an hour for my services. The going rate was $50 an hour and one of my competitors charged $75 an hour, but I thought that was outrageous. Of course, I didn't understand taxation, and the extra 15 percent that I had to pay the government for the privilege of being self-employed. Once I deducted all of the *real* costs, I figured out I was making 'burger wages.' About $8 an hour."

Actually, as someone at Working Capital pointed out to him, based on the hours he invested in the business he was earning only $4 an hour! With sales, marketing, and the management and upkeep of his business, Ev worked fifty hours a week. But his billings amounted to only half that time, about twenty-five hours a week.

"*That* was a revelation," Ev recalls painfully. "I worked out a spreadsheet on the computer and determined that I was always going to be operating at a loss."

Rather than reinvent the wheel, and spend his time and more of his money figuring out how to make his business profitable, Ev creatively investigated his competition, including the CAD houses in New York. Even if he raised his hourly rate to $50, it wouldn't make much difference. So what was he missing? Assuming that his competitors were making money, how were they doing it?

For one thing, as Ev's investigation proved, they didn't charge by the hour. They listed an hourly fee, but they charged by the project! As a comparison, if Victoria's Secret asked Lucky Dog Design to match colors, repeat a pattern, and apply the colors twelve ways for a line of underwear, the project would take Ev about four hours to complete. He would therefore bill $140 for the job. His competitors, however, would charge separately for each phase of the project. For example, matching colors might run $10 per color. Designing stripe patterns could cost $15 per stripe. Printing variable color combinations would cost $50 per combination. For the same job, Ev's competitors would bill $350, 150 percent more than Ev! Obviously *that* would make a difference to Ev's income.

It was especially advantageous because Ev was more experienced in computer graphics than most of his competitors. "I was good, and I was efficient," he explains. "I could do the same quality work as my competitors, but in half the time. That meant I could bill twice the volume of work."

Suddenly, Ev became more excited than he had ever been in the past about his business. Now there was no doubt that he could do what he loved *and* earn an impressive income. He continued looking at his business under a microscope, hoping to discover additional opportunities for improvement. "I examined everything related to the infrastructure of the business," he explains. "I looked at the work flow, the billing process, the invoicing, and I discovered I was wasting a tremendous amount of time. I reorganized the physical layout of the office to gain more efficiency, and then I realized that I had to invest in better computer equipment. It was taking me forty-five minutes to move a 500 megabyte file from one workstation to the next, but with higher computer capacity, that same job would take three minutes. After I crunched the numbers, it was clear that I could decrease my costs and become more profitable by upgrading my equipment."

Surprisingly, the upgrade also included another IRIS machine. He had originally purchased the smaller IRIS, but now he needed the larger machine. "It only increased my debt to the bank by $250 monthly," Ev explains, "but it tripled my daily capacity."

While adding overhead, Ev concentrated on decreasing costs. "After I bought the new IRIS I set up a printed spreadsheet to track our daily activity on the machine. The spreadsheet is color-coded so it's easy to record the kind of work I do at the time I'm doing it. If it's a proof, a promotional piece, or a production run, I keep track of the job. I can tell you, for example, that on April 5 I used three pieces of canvas, changed an ink set, and ran three proofs on watercolor paper. If the machine has a glitch and I have to waste a piece of paper, I track that, too. At the end of the month, I send the spreadsheet to my bookkeeper, and she calculates my cost of goods sold. My only regret is that I didn't do this kind of tracking from the first day that I started my business. It would have made a tremendous difference and saved me quite a bit of agony."

Ev's accountant, a CPA, also gave him a tool to help him better manage his business. "She set up an Excel form that allows us to calculate our sales and expenses and project as far ahead as we desire. She built some assumptions into the form so we can play pretend. We might anticipate doing a certain volume of business in a given month, but what would happen if we increased the volume by 5 percent, or we increased our fees by $5? Or what if we lost a client and we experienced a sales decrease of 8 percent? This tool shows us the outcome and it keeps us on track. If we're running behind our projections for the year, we know exactly what we have to do to get back to where we want to be."

What he usually has to do, of course, is increase sales. In that respect, Lisa has been a tremendous asset to the business. She and Ev joined six networking organizations. "We didn't have the money to spend on advertising," Ev explains, "so we learned to network. We got good at relationship marketing and asking for referrals." He encouraged the local artists who used ART to spread the word, and they happily obliged. "It didn't take long for the artist communities to hear about the amazing things that we could help them accomplish. We've already done work for Steven Spielberg—he filmed *The Love Letter* here. We became an extension of his art department. And recently, we added an art museum to our list of clients."

In 1998, ART managed to end the year with $56,000 in

sales. Working Capital awarded Ev the organization's Entrepreneur of the Year Award. The first quarter of the next year sales increased by 750 percent, and ART was on track to gross more than $120,000 in 1999. "Once we hit $215,000 in gross sales," says Ev, "we'll be forced to expand again. We'll need more equipment, and we'll need two employees to get the work done. It'll happen in the year 2000."

He's looking forward to it, of course. "We have yet to finish big," says Ev, "but we have every intention of doing so. We'll soon saturate the Cape Ann market and then we'll be ready to move into the regional marketplace. By the end of the year 2000, I expect ART to be the premier print provider in New England. And in 2001, we plan to expand nationally."

Ev points out, however, that his plans are dependent upon one single factor: *profitability*. "Whatever we do, the profits have to be there, or we'll change our plans," he explains. But by increasing sales and decreasing costs, Ev and Lisa intend to maintain ART's profits. Their business nearly perished once. For them, that was more than enough to learn this lesson.

CHAPTER ELEVEN

BE POSITIVE

America's Dean of Motivation, Zig Ziglar, failed seventeen times before succeeding in the speaking business. He's proof that the School of Hard Knocks won't fail anyone who maintains a positive attitude!

As I look back on nearly thirty-five years of building and expanding Subway, I realize that my best experience was gained in the School of Hard Knocks. By doing my daily work I learned by trial and error how to rent a good location, how to make a sign, how to advertise, how to take inventory, how to train employees, how to attract customers, how to cut costs, and how to create systems that would ultimately produce a streamlined, highly organized, and profitable company.

The daily routine of doing my work, of *doing things important to the business*, gave me the crucial experience that I lacked and needed to succeed as an entrepreneur. I didn't always learn by doing things right the first time. Often I learned by doing things wrong the first time and sometimes the second or even the third time. I'd have to step back, make adjustments, and try again and again to get on track. Often the work was frustrating, painful, routine, boring, and occasionally discouraging.

Over time I discovered that regardless of background, expertise, and education, many other entrepreneurs also earned their stripes by trial and error. They didn't have all the answers when they started their businesses and they didn't have the experiences they would need to build successful companies. They learned by doing the daily work.

Even very successful entrepreneurs continue to learn by doing their daily work. While being enrolled in the School of Hard Knocks is not always a pleasant experience, it is an important part of everyone's business development.

The school doesn't feed you the answers. It's more of a learn-as-you-go, trial-and-error system. The curriculum at the school is often grueling, and some entrepreneurs repeat it several times with different businesses before they succeed.

Hard knocks can discourage people, and they can even destroy the ambition of others. The key to avoiding discouragement is to remember that all of your experiences and all of those hard knocks will help you do better in the future.

You never graduate from the School of Hard Knocks because in business there are always more challenges. You may start your business with a destination in mind, and you may work extremely hard along the way, but you probably won't get to your destination in a straight line. In fact, sometimes you have to move backward before you can go forward again.

Problems arise, many of them unanticipated. There are supplier problems, cash flow problems, and people problems. Plus, there are new ideas, new technologies, new obstacles, new rules and regulations. Just when you think you've learned it all, the school knocks you back a grade. Discouraging though it may be, that's the way it works when you're an entrepreneur.

Even if yours is a very small one-person business that you're operating from home, or from a garage, or from a small office, you'll still be learning new lessons every day. The trick is not to allow the hard knocks to beat you down. Always stay positive about your business and learn your lessons as they are presented.

While you're learning from the School of Hard Knocks, you'll encounter many roadblocks and dead ends. It's as though the school deliberately traps you into making mistakes and delights in doing so. Some days you can feel lost, even hopeless, especially after hitting one wall after another. Many days, your best efforts will lead only to disappointment and the frustration may become overwhelming, especially in the early years of building a business.

Some entrepreneurs say that frustration is motivating and it encourages them to try harder and work smarter. Others, like me, want to avoid as many of those trying moments as possible. While I welcomed every challenge that the School of Hard Knocks set in my path, I was fortunate to understand the value of maintaining a positive attitude. Somehow I've always known that my attitude was my choice. While I could have developed negative feelings about every challenging situation, I chose to see every challenge as an opportunity to learn more.

Fortunately, I was able to endure the pain inflicted by the School of Hard Knocks as I struggled to figure out how to make my business work. I also recognized that it was important to look for the knowledge that every lesson delivered, even if it was simply the knowledge not to make the same mistake again.

Being positive helped me. It's still my attitude today, and I recommend that you always maintain a positive attitude.

Someone who has remained positive in spite of many challenges is Zig Ziglar. If the School of Hard Knocks granted diplomas, Zig would be among the first to receive one. Zig failed seventeen times before succeeding and for the last twenty-five years he has been known as one of America's leading motivational speakers and trainers. Zig has always emphasized the value of education and experience. But Zig would never accept a diploma from the School of Hard Knocks because that would be like saying he had nothing more to learn, and that's not Zig Ziglar. Zig is an American treasure who has developed one of the most positive attitudes in the world.

Zig Ziglar wasn't always a successful businessman. For sure the School of Hard Knocks beat him down as much as anyone, but he simply refused to stay down. By choosing hope over despair, Zig never yielded to failure, even though he had to pick himself up and start all over many times. Considering Zig's early career, it's amazing that he would eventually become a successful business owner, let alone the Dean of Motivation. But his positive attitude and keen mind, accompanied by a life of self-discipline and self-training, made all the difference.

"For two and a half years in the world of sales," says Zig Ziglar in the deep drawl that has become his trademark, "I just survived. Period." He was selling heavy duty, waterless cookware door-to-door. Or trying to. Of 7,000 sales representatives, he thinks he ranked number 3,000—or worse. "There was nothing whatsoever to distinguish me," he says.

To get started selling cookware in 1947, Zig had to buy a sample set of the product. "I borrowed $50 to buy myself a hat," he recalls. "A door-to-door salesman had to have a hat." He also bought a "cheap" briefcase and a suit of clothes, which cost $22.50. "I got a week of classroom training where I learned a canned sales talk to get inside a house to demonstrate my product." But the presentation wasn't very effective. "It took me ten days to get into the first house, and those were the days when everyone trusted everyone else. I almost quit on that tenth day." In fact, he came within one long city block of giving up. "I had been on the street knocking on doors for hours in Columbia, South Carolina. No one was interested. Then I hit Adelia Drive and I said to myself, 'I've been out here for ten days, and if I don't get inside a house to tell my story I'm going to quit when I get to the end of this street.'"

The next-to-the-last house on Adelia Drive belonged to a B. C. Dickert. When Mrs. Dickert answered her door, to be met by a properly clad and well-rehearsed Zig Ziglar, she said she just might be interested in some cookware. And so might her sister-in-law next door. "If she agrees to look at your cookware," Mrs. Dickert said to the astonished salesman, "call me and I'll come right over." The words were no sooner out of her mouth than Zig was running next door. There he met Mrs. Freeman. He introduced himself and repeated Mrs. Dickert's message.

"My husband comes home at six," said Mrs. Freeman, "so why don't you come back at seven and give us a demonstration." She assured him Mrs. Dickert would be there, too.

At seven o'clock sharp, Zig arrived to give the presentation of his life. Mr. and Mrs. Freeman, along with Mrs. Dickert, listened to his every word. When he arrived at his closing statement, the Freemans agreed to buy a set of the cookware. The cost was $61.45, but all that Zig required was a down payment of $16.45. "I wrote the order," Zig recalls, "and I was overwhelmed with my incredible success. I had some money for the first time in a long time, and I was patting myself on the back till my arm got sore." In all the excitement, he forgot about Mrs. Dickert. Then Mr. Freeman said, "Mr. Ziglar, I believe Mrs. Dickert would be interested in some cookware, too."

Zig turned to her and said, "Well, what about it, ma'am?" Mrs. Dickert said she hadn't brought her money. "But you just live next door," Zig said, surprising even himself. "Go get your money and I'll wait for you." And so she did.

"I tell you," says Zig, "we lived in an upstairs apartment at the time, and rushing home that night to tell my wife the good news I bet I didn't hit two steps going upstairs. We bought a couple quarts of ice cream to celebrate."

The double sale was Zig's first sign of encouragement as a cookware salesman, but it wasn't his first sales experience. He learned to sell as a child growing up in Yazoo City, Mississippi, the tenth of twelve children born into a farm family. "I asked my mom one time why so many children and she said, 'Son, where do you think I should have stopped?'"

172

There were seven boys and five girls in the family. However, when Zig was five, his father and his baby sister died within a week of each other. "After their deaths," says Zig, "we moved from a farm that was out in the delta to Yazoo City. My mom only had a fifth-grade education, but she was wonderfully wise, with great faith, and she was a hard worker. That's why we survived. We had five milk cows, several hogs and chickens, and a big garden. Every morning before school I milked the cows with my mother while my two older brothers tried to find some work with the highway department."

At age eight, Zig became a salesman. His first customers were his family's neighbors in Yazoo City. He sold them milk, eggs, and vegetables. When he was nine he advanced to selling bags of peanuts in downtown Yazoo City. For every nickel bag he sold he earned a penny. He also had a paper route, and in the fifth grade he started working after school at the local grocery store, and he remained with that job until he completed high school.

In 1944, Zig joined the Navy and was assigned to the Naval Unit at Millsaps College to prepare to enter flight training. However, the war was winding down, so all flight training for the Naval Air Corps was discontinued. He was transferred to the University of South Carolina; later, he went to the Great Lakes Naval Unit and then to Washington, D.C., and was discharged in June 1946.

After his discharge he returned to the University of South Carolina to continue his education. "I was not a student," he says. "I didn't excel in high school because I was working all the time. Even in college I was more interested in work and life than I was education. I really had no idea what I wanted to do. I had no plans for a career." It was at the University of South Carolina, however, while he was still in the Navy and living in a dormitory, that Zig spotted his first entrepreneurial idea. "At night," he explains, "young boys would knock on the dorm windows and sell us ice cream. We weren't allowed to go out of our rooms, so this was a terrific service that we all enjoyed. As

I got to thinking about it, I decided that once I was discharged from the Navy I would come back to the university and sell sandwiches, coffee cakes, and milk in the dormitories." In the fall of 1946 that's exactly what he did. It was his first business. "I was making $100 a week working at night," he recalls. "I'd probably still be there today if I could have made it a career."

One day, now as a married man, Zig responded to a newspaper ad for a cookware salesman. That began what he now refers to as an intensive, two-and-a-half-year struggle. "During this period of time," he recalls somberly, "I had my lights turned off, my telephone disconnected, and I had to turn in a car that I had bought and could no longer afford. When our first baby was born, the hospital bill came to $64, but I didn't have the money. I had to get out and make two sales to get my baby out of the hospital. They were tough times."

Even so, they were important times in the development of a budding salesman who would eventually become a successful businessman. "During those early years," Zig says, "it's important to understand that I was learning how to be a salesman. I learned how to get appointments and conduct demonstrations. I learned how to handle objections and close sales. In any business, you don't know everything that you will eventually need to know. But you know enough to start and then you pick up and learn as you go along. I needed experience and I was getting it. One of the things I learned during this time was that anything worth doing is worth doing poorly . . . until you can learn to do it well."

At the end of his two-and-a-half-year apprenticeship, Zig, now in his early twenties, was well trained. "The salesman was ready," he says, "but the man was not. In building a business, you start with the person and add the skills. I had the skills, but not the attitude." All of that was about to change, however, when he met P. C. Merrell, a supervisor in the cookware business.

"I was always a hard worker," says Zig. "I was pleasant and personable, most of the time. As a child, I had a lot of anger and I fought everything that moved. If I couldn't settle an argument in ten seconds or less, I'd just bust 'em one. I wasn't very smart about it, either, because I hit guys who I had to reach up to hit.

"In school I wasn't exactly the class clown, but I liked to make people laugh. And, even though I suffered from what experts later termed an inferiority complex, which resulted from being small for my age and having to work so much of the time, I had a good sense of humor. I was optimistic, but only in the sense that I would survive without ending up on government support."

Zig suspects that all of those factors—"plus maybe even something that I didn't see in myself"—attracted him to Merrell, who had written the company's training manuals and had set numerous sales records. "He was my hero," Zig says respectfully. "Mr. Merrell was a man of total integrity, and one of the top supervisors in our company."

What a surprise it was when Merrell pulled the struggling Zig Ziglar aside at a company meeting and told him that he had the ability to become the company's national sales champion if he would just believe in himself and work on an organized schedule. Zig had never heard such inspiring words before, certainly not in reference to himself. No one previously had ever encouraged him or spoken to him so assuredly. Why would they when, in the same organization, there were at least 4,000 other sales representatives outselling him?

"I'll never know why Mr. Merrell singled me out," says Zig, "but what matters is that I believed him. I went to that meeting a little guy from a small town . . . a little guy who had struggled to get ahead. But after Mr. Merrell talked to me, I left the meeting as someone who could do great things. *I could be the national champion.*"

That night, Zig conducted a cookware demonstration for three couples. "They were the easiest sales of my life," he reminisces. "My prospects were no longer dealing with a little guy from a little town. Now they were dealing with the national champion."

Well, not exactly, but close. Zig finished the year immediately behind the national champion, but second place was an incredible accomplishment, particularly for such a young man. He outperformed 6,998 other sales representatives! He received the best promotion the company offered, and was on his way to even greater accomplishments. Within two years, he became the youngest division supervisor in the company's sixty-six-year history.

"I've never forgotten that meeting with Mr. Merrell. It was proof to me that words spoken by one person can have a dramatic impact on the life of another. When Mr. Merrell helped me change the picture that I had of myself," says Zig, "everything got easier. Things didn't always go right, but when my attitude changed, my belief in myself changed and hope was born. And hope, as psychiatrist Alfred Adler said, is the foundational quality of all change. Hope is the great activator. If I have hope that I can make the sale, I'll make the call. Without hope I will not make the call."

Following Merrell's encouraging words and direction, Zig made an appointment with himself to knock on a door at 9:00 A.M. daily no matter what happened the day or the night before. "I committed myself to a regular schedule," he says. "I didn't sit around moping. I was inspired. I had responsibility, and I had learned from childhood to accept responsibility. So I went out there and knocked on those doors. I had a need and a desire, and that's all it takes to start a business. You don't need a lot of money. But you better believe in whatever you are going to do. Then be willing to do it, and work at it every day." In other words, do the daily work!

There is one more thing you better do, says the master of motivation. You better think positively. "This is so simple it's almost trite," says Zig, "but it's totally true. You are what you are and where you are because of what's going into your mind. You can change what you are and where you are by changing what goes into your mind. If you want a positive output, you have to have a positive input." But it may be easier said than done. "We're inundated with the negative," says Zig. "Negative news events, negative comments. It's easier to be negative than positive because there's so much reinforcement for the negative. Research indicates that half of us get here as pessimists and half of us as optimists. If you want to change that, you can. If you fill yourself with negativism, listen to negative news and read negative, violent, and smutty input, your self-talk will be negative and you will be negative. If you want a positive attitude, then you will have to choose to feed your mind with optimistic, hope-filled, motivational, enthusiastic information. Remember, the most important conversation you will have on any given day is the one you have with yourself. The most important opinion you have is the one you have of yourself. If it's not positive, the negative will take hold of you."

Zig says he's an optimist, as though there could be some doubt. He points out, however, that he works to maintain his optimism. "I do a lot of reading," he says. "In my car I seldom listen to the radio. I listen to audiotapes in my 'Automobile University.' At the moment, I'm listening to the old Jack Benny radio programs. They're absolutely hilarious. Laughter is a great motivator. It gives you a different outlook. You maintain the right attitude, or you acquire the right attitude, by deliberately listening to and reading inspirational material."

A positive attitude can also rub off from one person to another, says Zig. "I learned this lesson as a child," he continues. "When I was working in the grocery store during the Depression, the Kuhns Dime Store in Yazoo City sponsored a drawing for a cow. Now that's a big deal because a good cow cost $50 at the time. My boss sent me to the drawing with a rope. 'If anyone asks you why you've got that rope,' he said, 'you tell them it's to lead the cow home!' That was my first exposure to a positive attitude."

That positive attitude helped Zig set numerous sales and training records during his stint as a cookware salesman. One year, out of sixty-six divisions in the company, his South Carolina division finished third, behind New York and Kansas. "I had the number one salesman in the nation, the number one dealer in the nation, the number one field supervisor in the nation, and the number three field dealer in the nation. It was quite a record," he says. Later, Zig moved into the insurance industry and of thirty-one President's Club members in nine southern states, he had trained eleven of them. "People don't know it, but I've had more success as a trainer than as a salesman," he explains.

During these years, as part of his personal training, Zig read books and listened to phonograph recordings such as Earl Nightingale's *The Strangest Secret.* Frank Bettger's book, *How I Raised Myself from Failure to Success in Selling,* taught Zig about the value of enthusiasm. Later he read *The Magic of Thinking Big,* by David J. Schwartz, and the now classic *Power of Positive Thinking,* by Norman Vincent Peale. "It was Dr. Peale who taught me that it's not what happens to you, but how you handle what happens to you that will make the difference in your life."

Of course, he also attended professional seminars and it was on one of these occasions in 1952 that he heard the motivational speaker Bob Bales. "I had never seen anyone have so much fun, do so much good, and, I thought, make so much money," he recalls. "It all appealed to me enormously, and I decided I wanted to be in the same business. I wanted to become a speaker." He approached Bales to ask for his direction. "He was kind enough to tell me that I needed to get some birthdays behind me, because most people wouldn't be interested in listening to a twenty-five-year-old. 'Set some sales records first,' he told me, 'and then write to the Dale Carnegie people and see if you can associate with them.'"

Zig followed Bales's directions precisely. He worked hard and set more records. Then one day he sent a letter to the Dale Carnegie Institute to inquire about opportunities to become a speaker. "They kept the letter for several years," Zig says and smiles. "They kept it as an example of how not to write a letter. I said, 'I did this' and 'I did that.' I had a serious 'I' problem. But fortunately I had sent them my sales and training records, and they recognized that they were substantial. One day, John Mason, the Dale Carnegie sponsor for the Long Island area, reviewed my record and decided to invite me for an interview."

Soon thereafter the Ziglar family, now including two daughters, moved to New York and Zig went to work for Mason on Long Island. Within three months, however, he moved his family back south, but not because he didn't love the work. "It was the long commute that discouraged me," he says. "When I left home in the mornings my wife and daughters were asleep in bed. By the time I got home, my daughters were back in bed. And I wasn't about to let my girls be raised without a dad."

For the next five years, Zig says he became a "wandering generality." Building a speaking business on his own was difficult to do, and since he needed money to support his family he looked for other opportunities. As he explains it, he was in and out of seventeen different "deals." He sold life insurance, health insurance, investments, food supplements, cosmetics, china, flatware, vitamins, and a host of other opportunities, all the while looking for speaking gigs. "I was always looking for that get-rich-quick deal," he says. "But I was going broke fast."

Eventually, the cookware business rescued him, but only temporarily. "Harry Lemmons, the president of Saladmaster, gave me a chance to get back into the business," he says. Today, Lemmons's photograph hangs on Zig's Wall of Gratitude, along with nineteen other faces from his past. "Harry loaned me some money, bailed me out of my financial problems, and gave me a chance to sell stainless steel cookware." Zig quickly demonstrated that he still had the makings of a national champion. After a year, he placed first in sales and regained his financial stability.

Still, he dreamed about becoming a full-time speaker, and he accepted speaking opportunities as often as possible, sometimes driving a hundred miles one way to speak to a few people. His topic, early on, was sales. But gradually he made the transition to personal growth and development. "People needed encouragement fully as much as they needed sales instruction," he says. "And because encouragement played a major role in my life, I had a natural love for it. I can teach just about anyone how to sell. I could teach a twelve-year-old, or the biggest crook in town. But they'll never succeed until they acquire the character qualities. That was always a big part of my sales training. You've got to be the right kind of person to do the right thing in order to have all that life has to offer."

During this time, Zig learned the tools of the speaker's trade. "I developed the creativity and the style that I use today," he says. "I studied other speakers and watched what they were doing. I would pick up ideas and concepts, but I never copied anyone. Periodically someone comes up to me and says, 'I'm going to be the next Zig Ziglar.' I always laugh and say, 'And you're going to be a lousy one, too. If you can't make it being yourself, you can't make it being an imitation of anyone else.' The same is true for any business. You have to believe in yourself and your dream. You have to have a passion for it, and make the commitment to make it happen."

And for seventeen years, that's what Zig did. From 1952, when he first realized he wanted to start his own business as a speaker, until 1969, when he was forced to begin speaking full-time, he never gave up.

By 1968, he had left Saladmaster and moved to Dallas to accept the position of vice president of training for a multi-level marketing company that sold automotive products. It turned out he was the missing link in the company's success. "I started a training program for them and the business just exploded," Zig recalls. "Initially I worked with the company only one week a month," but later he was involved in training two weeks, then three, and finally four weeks each month. Not long thereafter several things happened, including some bad decisions by the company's management. In 1969, the company folded. At that point, Zig's only option was to make his living as a speaker.

The transition into the speaking business was anything but pleasant. For the next couple of years the Ziglar family zigged out of prosperity and zagged into financial peril. "One day, I went home and found a tax lien on my front door. It got pretty bad," he says. He managed to save the house, "but it was tough going until my speaking business kicked into gear."

That didn't happen until 1972. Zig can pinpoint the exact date. It was July 4. "That weekend," he explains, "I committed my life to Christ, and started teaching biblical principles. That's when my career exploded."

Since then, there's hardly a major business in America that hasn't invited Zig Ziglar to speak. IBM, General Motors, Ford, Mary Kay Cosmetics, Exxon, McDonald's, Holiday Inns, Amway Distributors, Hallmark Cards, General Mills, Home Interiors & Gifts, Chick-Fil-A, Peter Lowe's Success Seminars, and a host of other companies have invited him to grace their dais. Most have invited him back more than once. Nowadays, his speaking fee is $50,000 for U.S. engagements.

There was more to the speaking business than just being a speaker, however. In the early days Zig couldn't command a very big fee, and he often spoke for free. Eventually, however, he learned there was money to be made "in the back of the room" where an enthusiastic audience would purchase the speaker's tapes, books, videos, and manuals. Zig extended his reputation, and brand name, by producing these products. He also began writing books, including the best-seller *See You at the Top*. He's written sixteen nonfiction books and, at age seventy-three, he believes he has many more to write.

When asked about his plans to retire, Zig says he's "not going to ease up, let up, shut up, or give up" until he's "taken up." As a matter of fact, he says he's just getting "warmed up!"

Ask him how he's doing on any given day and he's likely to say, "Better than good."

True or false, it doesn't really matter. The School of Hard Knocks beats on Zig Ziglar every bit as much as it does the rest of us. He's simply learned how to succeed by being positive.

CHAPTER TWELVE

CONTINUOUSLY IMPROVE YOUR BUSINESS

Mary Ellen Sheets has never worried about planning her business. She simply tries to improve it every day. That philosophy has helped Two Men & A Truck enjoy enormous success.

To maximize the profits of a business you need to increase sales. To increase sales, you need more customers. To attract customers and keep them coming back, you need to continuously improve your business.

All successful businesses offer their customers something of value, but that's not enough. Customers constantly evaluate what they get against what they pay, and their criteria for making repeat purchases are very simple. They want everything: better, faster, and cheaper! Even if you're clever enough to build a perfect business the first time and your product or service is ideal for your customers, your position will eventually erode because the marketplace is not static. Your product or service may be unique, but it's not as though someone blew the whistle and stopped innovation. Sooner or later, and very soon if you're noticeably successful, other businesses will copy you. If they can provide a similar product or service better, faster, or cheaper, they're going to surpass you. Never forget that as a business owner you'll be in a constant race against an ever-improving marketplace, and no matter where you are in the hunt, making improvements is a daily necessity. Paul Orfalea, the founder of Kinko's, says, "The best definition of management I ever heard came from my wife. She said the role of management is to remove obstacles. People look at Kinko's and comment about how successful we are. But all I can think of are the obstacles. In a company, nothing is ever perfect, and I am never content."

Since we started Subway, we've never been content, either. We've made countless improvements, and we continue making them every year. The majority of these improvements are so subtle that they're not worth talking about. For example, we started out by selling seven variations of cold, footlong sandwiches. Then we offered half-size sandwiches. Later we introduced salads. We used to sell only white rolls, but then we added wheat rolls. And so on. At the end of any given year, we may have made 1,000 improvements. But we could look back and say that only ten of them were critical — that is, they resulted in meaningful changes. And of that number, only *one* was significant.

So you might ask: Why bother with 1,000 improvements if only ten really mattered? Why not focus on the ten? Or on the single most significant improvement?

If we knew in advance which improvements would deliver the greatest results then you're right. Why bother with the others? But you can't measure results until you've made the improvements, so you're forced to do everything as quickly as possible without throwing the company into chaos. For some entrepreneurs, including me, that's easier said than done. After we began franchising and we rented a small office, I frequently came up with new ideas. Dick Pilchen, who joined Subway early in our development and was instrumental in building our infrastructure, occupied the office next to mine. Many mornings I ran into Dick's office to share my latest "greatest" idea with him and ask him to implement it. Finally, after a few months, Dick said to me, "Fred, you have all these ideas, and they're all great, but it would be nice if you'd give me a chance to execute the *last* great idea before I start a new one! They're coming too fast and furious. I can't implement them that quickly, and our people can't keep up." After that, I realized it was important to think through my ideas before I shared them. I started prioritizing them, looking for the few that could potentially deliver the greatest results.

Many of our major improvements were not my ideas, however. They came from our employees and even our customers, and I suspect that's true of most businesses.

For example, when Pete, my mom, and I originally conducted our research prior to opening our first store, we had to decide how to cut our rolls. At Amato's, they sliced the rolls across the top, without separating the roll, and that's the style we used. With a single slit, we could spread open the roll and lay in the meat, cheese, and vegetables. It worked fine, until one day a customer gave us another idea. My mom was working in the store when a fellow came in from Philadelphia, a city where the submarine sandwich, or hoagie as they call it there, is a staple in the diets of many families. When this fellow ordered his sub, he asked mom to scoop out the dough in the middle of the roll, leaving just the outer shell of the bread. He said that's how it was done at the shop he visited in Philadelphia. So mom made the sandwich just as the customer ordered.

At our next Monday night meeting, we had a long discussion about this experience. Mom explained that she preferred scooping out the dough because it was easier to build the sandwich. She also thought less bread improved the taste of the sandwich. It provided a better balance of meat, cheese, vegetables, and bread.

Pete and I liked the idea, but we didn't think our customers would appreciate watching us dig out the guts of their

184

sandwich rolls. So we improved the idea. We developed the U Gouge, which has since become a trademark of a Subway sandwich. By making two slices on the top of the roll instead of one, we could remove the center section of the bread, thus creating a shell and cradle. That left plenty of space for the contents of the sandwich. As a goodwill gesture, we decided to donate the leftover chunks of bread to farmers to feed their livestock.

After we introduced the U Gouge, our customers frequently asked about the bread that we removed. "That's my bread," some customers would say. "Put it back on the sandwich!" But we said no, that's not how we make our sandwiches. This exchange was repeated untold times until we realized we were arguing with our customers, and that made no sense! So finally, weary of explaining ourselves, we decided to place the bread back on top of the sandwich. The customer could either eat it, or throw it away. That ended the arguments. And the customer got a superior sandwich.

Some years later, in the mid-1980s, we added another improvement that affected our rolls. This one was of major proportion. By now, we had opened franchises in many parts of the country, and I decided to tour some of our stores in the southern states. One Sunday in North Carolina, accompanied by Pete Slomiany], our Development Agent for the state, I arrived at a store in Wilmington at about three o'clock in the afternoon. I asked the young man behind the counter if the owner was available. "Oh no," he told me, "he's out picking up the bread."

"He is?" I said, a bit surprised. Usually rolls were delivered to our stores. "Well how far's the bakery?"

"It's forty miles away," the young man responded.

"Forty miles? He has to drive forty miles to pick up bread?" I had no idea this was going on.

"No, he doesn't have to drive that far," the employee continued. "He goes over to the bus terminal in town and picks it up there."

Pete then told me that this franchise couldn't find a local bakery that was willing to bake rolls to our specifications. The bakery shops in North Carolina, and as it turned out, other southern states, weren't familiar with our style of rolls. Even though any number of bakeries could have made these rolls, they chose not to because the demand by one or two stores wasn't great enough to make a special order worthwhile. As a result, this franchise was forced to rely on a bakery that bused the rolls to him two or three times a week. Obviously, the logistics of getting bread to the store were a challenge and product quality suffered as a result.

As I continued my tour, I discovered the challenge of finding local bakeries affected several franchisees. Many stores couldn't buy bread locally, and as a result, they were wasting a lot of time. In addition, their bread wasn't uniform—on any given day it varied slightly in size, shape, and taste—and sometimes it wasn't as fresh as we would have preferred.

Once I understood the situation my mind couldn't stop thinking about it. Where was the opportunity in this problem? How could we solve it? By the time the tour ended, I returned to my office with an idea that would fix the bread issue for everyone, while simultaneously contributing a major improvement to the operation of Subway. The idea was to bake bread daily right in our stores. It not only solved the accessibility issue, it also improved the products and provided the basis for a great promotional campaign: Fresh rolls baked daily at Subway! This was one of those rare ideas that would eventually lead to something even bigger than originally intended.

However, the idea was expensive and complex. By this time, there were only 300 Subway locations in twenty states, with merely a scattering of stores in most of those states. Except for Connecticut, we didn't have much depth in any one state. As a result of our expansion, it was now more difficult to make network-wide decisions because many different voices had to be heard and appreciated. In this case, the voices would be particularly intense because if we decided to bake our own bread, each franchisee would be asked to invest $5,000 per store for equipment and remodeling.

For most of the next year, we developed and tested our idea in Connecticut. We contacted oven manufacturers to find the appropriate baking system to work in our stores. We tested the process of making the dough, and then shipping it, either fresh or frozen. We researched zoning codes to be certain we wouldn't violate local laws, and we inspected the store leases to see what changes would be required. We documented every step of the process. We knew that our only hope for selling this idea to our franchisees would be to show them evidence that it made financial sense to bake bread in our stores. And, of course, if the evidence wasn't there, we would drop the idea.

It took longer to develop the idea than we had anticipated, but once our customers sampled bread baked on our premises, the response was overwhelmingly favorable. Our research demonstrated that we attracted more customers, and they came back more often. Sales and profits increased as a result. Clearly the idea was a winner. When we finally published the evidence, many franchisees immediately made plans to upgrade their stores. Some franchisees were less enthusiastic than others, but eventually everyone got on board and we were making bread in all of our stores. It's a feature that continues to pay for itself over and over again.

Baking bread gave us a competitive advantage, but over time others followed our lead and they started baking bread, too. For a while, however, we enjoyed the exclusivity of this major improvement.

As you build your business, always make it a point to continuously improve it. By doing so, you'll attract more customers, you'll keep them coming back, and you'll increase sales and profits.

Mary Ellen Sheets is a Michigan-based microentrepreneur who mastered the lesson of continuous improvement in her first year of business in 1984. She focused on turning her family business into a real system and once it was successful she realized that it was franchisable. If you were to meet this five-foot, three-inch blonde with spiked hair, bright blue eyes, teeny, artsy glasses and a terrific smile, you'd never guess what she does for a living. "I'm kind of odd," Mary Ellen says of herself.

Not so odd, however, that she's incapable of building a remarkable business, and improving it daily so that she, and the family members who help her run it, can continue to profit from it. "We've never had a business plan," says Mary Ellen. "People would say, 'What's your plan?' and we would say, 'We don't know. We just plan to keep on getting better, and growing!'"

Odd as it may be, here's Mary Ellen Sheets's story. It reminds me a lot of my own story, and the development of Subway.

You're forty-something, the mother of three teenagers, a systems analyst for the state of Michigan, and one day your marriage dissolves.

What do you do?

Do you invest $350 in a truck, quit your dependable but boring job, and start a moving company?

Only if you're the bold and free-spirited Mary Ellen Sheets.

"I just wanted to own a business, and have the freedom that a business can give you," Mary Ellen explains. As things turned out, she not only built a business for herself, but for her three children, too.

"As a kid, we lived by a river and a golf course, and we would dive into the river to retrieve golf balls and then sell them for spending money. I was always thinking of ways to make money and to have my own business," she explains.

Even so, for someone earning $40,000 a year, with great benefits and twenty years of seniority, quitting her job was a daring decision, to say the least. Of course everyone warned

188

her not to do it. "I told my mom I was going to quit my job," Mary Ellen continues, "and she told me I was going to lose it all. I was a single parent with a plum of a job—except that it wasn't very interesting—and everyone was worried about me, and telling me not to quit. I was scared to death, but I quit anyway. I don't know why I quit. Something inside me told me to do it. Just thinking about it now, it's still a frightening thing. But it turned out better than I could have imagined. It became the happiest time of my life."

It was in the early 1980s that Mary Ellen's husband left her behind in Lansing, Michigan. He also left behind a daughter in college, two sons in high school, and an old pickup truck. "My boys wanted to help me," Mary Ellen recalls, "so they decided to place an ad in the paper and start a moving service using their dad's truck. That's how they were going to make their spending money. I thought it was a great idea. I drew a logo for them—a truck with two stick men—and they ran it in their ad. They called the business Two Men & A Truck, and that was it. They got started with that ad in the newspaper."

The boys charged $25 an hour for their services, which they provided mostly on weekends and after school. For each hour they worked the boys paid themselves $10 each. They dropped the remaining $5 per hour into a bowl which they kept in the kitchen. They used that money to pay for gasoline, truck repairs, and advertising. "They never had to look for work," says Mary Ellen. "They were always busy." Sometimes too busy, or busier than they wanted to be. Occasionally the boys would make arrangements to move a customer's furniture, but then they wouldn't feel like working that day. So they'd call the customer and claim their truck had been stolen! "They were just teenage boys," says Mary Ellen. "But most of the time, they worked hard." For two years, in fact, until they graduated from high school, the boys continued their moving business.

"By 1985," Mary Ellen continues the story, "my boys were out of high school and they went to college in the Upper Peninsula of Michigan, which was about as far away from home as they could get and still live in the state. After they were gone, the business was supposed to end, but the phone kept ringing. People wanted to hire them. So one day I decided there wasn't any sense of losing the business. I bought a moving van for $350—that's all the money I ever invested in the business. I hired two guys, set up an answering machine, and every day at lunch I went home from work to return the calls and set up the moving appointments. At night there were more calls. One night there were twelve calls! It just kept getting busier. I continued working the business part-time for a few years, and then I decided I needed to quit my job and work the business full-time."

She had no business experience, knew nothing about bookkeeping—"I called bills 'ins' and 'outs'"—she had no business insurance, no workman's compensation, and—in a state that required moving companies to be licensed and regulated—no authority to move anyone! "It was a helluva deal," she says. "I moved people from Lansing to Detroit to Ohio and all over. And I loved it! I loved being my own boss and not reporting to anyone. I didn't like going to the office and working in a cubicle where I watched the clock, wondering if it was time to go home, or time to go on vacation. I worked with nice people, but I felt closed in and I didn't like that. Once I gave up my job and concentrated on my business, I worked longer hours than ever before, and I still do. But I love it. In the earliest days of my business I used to get up at two and three in the morning just to start working."

And there was plenty to do.

Like making forms. When Mary Ellen's boys began the business, she created the Moving Sheet. No one had to tell her to make the form. After all, she was a systems analyst. Whatever the boys were going to move—furniture, toys, garden equipment, appliances, boxes, etc.—she instinctively knew there had to be a way to track these possessions. "The form included the customer's name and address," Mary Ellen relates, "and it listed everything the boys moved, including where

190

they moved it to. But the funny thing is that the boys always made sure not to leave the Moving Sheet behind because if they broke something, or anything went wrong, they didn't want the customer to be able to track them down! Now, of course, we would never operate that way."

That one form has since grown to eighty-three forms, each one an improvement to Two Men & A Truck, says Mary Ellen. "When you don't have any money to spend on advertising, or to invest in new systems or equipment," she explains, "you tend to get creative on your own. I'm a forms junkie. If we ran into a problem, or we needed to control some aspect of our business, it wasn't hard for me to sit down and create a form to handle it. Then, I'd revise the forms every so often to improve them. When I worked for the state, I always had a computer, so it was easy for me to get up in the morning and create a new form. I was also great at juggling statistics. I created reports that helped me track the progress of my business."

Most of the time, however, Mary Ellen admits she made things up. "I didn't know how to run a business. I didn't know what I was doing, I just did things. I went to the grocery store one day and bought a little black book that was for tracking payrolls. I learned everything myself, and in the process I reinvented the wheel."

Within several years, Two Men & A Truck had expanded to four trucks and ten employees. Every year, Mary Ellen invested some of her profits in another truck. By this time, her business attracted some notoriety, especially from competitors. And they didn't like what they saw. One day, incredible though it sounds, one of Mary Ellen's trucks was forced off the highway and into a ditch by a police cruiser. Later, she found out that her competitors had complained that her trucks were traveling beyond the legal boundaries for a local moving company. The police were retaliating on behalf of her competitors.

"After that incident," says Mary Ellen, "I took a soup can, placed it on a map, drew a circle the size of the can, and I told my employees, 'Don't move anyone outside of this circle.' I thought that would take care of the problem."

But she was wrong. "One day I got a visit from a female police officer. I was a little nervous when I saw her, but she was dressed in a uniform and she was wearing makeup and blue eye shadow. I thought anyone who wears eye shadow can't hurt me, so I invited her in. She asked to go through our Moving Sheets because she said someone had reported that we were violating the state's transportation laws. And we had, although not intentionally. I was written up for seven misdemeanors for traveling outside of our area. It took me a year to get the mess straightened out in court, but I only had to pay $100 in fines, plus my attorney's fees. I learned a lot of things the hard way, but after that, I made sure we complied with all the laws."

Learning things the hard way came with plenty of disadvantages. "I had to give up a lot to build my business," Mary Ellen recalls. "One day I had a husband, a home, and a family, and then I was all alone. I had to sell our home because I didn't have a nest egg built up to carry me through. I couldn't pay myself for a long, long time after I got into the business full-time. Fortunately I had some money built up in a deferred compensation account with the state, but it wasn't enough. I was worried about my kids. They had to take out loans to get through school. It was the poorest we would ever be. I made a pot of coffee and used it all week long. I just warmed up the pot each day. It's an embarrassing thing, but it's what I had to do to get by. After my kids, my focus was on my business, getting it started, and then improving it to make it better."

Sometimes making it better seemed impossible. Like the day her men moved a freezer and didn't plug it in. "I got a threatening letter from our customer. She said we had spoiled everything in her freezer, and she wanted me to pay her $800! I didn't have any money, so I just ignored the letter. I wouldn't recommend doing that, but I'm thinking this is the end of my business, and fortunately I never heard from her again."

A couple of years later a customer called and complained that Two Men & A Truck had damaged his Formica furniture, which was hard to repair. "I tried to talk to this man," says Mary Ellen, "but he became irate and started screaming at me. He threatened, 'I'll take out an ad in the newspaper and explain what a horrible company you run!' I was so upset I called my brother and asked him what I should do. He said, 'Sell that stupid business.' That's not what I wanted to hear, so I got mad at my brother. And that's when I knew I was hooked on my business."

She still didn't have any money, but that didn't bother Mary Ellen. "Not at all," she says. "I was just happy not to be working in a job! When you don't have money, you do things that are fun to do without much money."

For example, you buy a houseboat! That's how Mary Ellen spent one summer. The boat cost $5,000, and since she didn't have that kind of money she financed it. Of course, it wasn't much of a boat. Mary Ellen called it *Pee Wee*, and friends sometimes referred to it as a "floating outhouse." But that's where she lived and worked and played, from the docks of Port Huron. She used a cellular phone to keep in touch with her land-bound employees and customers. "I was so proud of that boat," she says. "It was so peaceful and beautiful. I could work for hours on my business when I was on the boat."

Until the weekends, that is, when friends would board *Pee Wee* for some fun, and even a little danger. With Mary Ellen as captain, and Jimmy Buffett or Dr. Hook blaring over the sound system, *Pee Wee* ventured into the rolling waves of Lake Huron. More than once a summer storm stirred up the lake and the waves nearly rolled the boat. On those occasions Mary Ellen would bravely tell her nervous guests to open the front and back doors of the boat and let the waters rush through. Everything got soaked, but Mary Ellen would tell her friends not to worry. "*Pee Wee*'s made of Styrofoam. This boat can't sink," she'd say, and laugh hysterically. Eventually, everyone in Port Huron knew Mary Ellen Sheets. Even the Coast Guard.

"Whenever they saw *Pee Wee*," Mary Ellen reports, "they'd just roll their eyes, hoping we'd stay afloat."

As Mary Ellen continued building Two Men & A Truck, she was invited one day in the late 1980s to join a panel of business owners at a seminar at Michigan State University. She was introduced as the woman who had the nerve to start a business during the recession in Michigan.

"I had no idea!" Mary Ellen says. Others may have been dissuaded from starting a business if they had known about a recession. But it made no difference to Mary Ellen. "If there was a recession," she says, "I missed it."

On the panel that day, however, there was another woman who owned a franchise company called the Pet Nanny. After she heard Mary Ellen speak, she approached her and told her that she should consider franchising her business. "I said to her, 'But all I have are two men and a truck.' She got in my face and said, 'All I do is feed dogs, for God's sake. If I can franchise, so can you.'"

That was proof enough for Mary Ellen to contact an attorney to help her prepare her business for franchising. "I knew nothing about franchising, even for the first couple of years after we started franchising," she says, "but the idea made sense to me. I had created a system, and I knew the business would make money, so why not share it with other people? I saw it as an opportunity to improve what I was doing, and at the same time grow the business."

Now she had even more work to do. In addition to assisting her attorney, who had to write the legal documents required of franchise companies, she wrote an operations manual to explain the business step by step to her franchisees, once she had one. She created ads for franchise sales, she wrote newsletters, she developed more forms, she organized meetings and eventually training programs. "I did it all myself," she explains, "and it was overwhelming." But it was also successful.

Her daughter, Melanie, became the first franchisee. She had recently graduated from college and couldn't find a job.

So she moved to Atlanta and launched a Two Men & A Truck franchise. A second franchisee followed shortly thereafter. "He was a guy I was dating," says Mary Ellen. A couple of her movers recognized that Two Men & A Truck was a great business, so they borrowed money and bought their own franchises. Then, several newspaper articles about Mary Ellen and her franchise opportunity created numerous telephone calls from people who wanted to own a franchise.

By 1994, Mary Ellen had awarded thirty-five franchises and she thought she was just getting started when a telephone call changed her life, as well as her family's. The state of Michigan's Republican Committee had been watching Mary Ellen, and the leadership was recruiting her to run for the Michigan Senate. "Some of them got to know me," she explains, "when I testified on behalf of small moving companies when the state was looking into the deregulation of the trucking industry. I was so scared at the time that I was shaking before I testified and some of the members of the Republican Committee had to hold me up. Now they wanted to know if I'd run for the Senate. At first, I laughed because I knew nothing about politics. But they were serious. They introduced me to several senators and everyone said I was the perfect candidate. Plus they said I could still run my business. So I said yes."

But as soon as she opened her campaign office she regretted the decision. "It was ridiculous. It was not my thing. By this time I was making some money and I had a Mercedes. But I had to padlock it away so no one would see it. Driving anything but an American-made car wouldn't have helped my candidacy in the state of Michigan!"

There were other problems, too, that interfered with her lifestyle. "The committee members didn't like the way I dressed. They didn't like my hair. They wanted me to change it all and wear suits, which I did. But then I'd go to these chicken dinners and you could never sit down because you had to shake everyone's hand. I did this for two months in the spring and I was burned out. My friends were headed to Florida for a week's vacation and they wanted me to tag along because they knew I needed some time off. The committee told me to go ahead, but it would be my last break until after the summer. So I went to Florida, read books, relaxed, and when I came back to Michigan I looked in the mirror and said, 'Mary Ellen, what are you doing? Running for the Senate isn't you.' I called the Republican Committee and told them to find a new candidate. They weren't happy, but that's what they did." Her decision to call the Republican Committee is a good example of how important it is to make course corrections when you realize you're off track. It was a smart move for Mary Ellen to get out of politics once she realized it wasn't all that important to her.

Meanwhile, things had changed at Two Men & A Truck. Even though the Republican leadership had told Mary Ellen she could run for the Senate and simultaneously operate her business, she didn't believe them. When she agreed to become a candidate she consulted first with her family. She couldn't become a politician, she said, unless she knew the business was in good hands. And the best hands she knew belonged to her children.

By this time, Melanie had sold her Atlanta franchise and moved to Detroit where she opened another franchise of Two Men & A Truck. She had also accepted a job as a pharmaceutical representative and was earning $85,000 a year. But when Melanie heard about her mother's plans for the State Senate, she agreed to give up her job and oversee the franchise company. She would also maintain ownership of her franchise in Detroit, and commute to Lansing, the company's headquarters.

At the same time, Mary Ellen's son Jon had started a Two Men & A Truck in Grand Rapids. "He had already built a very successful business and he also had a family by this time. But he agreed to help me, too," Mary Ellen explains. "I needed him to run my local franchise, the business he and his brother had started. He agreed to come to Lansing two days a week to make sure that my franchise was operating smoothly."

And that's how Mary Ellen Sheets nearly worked herself out of a job. "By the time I gave up politics, my kids had taken over my business," she says. "I couldn't send them back to their homes, so I slid back into the business to do whatever needed to be done. There are always improvements to be made, and I'm the ideal person for that."

A couple of years later, life became nearly perfect for Mary Ellen. "We needed someone to handle our franchise sales," she explains. "So I called my son Brig, who lived in northern Michigan where he operated one of our franchises, and I asked him to come home. He sold his franchise, sold his house, and he and his wife and children relocated to Lansing. He's in charge of franchise sales and doing a great job. In fact, all three of my children are doing great jobs. They run a beautiful company."

By late 1999, there were eighty Two Men & A Truck franchises across the United States, and several in Canada. Of that number, seventeen of the franchisees, including Mary Ellen, had built businesses that grossed more than a million dollars. One franchisee was close to $2 million in gross sales. "It's sort of unbelievable," says Mary Ellen. "To think that it began so small. We've created more than 1,500 jobs for people and we've helped a bunch of franchisees attain lifestyles that they never thought they'd have. I see them coming to our annual meetings in fur coats, driving Jaguars, and talking about their kids going to expensive colleges, and they just built a second home . . . It's the best feeling in the world knowing that I've helped other people."

She plans to continue doing it, too. "That's what it's all about," says Mary Ellen. "I planted the seeds in the early days and we're still planting them. In this business, like every business, there's always room for improvement."

CHAPTER THIRTEEN

BELIEVE IN YOUR PEOPLE

David Schlessinger was fortunate when he launched Encore Books near the University of Pennsylvania. Even though he was a teenager, he intuitively knew that he would need other people to build his business. Consequently, he quickly assembled a young, dedicated team and together they created a retail phenomenon.

Just like David Schlessinger, I started in business as a teenager and I also knew that I would need help to run my store and to assist in building the business. However, even though I knew I'd need help, I never really appreciated how important and valuable every single team member would be to the building of a business.

Today I can tell you that job descriptions, proper levels of delegation to match the needs of the job, and the hiring of the right people for each job can make all the difference in your business. First, each job must be properly structured to suit the needs of your company. Then, you must delegate the correct amount of authority and responsibility to each job. Finally, you must hire the best people for your jobs, and then train and retain them. It's also important, of course, that you believe in your people!

How did I learn this valuable lesson? Frankly, it wasn't

easy. In spite of the fact that I had graduated with a degree in psychology, it took me years to "get it."

Even as a teenager I understood the general idea of hiring the right employees and training them properly. You probably have a general idea of how important these ideas are, too, but I would bet that you don't really know how valuable other people can be.

In the early days of building my business, belief in other people wasn't a subject that concerned me. For one thing, I didn't know it was important, and for another, my days were already full of challenging thoughts and ideas. There was always a lot of work to do. How to get the work done concerned me more than anything.

Fortunately, at least I understood that it was a good idea to categorize jobs and delegate them to other people. I knew I had to delegate in order to expand the business. The first week that I started Subway, I realized that I couldn't do all the work myself. That's when I recruited my high school friend Art Witkowski to help me build our first store and other friends to work in the store after we opened. With no formal training, and very little instruction from me, these first employees helped me get the work done. They didn't always do things the way I would have done them, and they didn't always make the right decisions. But they did the best they could. As we gained experience, we all performed better.

However, even though all my employees were working hard, I never gave them the chance to show what they could really do. We all seemed to be working on a series of tasks, but I seldom gave people broad authority to handle an area of responsibility, even though most every time I gave someone a task to do, they did it well.

I think most of us struggle with delegation. In the beginning we get involved with all of the jobs, we know what has to be done and we want everything done right, just the way we would do it, and we often think no one can do it as well as we can. We've all heard and tend to believe the phrase, "If you want something done right, do it yourself!"

Today I believe, "If you want something done as well as you can do it, do it yourself. But if you want it done even better, let someone else do it." That's right! I think most jobs in my organization can be done better by other people. Why? Sometimes they do a job better because of specialized knowledge, or because of their personality, or because of their problem-solving ability, or because of the way they focus on details, or because of their intelligence, or simply because of the amount of time they can devote to the job.

Also, I believe that too much involvement by me, or any boss, can be an obstacle to progress. If you think about reaching an objective in the same way you think about driving from here to there you'll get the picture.

For instance, if you wanted your employee to drive from New York to Los Angeles, you might give him a car, a budget, a map, and tell him when he's expected to arrive. Or, you might lay out the entire route, step by step. Or, you might tell him to stop every 100 miles to call in with a progress report and to discuss the journey before going forward. Or, you might not even tell him the final destination. You might simply tell him to drive west for fifty miles and then call in for further instructions. Finally, you might also want to get involved in the details of deciding where he should stay overnight. You might want to make the reservations for him and you might even want to be sure he buys the right gas at the right price.

I think you get the picture. Bosses can affect progress toward an objective. Sometimes they are like tollbooths, and even worse, sometimes they're like jackknifed tractor-trailers. Everyone that's moving toward the objective has to wait for *them* before anyone can proceed.

I'll give you three quick illustrations of how believing in people has really helped me in business.

I've already told you about Jim Smith from Baltimore and

how he became our first Development Agent. After taking the four-hour drive from Connecticut to Baltimore and touring the town I realized that we needed a local person to do the important jobs that were best done by someone in the field. I had to believe that someone else could handle these tasks, and Jim ultimately proved that he could. Today, we have 200 Development Agents like Jim Smith in North America and around the world.

My next enlightenment occurred when I couldn't return my phone calls quickly enough. In the beginning of our franchise operation, I was involved in almost every aspect of the business, from selling the franchises to training and supporting franchisees. As a result, the franchisees frequently called me when they had a question or faced a challenge. If I was unavailable for just a few hours the messages piled up. That created a major problem, because the calls wouldn't be returned fast enough. Even so, I kept trying my best to keep up, since I was the one who knew the most about the company, and I could do the very best job assisting them, or so I thought.

One afternoon I walked into my office and twelve phone message were waiting. Some were from the day before and others had come in during the morning. With my heavy upcoming schedule it looked like it might take a couple of days to return those calls and of course more calls would come in while I was calling the first group back.

I knew some temporary assistance was needed so I asked our newest employee to help out. Mary was a recent college graduate who was just learning the ropes. I gave her six of what looked like the easier calls and said, "Mary, I've got a dozen really important calls to return and my work is backed up. Please let these folks know that I'm really busy and that it may take a few days for me to get back to them. Also, find out what they need and see if you can help them in any way. While you're working on those perhaps I'll have a chance to get back to these others."

I had spent the next hour working on a project in my office when Mary returned.

"Did you reach them all?" I asked. When Mary explained that she had I was quite pleased.

"Were you able to find out what they called about?" I wanted to know. I was actually very surprised when she told me that every store owner had explained to her why they had called, what information they were looking for, and what advice they were seeking.

"Which are the urgent ones that I have to call back ASAP?"

When Mary told me that I didn't have to call any of them back I didn't believe her. I asked her in detail about every call and she explained that she was personally able to handle two of the calls on the spot, two required a little research, and two were handed over to others in the company who could give the advice the franchisees needed. I actually called two of the franchisees right then to see if they needed to talk to me further. Neither did. In fact, they told me how pleased they were with the help they got.

I should have been pleased, too, but my first reaction was complete and total surprise that someone so new to the company could handle my most important calls! How could that be?

So I turned over the other six calls to her to see what she could do with them. Same result.

After thinking through what happened with these calls I realized that the franchisees didn't really need to speak to me. They were simply calling for information and guidance, and what they really wanted was someone to spend the time and give them the best possible response.

Right then I gave Mary the permanent assignment of assisting the franchise owners who called in for help. Her job evolved into what is now known as our Franchisee Services Department, one of our most important teams at Subway headquarters. Since the establishment of this department, it's been much easier for Subway franchisees to get timely answers to their important questions. As Subway expanded the Franchisee Services Department also expanded, the team gained experience, and on any given day, most calls are routine for our coordinators, as we now call the people who work in that department. But not all of the calls were easy to handle and that leads to my third story.

Some calls from franchise owners were pretty sensitive because they involved a misunderstanding over the interpretation of a rule or conflict between people in the field. These calls often required a lot of time to work through and while I was happy to assist I found that I didn't have the best temperament to listen to the details of each problem, and I didn't have the time that each issue deserved.

For example, Subway requires its store owners to comply with specific operating procedures so that customers get a similar experience in every store. When we meet those standards customers return more often because they know what to expect from us. To ensure that the standards are met our Development Agents inspect every store each month and any store that is not up to standard gets marked "out of compliance." Franchisees who don't meet our operating standards can't open more stores, and they risk the termination of their franchise if they don't promptly correct the deficiencies.

Sometimes this inspection process creates a misunderstanding and the call might come in like this: "I'm getting marked out of compliance and I think my Development Agent is picking on me. He's misinterpreting the standards just to harass me. Help!"

Sometimes the store owners would skip over the Franchisee Services Department and call me directly. These calls were time-consuming, often requiring research that included asking questions of numerous people. The issues weren't always complex, but they seldom could be resolved with a single phone call. And now, many of these more difficult issues were piling up on my desk.

One day I went to lunch with a college professor and I told him about the calls that slipped through the cracks in our Franchisee Services Department and ended up on my desk.

"You need an ombudsman," he said.

That's a word that I had not heard before, but the professor told me it's a common position within colleges and universities. The role of the ombudsman is to investigate complaints of maladministration and resolve them.

Perfect!

When I returned to the office I designated one of our newer people to be Subway's first ombudsman. "These franchisees," I told her, referring to several message slips in my hand, "have certain problems. I want you to investigate the problems from their perspective and from Subway's perspective. Then, I want you to work to resolve the issues fairly for all concerned." With some guidance from me along the way she was able to work through every situation. Since that time the Subway Ombudsman Department has expanded to include several individuals who resolve all of these special issues without my intervention.

These three stories illustrate how other people easily handle important jobs that were formerly mine. As a business owner it's critical to understand that every person has important talents and their contributions can be even more valuable than your own.

Some people say it's hard to find good employees. I don't think that's true. Think about your own job experience. Did you ever start a job saying, "I'm going to do a really bad job here so that I'll get fired"? Of course not. Everyone has special talents. Please realize that when you hire them they really want to fit in and be part of your team.

Believe in people. Trust that people can do a great job and want to do well on the job. Work to put people into jobs that are well suited for them. Then, train them and allow them to

work toward important objectives without too much inter-
ference.

Leadership expert John Maxwell says that when we believe in people we motivate them to reach their potential.
"You can hire people to work for you," says Maxwell, author
of *Developing the Leaders Around You*, "but you must win their
hearts by believing in them in order to have them work with
you." He's right.

You also must equip people to make a contribution to
your business. Give them the resources and the support
they'll need to personally and professionally enhance their
role in your organization. Then, get out of their way so they
can get the job done.

Believing in people comes naturally for some and is a skill
that's acquired by others. At age eighteen David Schlessinger bought a small bookshop near the University of Pennsylvania campus in Philadelphia, where he was a student. He
had never owned a business before. Never managed people
before. He knew nothing about the bookstore business.
From his very first moment as a proprietor this young entrepreneur had to learn about believing in people. His story is
an inspiration for everyone who starts small and plans to finish big.

———————

David Schlessinger is a serial entrepreneur. In other words, he
thinks he knows a better way to build a business, and as soon
as he does, he moves on to the next idea. His obsession is the
adventure more than it is the money, the success, or even the
adulation of family and friends. Twice in twenty-five years,
after starting as a teenager with $10,000, David has built retail
empires. The first was in the book industry; the second in the
toy industry. Now in his mid-forties he has at least another
twenty-five years to continue his adventures. But ever faithful
to the style and temperament of a serial entrepreneur, he gives

no clues as to where he'll strike next. (A good hunch, however, is the Internet.)

"I just wanted to be free to lead a team to build great new concepts," says David, tall, dark, and bearded. "I love to create concepts that deliver value to the customer in a better way, and hopefully add something positive to the community."

Independent is a good word to describe David Schlessinger. No one quite understands the way he thinks. Look into his eyes, however, and you'll see the word *intense*. Whatever he does, he does it with passion.

Growing up in a comfortable Philadelphia suburb, life was good for the Schlessinger family. David's father was a prominent business attorney, and his mother became a literary agent after raising three children, the eldest being David. But there was no silver spoon in the Schlessinger home. David and his siblings were expected to earn their own way. Mom and dad would get them through college, but for everything else they were on their own. David learned exactly what that meant the year he wrecked his father's car. He had to pay the damages, and none of the money could come from his savings account. He earned the money in a steel mill where he was employed the summer between his freshman and sophomore years of college.

After high school graduation, David enrolled in a small Connecticut college with plans of studying to become a lawyer. But at the end of his freshman year, he wanted to be near his girlfriend back home, so he decided to return to Philadelphia and enroll at the University of Pennsylvania. That summer he labored in the steel mill and earned "a pile" of money. He not only worked double shifts, he volunteered to work on holidays. After he paid back his father, there was still plenty of money to fund his social life and add to his modest savings account. The mill's wages were so good, in fact, that he considered working full-time while going to college. But then the fatigue of double shifts caught up with him. He nearly wrecked his car again. That's when he decided it was better to quit the mill and concentrate on school.

But even then he had something else in mind to supplement his financial needs. After moving into the high-rise dormitory on the University of Pennsylvania campus he and a friend began plotting a strategy to earn money in the real estate market. At the time, center city Philadelphia presented countless opportunities for the renewal of real estate. "My friend and I talked about pooling our resources, buying an old house, fixing it up, and renting it for income," David recalls. "We read books that promised to teach us how to invest $3,000 and turn it into $3 million. We were going to make a fortune!"

While the search for an appropriate piece of real estate continued, one afternoon a Realtor suggested that David visit a small bookstore at 13th and Pine, near the Penn campus. The proprietor of the bookstore, Robert Marks, was thinking about franchising his concept, and the Realtor thought there might be an opportunity for David to get involved. Even though David wasn't interested in either a bookstore *or* franchising, he went for a look. Located next to a bar, Robert Marks Bookseller was a tiny, 200-square-foot shop jammed with books. Deep-discounting set the place apart from other bookstores. Most of the books were recent best-sellers that normally retailed for $10 to $15. But Marks sold them for $2 to $3.

Marks told David that he had discovered a source where he could buy books for 50 cents each. The source, David learned, was in the business of renting books to libraries. When a book ran its course and was no longer popular, the library returned the book and stopped paying the rental fee. All of these books, most of them still in good shape, ended up in a warehouse in Williamsport, Pennsylvania. "Marks was the only person who had access to the warehouse," David relates. "Somehow he charmed his way in and he could cherry-pick the best books. He selected books for two stores, one that he operated in

Philadelphia, and another that he owned in State College near the Penn State campus."

While David was excited to visit the store—he bought several hardback books, a luxury on his budget—and to hear Marks's engaging story, he didn't see an opportunity for himself. "I knew nothing about running a business, nothing about retail, and nothing about the book business," he explains. "Marks mentioned franchising, but that didn't interest me, either. I was thrilled to know that I could afford to buy these first-class books when I needed them, but that was the extent of my interest. Within a couple of days, I had forgotten about Marks."

But Marks hadn't forgotten about David. He called him a few weeks later with an unusual proposal. "Marks was in his early fifties at the time," says David, who was eighteen. "He was an eccentric kind of guy. He called to tell me that his parents had visited Philadelphia and they said it was too dangerous for him to live in the city! So he was moving to State College and selling his Philadelphia store. He wanted me to buy the store. He said the price was a firm $10,000, and he gave me three days to make a decision."

For someone who had no interest in business or a bookstore, David was curious enough to take a second look. "I don't know why I agreed to meet with Marks again. I didn't have $10,000, and buying a business was not on my mind. I was two thirds of the way into a semester, with plenty of work to keep me busy, but for some reason I was attracted to this opportunity. On my second visit I noticed that other than the books, there wasn't much in the store. The fixtures were old. The location was not ideal. But for every ten people who walked past the store, three or four of them stopped to shop, and 90 percent of the time they left with an armful of books. Everyone loved the store, especially college kids. Curiosity tempted you to stop in and browse for a few good books. It was fun to buy the books at discount."

In spite of all that, the store wasn't making much money. By David's analysis, and his father's verification, the store earned about $100 a day, after paying the employees and the rent, which ran $225 a month. "For $10,000," David's father told him, "you won't be getting your money's worth. The earnings aren't there. But if you think the source for the books is valuable, then it might be a good investment." He gave his blessing for David to proceed.

By this time, David was feeling comfortable with the idea of owning a business, and he decided to agree to Marks's terms. "I only had $7,000 in my savings," he explains. "Marks said he wouldn't negotiate the sale price, so I had to come up with another $3,000. I borrowed half of it from my eleven-year-old brother, Andrew, and half of it from my fourteen-year-old sister, Marjorie. I knew it was a risk, but at worst case if the business failed I'd just have to pay back my brother and sister. I'd still be in school, and I'd still go to law school. So I really didn't have much to lose."

On December 16, 1973, ownership of Robert Marks Bookseller was transferred to young David Schlessinger. He promptly changed the name to Encore Books. "Marks helped me come up with the name," he recalls. "We were brainstorming one day and we said we were selling books that were making a second appearance. From that line of thought we landed on the name Encore." Little did he know that Encore would soon become a recognizable brand name, eventually to become a chain of 100 stores.

David's timing was perfect. The Christmas season is one of the best times to own a bookstore. Sales tripled during the holidays, from several hundred dollars a week to a few thousand. At first, David wasn't sure how to handle the money. "I really didn't know what I was doing. I used to carry the cash back to my dorm room every night. I stacked it on my bed and after a few days I had collected several thousands of dollars. I said to a friend, 'What do I do with this? What kind of a bank account do I open for a business?'" Fortunately a call to his father set him straight.

As David settled into the business, Marks provided assistance from afar. Mostly, he continued buying the inventory for the store, making every effort to provide a good selection of books. He charged David 62 cents per book. Meanwhile, in spite of his naïveté, David concentrated on boosting sales, serving customers, and operating the business, all the while remaining a student at Penn. "I wanted to build the best bookstore in the city of Philadelphia," he says, "but I had no master plan or vision at the time. I didn't have a written mission statement. I didn't have long-term goals. I had no idea what the business could become." What he did have, however, was an obsession to build a successful business. Even without a plan for what he hoped to build, no sacrifice was too great a price to pay for this adventure. That included a law degree, or for that matter, any college degree.

"I was working more than forty hours a week," David recalls, "and keeping up at Penn was a challenge. Beginning that second semester, I started looking for the easy courses. I had a friend who took great notes and I registered in as many courses with him as possible." Often forced to choose between attending class or tending to the business, the business won. "But as long as I had some time to study, and I could rely on my friend's notes before exams, I could maintain a decent grade point average." Clearly, however, David was now less intense about school.

At Encore, David worked alongside three employees. "When I bought the store, I kept Marks's employees, and that was a necessity. They were all older than I was and they knew the business. I quickly learned to rely on them, especially when I had to go to class or I couldn't be in the store. I could stack shelves, serve the customers, and run the cash register, but I knew that I couldn't do it all on my own, even though I wanted to. I can't say that I was comfortable relying on people I didn't know very well. It required a lot of trust, and that was difficult. But at this point it was either sink or swim. So I learned how to delegate from day one."

He also learned the importance of building and managing

systems, especially as he thought about expanding the business. At first, he had every intention of operating only a single store, at least until he graduated from college. But within a few months, those plans changed. He needed more space, and a street with more foot traffic, so in May 1974, less than six months after acquiring the business, he moved Encore to Walnut Street. "I leased 1,000 square feet of space in a highly commercial area of the city with many shops and lots of office buildings. The rent jumped to $750 a month, and that was scary, but instead of a couple hundred people passing by a day, we now had a few thousand. More people meant more book sales." The extra space provided the opportunity to broaden the inventory, so in addition to a larger variety of used books, David introduced closeouts, or remaindered books that could be purchased for pennies on the dollar.

Of course, now he also needed additional staff. "It was very obvious to me that building a team of people was critically important. There wasn't any other way to develop the business successfully. And yet, without much money to pay people, hiring good people was a struggle. So I did what came naturally to me. I treated people like members of my family." In fact, many of the employees were family! "Initially, my business and family were totally interchangeable," David continues. "Every member of my immediate family—including aunts, uncles, and cousins—worked full-time, or just pitched in to help make Encore a success." David also employed his college friends, at least a dozen of them at different times, he estimates.

"When I hired employees, it was first a matter of painstakingly finding the best, most trustworthy people to invite into my business. Then, I trained them in my philosophy that we're a family committed to serving the customer at the highest level. Finally, I retained them by treating them the way I wanted to be treated. Like a family, we celebrated our milestones with parties. I gave them awards for their accomplishments and I paid them to the best of my ability. Our salaries were never as good as the chain bookstores, but fortunately

211

the book business appeals to a lot of people. Once they were on board, it was easy to get them excited and to get them committed to the business. Soon they were initiated into the family feeling, and that fostered a real team commitment and esprit de corps."

It helped, no doubt, that everyone who worked at Encore saw David Schlessinger as the model employer and manager. "Even though I was without an explicit mission or a vision for my business, I knew I wanted to be the best regional bookstore. Details were very important to me, so I created checklists for everything, from cleanliness to friendliness, from receiving inventory to placing books on display. I committed myself to these checklists, and when people saw my concern and interest for doing things right, they committed themselves to the same details. One of my earliest hires was a woman who had worked for 7-Eleven. Her job there included traveling from store to store checking the lunch meat, making sure it was in the right place, that it had not spoiled, and that everything was perfect for the customer. I knew if she was checking bologna at 7-Eleven, she would be perfect for Encore. Following those checklists, paying attention to details, and living up to the highest standards, that's part of the reason we became so successful."

Everyone knew that as the leader, David played by the rules. That made it easier for others to play by the rules. Anyone who violated the rules simply wasn't a good fit, and they didn't survive in Encore's culture. The fall-out occasionally surprised David, especially because he wanted to trust people, and delegate as much as possible to them. "There was a salesclerk who really disappointed me," he recalls. This fellow, according to David, had a full-time job with a reputable organization. "That gave me a feeling of comfort about him. But one day I watched him interact with some of his friends in the store. They picked up an armful of travel guides and walked out. I didn't see them pay for the books, so when the salesclerk went to lunch, I checked the register tape, and he had not rung up the sale. It should have been a $30 to $50 sale. When the salesclerk returned from lunch I confronted him and he denied it. He said he had charged them a discount because we gave substantial discounts to large companies and organizations, which wasn't true. But even with a discount he couldn't show me that he had rung up the sale. Again I said he hadn't fully charged his friends for the books, and he continued to insist that he had. This went on for quite some time until he finally admitted the truth. I said he could no longer work for Encore. He asked me for a second chance, but I said no. This was all very difficult and intimidating for me because he was older than me. But I stuck to my guns. He left angry. He told me that if I couldn't give people a second chance then I had a bigger problem. It was a telling lesson for me. In a retail business everything is built on trust, yet it was clear that even seemingly trustworthy people could sometimes let you down. That's when I realized the best way to avoid these types of problems was to treat employees like part of the family so that their loyalty would be strengthened, and build good systems that would expose future transgressions."

David's theories worked. Through the years he recruited a talented and dependable staff. "They were a great group of people," he recalls fondly. "Usually when they joined Encore it was their first or second job. So they were young and inexperienced, but they were willing to work hard. I took the time to get to know them, and that seemed to make up for the modest wages that I could afford. I never asked any of them to do anything that I wouldn't do, including working right through the night to set up a store, or until my hands were swollen, as happened once. This wasn't just a job, and I never treated it like that. As a result, they didn't either. Many of them would have walked through walls to get their jobs done."

The dedication encouraged David to believe in his people and to delegate work to them. But even then it wasn't easy. "I really didn't delegate enough of the work at higher levels, and I would encourage others to do so," he says. "I needed better budgeting and planning. I needed a president or chief operating officer to take on some of my operating responsibilities. I could have used a board of directors to help me think strategically at a higher level."

As it was, it seemed that he performed spectacularly thinking at his own level. After relocating his first store, sales more than doubled to $250,000. He was on track to hit a net profit of $40,000. His parents, who monitored his progress, especially after his father signed a bank note to help relocate the business, decided they wanted to open a store for David's mother to manage. His parents, of course, funded the operation while David provided the operational system. "My mother's store was on Chestnut Street, in another commercial section of the city, and it worked so well that I got interested in opening more stores." Soon, David opened a third store on the University of Pennsylvania campus, and then he trekked across the Delaware River to open a store in suburban Cherry Hill, New Jersey.

"By this time," David explains, "I was beginning to understand the dynamics of the business, but it still wouldn't come together for several years. I needed six years just to learn what I was doing." One of the facts he understood was that his stores depended on foot traffic. Also, in retail jargon, they were impulse stores, and not destination stores. "We attracted people secondhand," David explains. "They were already out shopping for something else. When they saw the Encore sign, they stopped in to look around. However, they weren't coming to us first. We weren't a shopping mall concept, so we couldn't go there."

Yet, David wanted to follow the money, which meant that he needed to expand his business to suburbia. To do that, Encore would have to become a destination store. That meant a full-line store, with new books, hardcovers, paperbacks, magazines, and even gift items. A mass-merchandised store, properly promoted, could draw customers firsthand.

Nearing the end of the 1970s, regional bookstore chains

popped up in other parts of the country, some of them backed by major book companies. One or two of these chains, David suspected, would eventually move into the Philadelphia market. With four Encore stores open, David found himself at a crossroads. Would Encore remain a closeout business, or become a full-line bookstore, capable of competing with newcomers?

"The Cherry Hill store," David relates, "was breaking even at best and it wasn't helping us financially. The business didn't have the foot traffic that we had in Philadelphia. I realized it wasn't going to work unless we aggressively advertised to attract more customers. At the same time, I noticed the suburban buyers weren't as sophisticated as the city buyers. The suburban customer wasn't willing to stop in to see if they could get lucky and find a great book at a low price. They needed a reason to come to us. One day I heard a woman say to her companion that she wasn't going to Encore because 'they just sell used books there.' That's when I decided to get all of the used books out of the store and we began to evolve into a full-line bookstore."

In 1980, committed to a vision where there had been no vision before, David opened three new stores with no used books. He converted two of his existing stores to the mass-merchandised concept, and kept one store for closeout sales only. "It was during this time," he says, "that I worked for thirty-five days straight without a break, and at one time for thirty-six hours without stopping."

Why?

Because he was scared.

"Everything was now at risk," he explains. "My parents invested money to help me, and so did several of their friends. Everything was at jeopardy with this new concept—our future depended on the mass-merchandised bookstore, and that concept was entirely new to me."

As it turned out, the business struggled financially for a year, but in the second year after the conversion, the business began making more money than it ever had before. Helping matters was a bold advertising campaign that trumpeted the benefits of the new Encore—i.e., new books at discounted prices—and customers eagerly responded. Enthusiastically, David began opening three to four new stores annually.

Success created a cultlike admiration for David Schlessinger in the business and book communities of Philadelphia. Authors wanted to befriend him, cognizant of his powerful marketing empire. Business leaders courted him, curious about the whiz kid's next move. Even the president of the University of Pennsylvania made note of his success, particularly because David was one who got away. He never completed his degree. "After three years at Penn," David explains, "I had a 3-point-something grade average and one credit more than was needed to graduate. So I planned to march in the commencement ceremony. But then the university reminded me that I had not made up an incomplete, and until I did I could not get my diploma. I said I would enroll in another class during the summer, so I was allowed to wear a cap and gown and participate in the graduation ceremony, which I wanted to do for my parents. That summer, I enrolled in an art history course, but it was far more difficult than I had time to invest in it, so I dropped out. Later, I petitioned Penn to grant me a diploma. I explained that I had started a business in my sophomore year, and I was willing to write a case study about the start-up if they would give me credit for it, but the university turned me down. At that point, I decided I didn't need a degree to succeed in business."

Obviously he was right, but the situation was still somewhat bothersome to Sheldon Hackney, Penn's president. One day, at the height of David's success, Hackney wrote the former student a letter. "He was really very humorous," says David. "I had never met him, but he said I was not a good advertisement for higher education in general, and not for the University of Pennsylvania in particular. So he invited me to return to college and complete my degree. He asked me to enroll in a course of my choice—he even offered to pay half the fee—and upon successful completion, Penn would then grant me a degree. The letter was so skillfully written that I decided I couldn't turn him down."

David enrolled in an English course that sounded particularly interesting and useful. But once again, scheduling conflicts frequently arose and David always chose his business over school. Since the class met weekly, by skipping one session David missed an entire week of information. Leading up to the final exam, however, there was still hope that David would pass the course and Penn would grant him a degree.

At this same time, Rite Aid, a large drugstore chain based in Harrisburg, Pennsylvania, contacted David with interest in buying Encore. "Rite Aid had already purchased a couple of other niche businesses," David relates, "and now they were looking at the book business. On the day of my final exam, I was invited to Harrisburg to get serious about the acquisition. I thought I could fly over there—it's only 100 miles from Philadelphia—and get back by the end of the day to take my final exam at six o'clock. But late in the afternoon we still had not worked out the details of the purchase, although we were getting close. The chairman of Rite Aid then asked if I'd like to stay for dinner before I flew home. Now I'm thinking, do I tell him that I have to get back to Philadelphia to take an exam? Or do I just keep quiet, spend some additional time with him, and hope to work out the terms of our deal?"

There really wasn't a choice. David stayed for dinner. And that night Rite Aid agreed to pay him a seven-figure sum for his twenty-store chain.

"I wasn't looking to sell Encore," David explains, "but when the opportunity came along, I decided to consider it. For a dozen years, I had only done one thing in my life, and I didn't want to do just one thing. Not that there's anything wrong with that. But I decided to stop and look for a new direction. I was obsessed with Encore. I had a tremendous passion for the business. But I had also begun to feel tremendous pressure

START SMALL, FINISH BIG

about the debt, which was considerable. My parents had personally guaranteed my loans, and their house was on the line. If my business took a downturn, my parents risked losing quite a bit of money, and that wasn't a good feeling. I wanted to clear the debt as much as anything else. So when Rite Aid approached me, it was the right thing to do for me and my family."

As part of the deal with Rite Aid, David became an employee of the corporation and continued to expand Encore. But within a couple of years boredom set in, and then he gave up the book business for good. "After so many years," he says, "I was thrilled to be able to travel and to spend time with my wife." He bought a house on the beach, he studied French, he learned how to hit a tennis ball, and for a couple of years he drifted, though he always intended to develop another business.

"Once I started looking for a new challenge," says David, "I wanted to build something I could believe in. I was frustrated because for a long time I couldn't find anything meaningful. I kept looking at niche markets, but nothing appealed to me. During this time my wife and I were planning to start a family and I realized that shopping for children was a hassle. If you wanted to buy them something really interesting, you had to rely on catalogues. There weren't any retail businesses that served the specialty educational toy market."

Voilà!

David envisioned a superstore stocked with top-quality children's toys, games, books, and multimedia products. The business would have a unique mission in its dedication to "the best for children," and a passionate commitment to its customers. In 1991, David opened his brainchild in suburban Philadelphia under the name Zany Brainy. Within a year, the store averaged 50 percent higher annual sales per square foot than Toys "R" Us, and David began his expansion program. Again, he credits the people who helped him build a second successful business. "By this time," he acknowledges, "I had learned the art of delegation. I hired people in advance of needing them, rather than just to survive, as I had to do at Encore. But everything I learned at Encore, I brought to Zany Brainy."

Within half a dozen years, the Zany Brainy chain included fifty-one locations nationwide with annual sales in excess of $100 million. And then, almost on cue, David decided to move on.

Early in 1998, he felt so confident about his management team that he turned the operation of Zany Brainy over to them and he and his family moved to New Mexico to begin a sabbatical. David needed time to think; time to prepare for his next strategic move. "When I'm building a business," David explains, "I believe in giving it a 100 percent pure, unadulterated commitment. But during the downtime between businesses, I give 100 percent to the intellectual and spiritual renourishment of my family."

Eventually, David plans to return to Philadelphia and undoubtedly to begin his next serial move. He wouldn't say, of course, what he plans to do next. But whatever it is, people will be part of the venture.

CHAPTER FOURTEEN

NEVER RUN OUT OF MONEY. BORROW BEFORE YOU NEED TO.

Earl Tate loves to spend money! So much so that it nearly destroyed his business career. Twice he lost his business for lack of money. But now he's back in the game, and this time he's learned his lesson! He says he won't run out of money again.

Here's a scary thought. Even if your business does well, you may run short of money. Even worse, you may run out of money and fail as a result, even though everything in your business appears to be going well. How could this happen? How can this be avoided?

Extra money is almost always needed in business. If your business is good and you attract new customers, cash may be tight as you wait for them to pay you. Also, you might need to add capacity, or you may want to open a second location. If business is bad you'll need some extra money to tide you over while you correct the situation.

That's why the most important rule of business is to always have cash in the bank and to never, ever run out of money. Keep your expenses low, collect any money due you as soon as possible, and borrow money before you need to.

In business, proper borrowing practices can help, but most small business owners don't understand how banks work, and they don't know how to think about borrowing. Before we delve into this topic, let's examine your personal thoughts about these subjects. You can begin to sort out your thoughts by quickly answering these questions: When is it good to borrow money? What is the limit of how much you should borrow? How much will interest payments impact profits? How does a bank decide on who to loan to?

I grew up with conservative ideas about borrowing. Years ago I would have said that banks loan money to businesses that need loans, and that businesses should borrow as little money as possible, and only when absolutely necessary because interest payments can really hurt profits.

Today I say that banks never loan money to businesses that *need* to borrow. I tell business owners to borrow as much money as possible, and to borrow well before they need the money. I also tell them not to worry so much about the interest payments because they can always use the excess money to earn some interest, and of course, they can always pay off the loan with the cash they have. While there's a cost to borrowing, it's nowhere near the cost of running out of money.

Allow me to tell you about my first real experience in borrowing. Except for Pete's initial loan, I didn't borrow any additional money to open the first dozen Subway stores. We never kept any cash in the bank and we used every cent of profit, greatly enhanced by credit from our vendors, to totally finance our development during the first six or seven years of business. It actually felt quite good to expand without debt, until it occurred to me that our future growth was limited by the amount of profit that we could generate.

By that time we had developed a lot of good systems and we needed money to grow more quickly to reach our goal of thirty-two stores in ten years. That's when I decided to visit my bank to borrow some money.

Up to this time, I had only visited my bank to *deposit*

money. Given my natural reluctance to become a borrower, I really didn't know what to expect. The bank was in a huge building in downtown Bridgeport. I arrived without an appointment and was directed to a thickly carpeted section of the bank that was reserved for private conversations, such as the one I hoped to have. There I met a kindly, white-haired gentleman who was perfectly dressed in a suit, starched shirt, and a conservative tie. Stepping up to his large mahogany desk, I felt like I was about to talk to God!

I explained to the gentleman that I had come to borrow some money. He invited me to sit down and to tell him about my business. I told him about every store we owned and how each one was doing, including what it cost to make sandwiches and the prices at which we sold them. I told him why we needed to borrow some money, and that we had been the bank's loyal customers for years.

When I finished, the gentleman smiled and calmly asked to see my financial statement. I didn't understand. Hadn't I just given him my financial statement? Could you believe that by this time I was a college graduate, I had been in business for over six years, I had a dozen stores in operation, and I didn't even know what a financial statement was?

He then taught me about financial statements, explained that having one was a requirement to borrow money, and said the statement should be prepared by an accountant. That was a problem because we didn't have an accountant. Up to that time, Pete and I had handled paying the taxes ourselves and we had never even thought about hiring an accountant. But if the bank needed a financial statement prepared by an accountant, then I would get one.

"Can you refer me to an accountant?" I asked the banker.

He said he couldn't, but he assured me there were many qualified accountants around town.

"Where's the closest one?" I asked, standing up to leave.

He nodded to the side door of the bank. "There's an accountant right across the street," he said.

I thanked him for his time, headed out the side door, and a few moments later hired our first accountant.

Several months after this experience, having gathered the appropriate data for our accountant to produce the critical financial statement, I returned to the bank expecting to borrow some money. The same gentleman was waiting for me when I arrived. He reviewed my financial statement, appeared to be impressed that a twenty-four-year-old kid had built a substantial business, but in the final analysis he rejected my appeal for a loan.

Why? I had a modestly successful business, and a professionally prepared financial statement to prove it. How could borrowing money be so difficult? I was about to discover the rules of borrowing. I learned . . . and you must always remember . . . that bank loan officers have two important rules to live by:

Rule #1—If you *need* money, you can't have any.

Rule #2—If you don't need money, you can have what you don't need.

At first, these rules didn't make much sense to me and they probably don't make much sense to you. However, these are the rules, and you must commit them to memory.

Since my first borrowing experience I've watched this lesson repeat itself many times. As an example, a Subway franchisee might need about $100,000 to open his first store and he might have $100,000 in savings. The tendency for many of our new owners is to use savings to get started. They want to be debt-free, they want to keep their monthly expenses low, and it makes no sense to them to borrow start-up money and pay interest while their savings are tucked away in stocks, bonds, and certificates of deposit. The franchisee reasons, "I'll start with my own money and I'll borrow when I *need* money for my second store."

And that's when he learns how borrowing really works. After about six months in business he might want to open a second store. Armed with a healthy financial statement, he goes to the bank to tell his story and ask for a loan. When he finishes, the bank's loan officer will look at him and say something like this, "Mr. Franchisee, you made the right decision to join Subway. It's a fabulous company with an amazing track record for growth. They obviously have a terrific product, an effective operating plan, and great control systems. I've known Subway for many years and, in fact, I'm a loyal customer at your store. You give great service and your store is spotless. As soon as you can come in with a longer track record, perhaps a few years of operating statements, I will give your loan request the highest possible consideration."

In other words, the banker's answer is a polite no.

Why? You know why, and now the franchisee knows, too. When you *need* to borrow money, you can't have any.

The mistake was in the timing. Had the franchisee visited with the banker before he started his business—when he still had his own money—the loan would have been granted promptly. The franchisee would have said, "Mr. Banker, I just joined Subway and it's going to cost about $100,000 to open my first store. And look, I have the money, I don't need to borrow, but I'd like to borrow $100,000. Can I have it?"

Because of Rule #2—"If you don't need money, you can have what you don't need"—the banker would have jumped at the opportunity to make the loan.

If you still question the wisdom of borrowing money and paying interest, take a few minutes to examine the financial statements of some of the world's largest companies. These giant enterprises hire the best and brightest business leaders that money can buy, and they also install top-notch accounting officers to oversee their finances.

Some of the numbers on the financial statement might look something like this. Cash in bank accounts: $3.0 billion. Money borrowed from others upon which interest is paid: $2.0 billion.

Seems like a no-brainer, doesn't it? Shouldn't they take

that $2.0 billion and pay down their debt? If they're paying 10 percent interest that one step alone would save the company $200 million per year!

Why don't they do it? Simple. Because that's not the way business is done. The best brains in business know that you can never risk running out of money, and that you can't even appear to need money, because if you do, you won't be able to borrow it.

Borrow all the money you can before you need it, but be careful with what you borrow. Don't take on an excessive amount of debt; don't use borrowing as a crutch to compensate for poor business practices; don't overextend yourself; and don't borrow simply for the sake of borrowing.

A charming microentrepreneur in Boston has learned this lesson the hard way—more than once. Earl Tate, the founder of Staffing Solutions, a temporary and permanent employment firm, says he traded his "body, hard work, sweat, and skills" for the opportunity to get into business. Twice he lost his business, or at least a part of it, because he ran out of money. But now, Earl is back in the game, and this time, he says, it's for good.

Earl Tate was born into a family of twelve children and he was the only one to graduate from high school, and then go on to college. "My career goal," he says, "was to earn $35,000 a year. From the ghetto that I came from, that would have been a big deal. I had no desire to become an entrepreneur. I looked forward to marrying a good woman, buying a home, starting a family, and enjoying my life."

By the time he was thirty, all of Earl's dreams had come true. As a medical equipment salesman, he earned more than $35,000 a year. He bought a home, and he and his family were enjoying the good life in Boston, Massachusetts. Then a friend, who had been one of his college professors, offered him the opportunity to join his business as a partner. Without investing any money, Earl could earn one-third ownership of Exclusive Temporaries, a booming New Orleans–based employment agency. "At first," Earl explains, "I wasn't interested. I liked my life the way it was. But then, once you accomplish a dream, there's always a bigger dream. And so when I went to New Orleans to take a look at the business, I decided it was the thing to do, even though I'd have to take a cut in pay. It was an opportunity to work with young people, and I especially liked that."

Little did he realize, however, that the decision would nearly ruin him financially and personally. "I lost my home, my family, most of my cars, and the material things that I had acquired," he says painfully. He also was forced to file for personal bankruptcy. But he doesn't dwell on the past. "It doesn't make me smile," says the man whose friends say he's always smiling. "But I'm going to be okay. I brought it all upon myself. Now I'm bouncing back. I've learned from my mistakes, and I'm going to be okay."

Earl says he made numerous mistakes as a young entrepreneur, but the fatal mistake was running out of money. "I had a booming business, growing by as much as 40 percent a year," he explains. "But you can have all the growth and revenue in the world. If you ain't got money, you're out of business." That's especially true in the employee leasing industry, which is driven by cash flow. When a customer needs an employee, the leasing company provides the employee and pays the employee's wages and benefits. Then the leasing company invoices the customer at a marked-up price. It may be thirty days or more until the leasing company collects its money. Consequently, the leasing company depends on cash flow to finance its accounts receivable.

When Earl accepted his friend's offer to join Exclusive Temporaries, it didn't seem possible that they would ever run out of money. Earl opened the company's Boston office and managed it while also serving as national sales director for Exclusive Temporaries' four existing offices. "In the first year, our

Boston office hit $1 million in sales," he recalls. "It was phe-nomenal. Unbelievable, really. But I worked at it night and day. When Boston's revenue reached $1.3 million in sales, I started opening additional locations. The company was sol-vent. We had money in the bank, so borrowing money to pay for our expansion wasn't a problem. For five to six weeks at a time, I went on the road, leaving my family on Sunday nights and not returning to Boston until the next Friday. Within five years we had thirty offices generating $30 million in revenue. That was gigantic. And I owned one third of it!"

By 1987, six years into the business, Exclusive Temporaries was approaching $40 million in sales when suddenly trouble appeared on the corporate balance sheet. "My partners always ran the business like a mom-and-pop shop," explains Earl. "They didn't see the need for a fax machine, for example, but that didn't bother me. They were being fiscally conservative, and I didn't mind because I owned a third of the company. But then I learned we were $2 million behind in paying our taxes. Our employment taxes had not been paid."

It was an unfortunate though common story in business. When bills start to mount and cash flow disappears, business owners are forced to cut *something*. That's when they're likely to skip paying the government, and that's almost always a mis-take. If the government doesn't catch them and punish them, there's a good chance someone else will, as Earl and his part-ners were about to discover.

"When I started investigating the situation," Earl contin-ues, "my partners turned on me. I demanded to see certain records, but I was told they were 'missing.' When I applied some pressure, noting that I was a partner, my friend said our agreement was only as good as the paper it had been written on. As far as he was concerned, he owned the company and that's the way it would be. During the struggle, the bank got wind of our IRS problem and decided to call in our loan before the government levied our accounts. That's when things began to unravel. We were out of money." Exclusive Temporaries was forced to close nearly all its branches, including those Earl had opened.

But Earl wasn't about to give up. He had worked too hard and come too far to fall behind now. Boldly, he decided to keep the Boston location, rename the business Staffing Solutions, and start again. "I didn't have any money," he says, "but at least I had thirty-four clients that generated nearly $3 million in revenue. I visited each one of them and asked, 'Will you help me?' Most of them were good friends by this time and I was able to convince them to pay my invoices immediately rather than make me wait ten to thirty days for payment. I would look for new accounts on Mondays, but on Tuesdays and Wednesdays I walked or drove to every customer's location with an invoice. They would each give me a check on the spot and I would deposit the checks in my account so that I could make Friday's payroll. I convinced the bank not to wait the traditional three days for the checks to clear.

"On Fridays, I parked myself at the bank and every time one of my temps came in to cash their check I was there to ward off problems, such as insufficient funds. I was fairly well known in the Boston business community. Even during the years that the business consumed my time, I still served on several boards and participated in political functions. I knew that was important. I was well connected, and as a result I had a personal relationship with the CEO of the only predominantly black bank in the city. I couldn't qualify for a formal loan, but when I needed funds, the CEO would advance the bank's money temporarily to cover my checks. Once I deposited money, the bank got its funds back. It was an unusual, and great relationship."

During this time, Earl's constant companion was stress. "It was one of the most challenging periods of my life," he says. "But in spite of the problems, I survived." After nearly a year of rebuilding, Earl could recognize some progress. "I had everyone trained. My clients continued to pay me without delay, and the bank told me that I didn't have to show up anymore on Fridays. 'You don't need to be here, Earl,' they said. 'We'll cover the checks.'"

Within a couple of years, determination put him back on his feet. Earl boosted his company's sales to $4.5 million and he soon felt confident that the darkest days were behind him. "I started spending money again," he says. He especially liked taking care of his family in a sometimes lavish manner, and he loved buying nice clothes for himself. When a large Boston bank decided to assist minority-owned businesses by offering loans at attractive rates of interest, Earl was smitten. "When they called on me," he says, "I decided to go with them. Even though I had a carte blanche relationship with the black bank, this new bank was bigger. They offered me immediate access to money—money that I could use to build the business faster." Money that he could use to enjoy life a little more.

"The odd thing," he says, "is that the big bank never asked for a cash flow statement. They asked for an income statement, but they never monitored my financial situation. They eventually gave me access to $500,000, but they didn't seem interested in how I was spending the money. Nor were they interested in helping me understand *how* to spend the money." The latter was a serious problem, though Earl wouldn't have admitted it at the time. He couldn't. He was a spendthrift who had suffered long enough, and he was now eager to make up for lost time. Even though he had learned the lesson about not running out of money, he apparently had not learned it well enough.

When Earl switched banks, he was assigned to a senior loan officer who was well respected in the Boston banking community. "He had signature authority up to half a million dollars," Earl explains, "but he only gave me a loan for $250,000, because that's what I asked for. Had I asked for half a million, and provided the proper support, which I could have done, he would have approved the larger amount. But as it was, he loaned me $250,000 to pay off debt and buy new computer and training equipment. Then he approved a revolving credit line of $250,000 for my ongoing cash needs."

Unfortunately, it wasn't enough money to support a rapidly expanding and by now $6 million company. "I could have borrowed more, and I should have borrowed more. Our cash needs were much greater than the credit line permitted. However, I didn't know it. My in-house accounting staff didn't know it. And the bank didn't know it, either. I can't say to the Boston banking community that I wasn't given the chance to borrow money, because I was. But did my bank really do the kind of analysis that they said they needed to do? Did they do all they promised to watch their money? No. The bank was more interested in marketing to minority entrepreneurs and making us a part of their portfolio than they were in really helping us. They didn't look at my receivables. They didn't ask for a cash flow statement. Clearly these checks and balances are required by a good banking relationship, but in my case, at the time, they just didn't happen." Of course, the bottom line is that it was Earl's responsibility to know his company's cash needs and to provide accountability.

In the absence of accountability, Earl launched a personal spending spree. He didn't do it selfishly. He didn't do it with even a hint of knowledge that he would destroy his business a second time. But he admits that he did it foolishly. "I'm not ashamed of what I did," he says, "but at age forty-eight, I'm not proud of it."

The first thing he did was increase his salary from $90,000 a year to $140,000. "I knew the business could afford it," he explains, "because the money was there." However, the money was there because the bank had approved his quarter-million-dollar loan, and his credit line. "The additional money camouflaged the real cash situation in my business. Yes, the money was there, but where was it coming from?"

He didn't take the time to look. He had suffered long enough, and the money was his payback. He bought a new home. Then he gave his wife a Jaguar, which cost the company

$1,049 a month. "She used to drive a Chevrolet," he says, "but she was a board member and so we gave her the car as a gift." The Jag soon became one of many decisions that he regretted. "When I peel through the onion and look at what I should have done differently," Earl says reflectively, "I should have stopped all the personal spending. I sucked money out of the business. I have 200 golf sweaters in my closet and I've probably worn twenty of them in the last five years. I have twenty-five suits and I could go to work every day for a month with a different one, but why? We used to take elaborate vacations. Rather than go to Disney World, we flew to Hawaii for three weeks, first class. Then we'd turn around and go to Bermuda for two weeks. I worked hard, from 6:00 A.M. until 10:00 P.M., and so I felt the need to reward myself and my family. But I would have been better off buying a summer property or investing my income in mutual funds. It just never occurred to me that the money would stop coming in."

But, of course, it did.

Had Earl spent some time reading his company's income statement he might have recognized the disaster before it occurred. But he wasn't interested in those facts at the time. "Most entrepreneurs own a company so that they can do things they couldn't do with the salary paid by a conventional career," he explains. "And I don't say don't do them. However, you can only do them when you're fiscally responsible. That's something every person in the world should learn, but there aren't any schools, not even graduate schools, that teach you how to manage your money. I had an absolute taste for living well and enjoying life, and that was my downfall."

Even though Earl's extravagance stretched the company's cash flow, it was difficult to notice because his company was rapidly expanding. Fast growth also contributed to the company's demise. "The bank told us we were growing too fast," says Earl. "But how do you tell an entrepreneur that his business is growing too fast when the revenue is coming in, and that's what it's all about?"

But that's *not* what it's all about, as Earl would soon recognize. It's enough of a challenge to manage a business while you're working in it. When you're flying from one vacation spot to the next, it's nearly impossible. When you're undercapitalized, it *is* impossible. Invoices that were once paid on the spot were now delayed by thirty to forty days. Earl's false confidence, and his preoccupation with growth and hard work, for which he rewarded himself with more of the good life, prevented him from doing anything about it.

And then it happened. The darkest days of Earl's life were about to reveal themselves.

"We suffered several months of losses," Earl recalls, the pain still noticeably in his voice, "and when I couldn't turn it around fast enough our cash flow disappeared very quickly. Our expenses sucked up whatever we had. Even if I hadn't spent so much money personally, we were still underfunded by at least $400,000 to $500,000. Then, when business dropped off, we simply didn't have the money to weather the storm."

At a time when he needed him most, Earl's loan officer had already moved on to another job. The timing was unfortunate. Worse yet, a larger bank was acquiring his bank, and no one of any authority was willing to speak up for him. The first sign of darkness occurred when the bank called his loans. "We were more than ninety days' delinquent at the time," he says. "The bank wasn't interested in working with me. Minority-owned businesses were not a priority anymore. They literally pulled the plug on $500,000 overnight. We had $130,000 a week in billings, but again, no money."

He was back to square one, although this time the circumstances were even more bleak. The bank forced him into personal bankruptcy. His marriage of twenty years ended in divorce. "I can't tell you the pain and the awful stuff that I went through," he says sadly. "I didn't realize that even when you're involved in your community, and you spend time with some of the better-known CEOs in town, if you don't keep a strong company they'll forget who you are in five minutes. It's amazing how quickly they'll stop dealing with you when they don't view you as a player of any significant value. They'll leave you out to die."

He pauses, then continues, "I never set out to hurt my wife, my family, myself, or my company. I hadn't ever planned on destroying my credit rating, because that was so important to me. So how do I come to terms with the fact that my greed got me into trouble? How do I explain that I once had a net worth of nearly $3 million, and now it's about $60,000? I sucked the money out of my business. Fiscally responsible people don't do that."

And yet, Earl instinctively knew that he wasn't a bad man. "Sometimes I ask too many questions," he says, coming back strong. "I'm a good and decent person. I made mistakes. Many mistakes. I assume responsibility for them all. There was no excuse not to be better prepared. I can say I was a kid from the ghetto and my parents never taught me how to manage money, but it was *my* responsibility. I didn't have the where-withal to keep my focus on the business, and I paid an enormous price for it. What happened to me was a tragedy, but I quit making excuses a long time ago. I quit feeling sorry for myself, and I quit beating myself up beyond repair."

In the midst of his turmoil, he decided the only way to salvage the business—to salvage himself—was to start again. "I still had a good relationship with my customers," he explains, "and so I went back to see them. I told them there was no reason to stay with my company, we were bankrupt. But I asked them if they would stay with me if I reorganized the business. Eighty-five percent of the customers said, 'Earl, you're a great guy, and wherever you go, we'll go with you.' But they also told me they expected better service this time around. They wanted their needs, and not mine, to come first. They also expected a better price."

Earl rose to the challenge, even though he had no money to pay his employees, including the temporaries he contracted out to his clients. His only option was factoring. A factor finances business accounts, usually at a high rate of interest. Earl arranged for a factor to buy Staffing Solutions' receivables. In turn, the factor would immediately pay the company a discounted value for each invoice. Earl could then use the money to meet his weekly payroll and other obligations. It might not have been the best solution, but for Earl, there was no other solution.

Since the bankruptcy, there hasn't been another solution. "We're on our way back," says Earl, wiser this time for the experience. "The company has climbed back to nearly $3 million in revenue, and we're profitable, but we're still being factored. We're netting 3 percent after expenses and taxes and that's not as good as it ought to be, but we're coming out of the woods. It appears that resilience is paying off and we're making small steps back to some significant success. We've certainly had the opportunity to do what most black males would never get a chance at—a second or third time at bat. We would have been five to six times this size if I hadn't lost the momentum. But considering the pain and anguish that I've been through, I consider myself fortunate to have bounced back this far in so little time. Now I have a chance to prove myself again. This time, I'll do it a lot better because I'll have the skills."

As part of his rebuilding program, Earl says he has committed himself to learn the disciplines of success. "The disciplines weren't all there the first and second time," he explains, "so now I'm learning a new discipline every six months. What's really most gratifying to me is to sit down each month and really look at my cash flow statement and be able to understand it. Profit is great, but what are our expenses doing to the profit? If we make this move, how will that impact the company six months or a year from now? I'm doing more planning on paper, and more processing before I attempt to share an idea with someone. I take out a yellow pad and I list the pros and cons of decisions in advance. Rather than rush out and buy a new computer, or new software, I determine how that purchase will make a difference, and then I make the decision to buy it or wait. I've enrolled in a basic accounting course. I'm going to learn about finances. It may take me three or four years, and it's exhausting to work all day and go to school, but I'm determined to understand it. I'm not going to get caught unprepared again."

Meanwhile, an outspoken Earl is sharing his gospel with other entrepreneurs. Working Capital, the Boston-based microlending organization, which has loaned more than $2.5 million to help revitalize poor communities, tapped him for its board of directors in 1998. At first, he turned a deaf ear to the organization. He said he wasn't fit to be a board member. After all, he had recently filed bankruptcy. "I'm not your guy," he said. "I don't have the time, and you don't want me."

Quite the contrary. He was precisely the type of person Working Capital needed to meet with its growing membership. "They told me that several banks had recommended me to them because of my resilience," he recalls. "They told me, 'You will overcome what you've been through and you will have some incredible lessons to share with other people.' It took about eight months for me to come around, and then I started mentoring a young man who I hope I can help save from the problems I've faced. The mentoring has been a good healing process for me. It appears that my contributions could be significant."

What does he tell new entrepreneurs? "I tell them to learn everything they can about their industry. I tell them to hire a good accountant, someone they can trust and talk to; someone who will read the warning signals and not be afraid to tell them. I advise them to budget, and to set controls in place and not violate them. I tell them to live within their means. I would not ever live beyond 50 percent of my income again. I help them understand the value of money, and the responsibility that they have to their staff, and their customers. I tell them to build relationships with bankers, and I tell them to always prove that they are honorable people by paying their debts and keeping themselves in good standing."

And, oh yes, he tells them one more thing: *Never run out of money.*

CHAPTER FIFTEEN

ATTRACT NEW CUSTOMERS EVERY DAY

Terri Bowersock has a knack for attracting new customers to her retail consignment business. So far, she's built a $16 million empire, but she's just getting started.

Attracting new customers is half the job of building a successful business and no one knows that better than Todd Carpenter, a Subway Development Agent in Nebraska. I was at a regional franchisee meeting in Denver some years ago and several times people came up and told me to be sure to meet Todd, who at that time owned one Subway shop. Finally I asked, "What's the story with this guy? I want to meet him, but why do so many people think I should?"

It turned out that Todd was a young man in his early twenties and when he opened his store in a little town in western Nebraska he started out doing just $2,000 a week in gross sales. Not a big deal by Subway's standards. However, within eight months he increased sales to $8,000 a week! That won the attention, and admiration, of many other owners in the area.

How'd he do it?

As Todd would say, it was pretty simple. He used the process of Awareness, Trial, and Usage.

Every day, Todd worked in his store during lunchtime, and every afternoon he prospected from door-to-door in the neighborhoods around his store. Most people who own a sandwich shop, or most any business with a storefront, don't take the time to go door-to-door and introduce themselves. But Todd did.

"Hi, I'm Todd Carpenter. I own Subway on Main Street," he would say to the people who answered this polite knock. Checking for *awareness* he would ask, "Have you been to my store?"

If the answer was no, Todd would continue, "Well, as I said, I'm the owner, and I'd like to invite you to come over for lunch." The *trial*. As he talked, he reached into his back pocket and pulled out a coupon, good for a free lunch. "I'm in the store every day," he said with a smile. "So I'll be looking for you." He would then describe the exact location of the store.

If someone said yes, they had been to the store, Todd would ask, "How did you like it?" If they said they enjoyed it, or words to that effect, Todd would respond, "Oh, I'm happy to hear that. I'm the owner, so I like to know about satisfied customers." Then he'd reach into his other back pocket and pull out a different coupon and explain: "I'm in the store every day, so please come back again." The *usage*. "And here, I'd like you to use this coupon. It's good for a free sandwich for a friend. When you buy one sandwich, you can get another one free. Come back soon, and be sure to say hello."

On the rare occasion when someone said they had tried the store and didn't like it, or they had a bad experience, Todd would listen to their complaint and then say, "I'm sorry. Please forgive me. I'm the owner, and I'd like you to give us another try." He would then extend a coupon for a free lunch and encourage the person to return.

No matter what, Todd always made sure everyone got a coupon to visit Subway.

Todd's neighborhood walks required a daily effort. Indeed, the effort and discipline required may be the most difficult part of attracting new customers. I wouldn't describe Todd as a "born" salesman. He's a humble, hardworking, down-to-earth young man, now about thirty years old. It was just as much a struggle for him to do this door-to-door prospecting as it would be for most people. But because he methodically introduced his business to thousands of individuals and households over a period of time—inducing them to try his products, and return again and again—Todd built a loyal customer base, and a successful business. It wasn't long before he opened additional stores, and eventually he became a Development Agent, which meant that he would be responsible for the development of numerous stores. Todd now oversees seventy-seven Subway shops throughout his territory, which covers most of Nebraska. He's a terrific example not only for Subway franchisees, but also for everyone who's trying to build a successful business. Todd understood the importance of attracting customers every day, and he went out of his way to do it.

When I travel around the world and meet with Subway franchisees, one of them will sometimes say to me, "My sales are lower this year than last year. Why do you think that's happening, Fred?" My standard answer is: "Because you have fewer customers this year." As simple as it sounds, the idea that more customers equals more sales, and fewer customers equals fewer sales, often escapes many entrepreneurs. For some odd reason—maybe because it is so simple—it's a rule that's easy to overlook. But if you want a lot of sales, you need to attract a lot of new customers and to keep them coming back. That's why it's important to learn how to create Awareness, to gain Trial, and earn Usage.

Most people would agree there's nothing complex about Awareness, Trial, and Usage. In spite of that, it took thirty years of building a business for me to be able to verbalize the process. Suddenly one day it hit me: *Of course that's the way it works!* Make them aware. Get them to try it. And keep them coming back. It's not rocket science, but until a few years ago, I couldn't explain it that clearly. Intuitively I understood the process—I think most entrepreneurs do—but it was difficult to sort out the steps, and then teach the process to someone else.

When I started Subway, I knew very little about attracting customers. But I learned fast. During the week that I was building our first store, I looked out the window one day and realized we had selected a crummy location. Even though our store was less than a football field away from a busy intersection, people could not see our store from the street because it was tucked into the back of a shopping center. How would anyone find us? If they couldn't see the store, how would they become aware of the store? If they weren't aware of the store, how could we expect them to try our products? That's when I decided that I had to create awareness, even though I didn't use that word. I created a promotional flyer with a map pointing to the store, printed a few hundred copies, and for several days prior to the store's opening, I stood at the intersection and introduced myself to motorists as they stopped for the traffic light.

"I'm opening a new sandwich shop on Saturday. Will you come?" I would ask while handing a flyer into the car through the passenger window. Most cars at that time didn't have air conditioning and since it was summer the windows were open.

"Where is it?" was the usual response.

"It's right over there," I'd say, pointing to the back of the parking lot.

Most people responded affirmatively. "Sure, we'll stop by," they'd say, and I would smile and head for the next car. While I wouldn't know the effect of this promotion for several days, I had the feeling it would be successful because several factors worked in my favor. First, the promotion was aimed at a specific, local market. Almost everyone who stopped at that intersection lived nearby, so they were likely to come to my store for a sandwich. Second, I used the word "new." Everyone likes to hear about something new. Third, I asked for a commitment and usually got one. And finally, I was ambitious. Most of the people I met probably admired the fact that I was out there trying to build a business.

Of course, there were other things I could have done to create awareness. I could have purchased a billboard, or a series of ads in the local newspaper, or several spots on a radio station. But not with start-up capital of $1,000! Handing out flyers was all I could afford to do. And it turned out to be a good idea, especially for a local sandwich shop. Using other forms of media would not have targeted my market as effectively.

I didn't know anything about trial at the time, so I didn't include coupons with the flyer, or offer a special price for our Grand Opening. In a way, though, the flyers automatically induced trial. Each time I handed out a flyer, and said that my store was opening on Saturday, I personally asked the motorists, "Will you come?" Most of them said yes. And many of them did. Our opening day was the busiest day *ever* at that store.

Later, realizing that it was necessary to give people a reason to try our products, we introduced an Anniversary Special. However, we didn't stage this sale at the time of our real anniversary, which occurred during the busy summer months. We waited until February when the customer count in our store was traditionally low due to the cold weather. Also, we timed the sale with Lincoln's Birthday when it made sense to offer a "penny sale," which enabled customers to buy one sandwich and get a second one for a penny. We didn't make any profit that day, but we created excitement, and that created awareness and trial. If all went well—that is, we did a good job of servicing the customers, and they enjoyed our products—trial would lead to usage, and these one-time buyers would return again and again and become loyal customers.

Even without anyone telling me, I knew that customers wanted only four things from my business—in fact, they wanted these same four things from any restaurant:

1. Good food.
2. A clean store.
3. Good service.
4. A good deal.

The extent to which we met and exceeded those expectations drove usage and increased the frequency of usage. That's true for any business, although customer expectations differ by type of business. As I discovered, it's sometimes easier to be aware of what should be done than to actually execute on them consistently and with expertise. In our case, we did a terrible job of execution!

Basically, I knew how to complete the transaction. When someone came into the store, I could take the order, get it straight, make the sandwich, and hand it over the counter. And I did it fast. Accuracy and speed seemed really important to me. I collected the money, smiled, said thank you, and that was it. I didn't think much about the kind of service I rendered. I knew to keep the store clean, and I would clean up between customers and after the store was closed. But as a kid, I wasn't really very good at it.

I also knew it was important to serve sandwiches with fresh rolls, but the truth was, I didn't always do it. A customer might get a really fresh roll one day, and a not-so-fresh roll the next day. Many nights I closed the store with leftover bread. At the time, our rolls cost 60 cents a dozen, or a nickel each. Since we didn't have much money, and our first store wasn't making money, it was important to sell all of our inventory and not waste it. However, because of weather conditions and other factors that affect sales, it wasn't easy to judge how much bread to order. So if Monday was a slow sales day, and we didn't sell all of our bread, I'd wrap up the leftover rolls and save them for Tuesday. The quality of the bread wasn't as good on Tuesday, but you couldn't always tell.

Of course, it was a mistake to sell leftover bread. Saving a nickel was a short-term gain that created a long-term loss. But when you're under financial stress, and you come up against a decision like selling old bread or throwing it away, it's easy to make the wrong choice.

Few lessons are more important than Attract New Customers Every Day because customers *are* your business. They're truly your only asset as a business owner. Management professor Peter Drucker says that a business has but one purpose: to create a customer. The value of your business is directly proportionate to the number of customers you capture and keep.

The quickest way to build a successful business is not merely to meet your customers' expectations, but to exceed them. Then, they'll return repeatedly and spend more of their money on your products and services. Some customers will become occasional users of your business. Others will become frequent users. And at least a few will become missionaries. It's important to develop as many missionary customers as you can because they are relentless promoters. They'll recommend your business to all of their friends, and not in a cavalier manner, either. They like sharing good information, and once they do, they want their friends to confirm their good judgment.

"Have you tried the new restaurant in town?" they'll ask.

If you say no, they'll say, "Oh, you've got to try it. It's really good."

If you say yes, they'll ask you how you enjoyed it. If you say you didn't like it, they'll tell you to try it again because something must have gone wrong that day. "Usually, it's just great!"

242

Missionary customers are terrific salespeople, and every business needs to develop them. By their enthusiasm and word of mouth they will generate more customers and sales for your business. And that means more profit!

As a business owner, your goal is to attract new customers every day and the principles of Awareness, Trial, and Usage work every time. Just ask Subway's Todd Carpenter.

Or ask Terri Bowersock. She started Terri's Consign & Design Furnishings in Phoenix, Arizona, in 1979. Today, she oversees a $16-million-plus business, and she'll tell you that much of her success is due to her ability to attract new customers every day. You'll see what I mean in the following profile.

———

"I started my business because I couldn't fill out a job application," says Terri Bowersock, who now owns seven businesses, among them Terri's Consign & Design Furnishings. Kenny Rogers, the Beach Boys, Alice Cooper, Willie Mays, Hugh Downs, Walter Cronkite, and Geordie Hormel (of the Hormel Meats family) are among her customers. Not long ago she appeared on *Oprah* to tell her story, and she has been featured in numerous publications including *Woman's World* and even the *National Enquirer*. She has won a roomful of awards, including *Entrepreneur*'s Entrepreneurial Woman of the Year (1998), Avon's Women of Enterprise Award (1998), Phoenix Small Business Person of the Year (1997), the Blue Chip Entrepreneur Award (1996), Impact for Enterprising Women (1995), and *Inc.* magazine's Socially Responsible Entrepreneur of the Year (1992 and 1994), among many others.

The awards are even more important to Terri than her magnificent financial success, estimated in the millions of dollars. "It's important for entrepreneurs to know what drives them," she says, speaking at record speed, the norm for this contagiously enthusiastic woman. "For me, it's not financial success. It's fame! I wanted all my teachers, friends, and family to know that I was smart. My drive and determination is motivated by years of desire to prove that I am smart."

Through twelve years of school, Terri was told she was anything but smart. "You know the dumb kid who had to sit in front of the teacher's desk? That was me," she explains, still stung by the experience. "People made fun of me all the time I was in school. Teachers hurt me. One of them used to use a yardstick to hit me in the back of my head and tell me that I was as dumb as a cue ball. Friends called me dummy and stupid. When teachers graded our papers, I always hid mine because it came back with red ink all over the damn thing. To this day I hate red pens. I won't allow one in my office."

Like several of the microentrepreneurs profiled in this book, Terri is dyslexic, though she didn't know it until after graduation. "When I went to school it was totally based on reading and testing. It didn't make me feel good about who I was. I always felt stupid. During a test, I'd sit there and watch the other students. When they were done, I'd act like I was done, too, even though I was still on question number five. When we had to take turns reading, I would calculate how many students were in front of me, and then I'd act up right before it was my turn so that I could get kicked out of class. I couldn't read. I still want to know who invented spelling bees because they tortured me! I could only get through a spelling test by cheating, and I remember the teacher saying, 'Cheaters are bad people.'"

Later, when she discovered her dyslexia, Terri asked her mother, Loretta, why she didn't tell her teachers she needed help. "My mother said I was good at hiding the dyslexia and conning my way through school. By the time I was a teenager, mom thought I had gotten over it. Somehow I managed to pull down Cs. Once I got a B in something that was really easy. I was cunning and witty and that's how I managed to get through school."

She hadn't really fooled her mother, however. Loretta Bowersock knew that her teenage daughter was basically unemployable. "She realized that the only way I could make it was in my own business," says Terri. "Once I started filling out job applications, my mother could see that I couldn't do it." But that didn't bother Loretta because she was an entrepreneur in her own right. She and her husband had divorced when their daughter was eight. "My mother had to step in and be entrepreneurial to help us survive," explains Terri. "She developed her tennis skills and became a pro." Loretta worked for a couple of resorts in Phoenix and Tempe, and at one point she also ran a tennis shop.

While she was a senior in high school, Terri started a window washing business. "My mother had paid $20 to get a special corn starch and water formula for cleaning windows. It really works! She bought the formula from a cleaning lady who was moving out of state. So I made up some calling cards and started knocking on neighborhood doors looking for jobs. I got pretty busy, and that was the first time I realized that if I wanted to do something, I could."

Shortly before graduation, when Terri needed to make some additional money to pay for a summer vacation, her mother suggested that the two of them sell sandwiches to golfers at a nearby golf course. "We got up every morning and made great sandwiches, and then we went to the golf course and sold them. You had to be *good* to sell to golfers," Terri says. She honed her sales skills on tees and greens. "I would drive my golf cart up behind a foursome, tell them a joke to get them laughing, and then they'd buy my sandwiches. We didn't make a lot of money, but it paid for my vacation."

One day Loretta Bowersock came home with the delightful news that she had arranged for her daughter to operate the Closet Emporium, a tiny gift shop at a Phoenix resort. "That's where I learned retailing," says Bowersock, hinting that it wasn't all that simple. "I ordered tennis shoe laces and put them all out on the shelves and priced them. But it was only later I realized that you had to add a profit to the price!"

In spite of her inexperience, Terri was a natural at attracting customers. "That's what business is all about," she says, a smile stretching across a pleasant face framed in reddish brown, shoulder-length hair. "You don't have anything without customers. So I learned to develop a style to attract them. I always had a gimmick. For example, candy and cigarette sales were very important to the success of my gift shop. They brought in a lot of dollars. But one day the hotel put a cigarette machine outside my shop. I started losing customers. So I came up with an idea. When local businessmen or out-of-town guests came into the gift shop to buy cigarettes, I would say, 'I'll memorize the brand you smoke and the next time you come in to the hotel, you have to buy your cigarettes from me. If I don't know your brand, then you can use the cigarette machine.' I was really good at memorizing. I couldn't remember the names of the guests, but I recognized them by their brands." The customers eagerly responded to the game. "They'd walk in and say, 'Okay, what brand is it?' I always got it right. That was the beginning of my education in marketing."

After operating the Closet Emporium for four years, Terri wanted something more to fulfill her life. "I was twenty-two and I didn't feel like I was going to become anyone in a gift shop. If I was going to prove that I wasn't stupid, I had to do something other than own a little gift shop."

One Christmas she went to visit her father, an Air Force officer in Kansas City, and he introduced her to a couple of lady friends who owned a consignment shop. "Their husbands had told them that they were in trouble if they bought any more silver or china, but they couldn't help themselves," Terri explains. "So they started selling off their extra stuff and they raised money for charities, and also for themselves so that they could buy more silver and china!" When she met the women she paid close attention to their description of their business. Essentially, the way they explained it, they invited people to consign their furnishings and accessories to their shop. When the items sold, the women would keep 50 percent of the sale price and give the consignor 50 percent. "It was so simple," recalls Terri, "I said, 'I can do that!'" The women agreed and they coached her while she visited her father.

"My brain went to work processing the whole consignment idea and by midnight I was on the phone with my mother. I told her, 'We're going to be rich!' Then I explained what I planned to do, and mother said, 'It sounds like Sanford & Son. Go back to the drawing board. I don't want to sell used furniture. I'm going to sleep and I'll talk to you when you get home."

Terri wasn't about to be dissuaded, not even by the woman she loved most in her life. "I knew I'd have to do a sales job on my mom," she recalls, but meanwhile she created a business plan. "I did it in crayons and colored pencils. I visually designed the building and how we could lay it out. I knew it would have to look good for my mom. The drawing included a house with a chimney. I wanted to give the impression that it was 'From your house to our house.' I even drew the cash register and the checkout counter."

Returning to Phoenix after Christmas 1979, Terri tried to sell her mother on the idea, but she didn't succeed for several months. "My mother really doesn't believe in saying no, but this took some convincing." Meanwhile, Terri hopped on her motorcycle and drove off in search of a suitable building to open Terri's Consign & Design Furnishings. She found the perfect location in Tempe. The building resembled a house, and it was available immediately. Since she couldn't read, she pretended to read the lease. She recalls thinking to herself, *How long would it take a normal person to read through this lease?* When a reasonable time had lapsed, she nodded her head knowingly, grabbed a pen, and signed the lease. She then borrowed $2,000 from her grandmother to pay the first month's rent and to add some decor to the shop.

Her first consignment came from her mother's home. "I took my bedroom furniture and my mother's living room furniture, arranged it in my new store, and opened the doors. And people actually came in. At first they'd ask me, 'What's this all about?' and in my naturally enthusiastic way I told them about my business and invited them to bring me their furniture. 'I'll sell it for you,' I explained, 'and then I'll give you a check.'"

A day or two after opening the shop a woman came in and looked at Terri's bedroom mirror, which she had possessed since childhood. "I'll buy this," the woman said.

"You will?" Terri quickly responded. She grabbed a little tin cash box where she kept sales slips and wrote up the order. "The woman reminded me not to forget the sales tax," Terri recalls. "The price was $35. Fortunately I had a little plastic card that showed me how much to charge for tax because I wouldn't have been able to figure it out myself. I was so excited. The woman said, 'Is this your first sale?' I admitted that it was and she signed a dollar bill and hung it on my wall to remind me of her."

Since Terri had moved her bedroom furniture out of her mother's house, if she wanted to continue sleeping in a bed she had no choice but to move into the back of her store. "I couldn't afford to live anywhere else," she explains in her adventuresome voice. "It really wasn't a very good idea because I worked too many hours. People would drive up after hours and I never wanted to turn them away."

But living at the store also had some advantages. One day Terri baked bread. The aroma added an attractive flavor to the shop. Another morning she baked cinnamon rolls and her customers responded enthusiastically. After that, baking became part of her routine. She also cooked dinner in the store every night, adding yet another homelike quality. "This was my home," she says, "and my customers began to feel like they were my guests. That kept them coming back. Plus, one of the lucky things about this business is that we are always getting something new. It's like a treasure hunt. Customers come in week after week because they love seeing our new stuff, or they want to sell stuff. They tell their friends about us. That kind of energy is infectious and it helps to build a business."

Attracting consignments wasn't much of a challenge for

this enthusiastic microentrepreneur. "I told everyone to bring me their furniture. When I saw a garage sale, I invited the people to bring their leftovers to me. We hung door hangers on nice homes, inviting the owners to give us their 'gently used' stuff. My grandmother helped me do that."

Terri discovered that the work was hard. She spent long days picking up furniture in the morning, selling it during the day, and delivering it at night. "After several months," she says, "I knew I couldn't run the business myself. I needed help. So again I started selling the idea to my mom. I told her, 'Mom, teaching tennis is going to give you skin cancer. You're out in the sun all the time. You're getting really dark and it's not good for you. You should come into the furniture business with me.' And that's how I talked her into it. Not long afterward we had to deliver a sleeper sofa to the third floor of an apartment complex and after we climbed the stairs my mother looked at me and said, 'I'd rather have skin cancer!'"

Loretta Bowersock added a classy distinction to the warehouse. "My mother knew how to decorate," explains Terri. "She's a natural. She's the type who dresses up just to go out and pick up the newspaper. I think she was a queen in a past life. Our home always looked great and mom knew how to put together a *look*. She didn't just wear a dress, she would add a scarf, or something. She made it, in her word, *purty*."

While her daughter was satisfied with any arrangement of the furniture in the store—"I would have had an old junk store," she says—Loretta insisted on bringing in brand-name furniture and accessories. "This isn't going to look like Sanford & Son," she told her daughter repeatedly. "We are the rich man's consignment shop." Later, when Terri began using television commercials to promote her business, she would say, "You can trust my mom. She's checked it over and made sure it's good for you."

Business at Terri's Consign & Design Furnishings started out slow, with $4,000 in sales the first month. But the numbers quickly increased, especially after Terri created her marketing plans. "This was really the beginning of my success," she explains as she begins talking about her promotional ideas. "Our shop was located on a busy street. Traffic moved at fifty to sixty miles per hour and I knew I had to slow it down to attract more customers. So I decided to place some furniture outside to call attention to the store. But the real draw was a mannequin that my mother had given me. I dressed the mannequin in a tennis skirt and placed her among the furniture so that it looked like a lady standing in her living room. As trucks came by they would honk their horns and wave."

As luck would have it, a truck hit the mannequin one day and broke both of its arms. Instead of fretting over it, Terri immediately recognized an opportunity. She called the editorial department of the local newspaper and shouted into the phone, *There's been a mannequin accident. Come right away!*" A reporter did. "I said it so hysterically," Terri explains, now laughing, "that the reporter rushed over to see what had happened. I played it to the hilt. When the reporter heard the story, he laughed and he wrote an article for the local newspaper." A photograph of the armless mannequin accompanied the article. "*Farewell to Arms*" read the caption under the photo. "The mannequin is not for sale," the caption explained, "and new arms have been ordered for her."

"The article *really* helped me attract customers," says Terri, confirming the power of the media in her mind. "I don't know how I got the ability to market, except that when God takes a gift away," referring to her dyslexia, "he gives a gift. So it's a natural for me. I tell my story and I'm good at it. I don't think about these things. My mannequin got hit and I instinctively knew to call a reporter."

Just when business was building, however, Terri ran into her first major challenge. Fake reading that lease proved to be a huge mistake. There was a question about the legality of the lease and whether the lessor had the authority to sublet. "I was paying the rent to him, but he wasn't paying the landlord. So suddenly I got evicted!"

It was a dark moment for her. She started doubting herself, especially her ability. "I thought, *God, am I stupid! How could I have done that?*" One night she went to bed believing that her business was over. But when she woke up, her attitude had changed. "I decided that if I let go of the business, there wouldn't be a Terri's to shop at. That's when I really understood the value of my business. I valued it too much to give it up."

Forced to find a new location, and hoping not to repeat the move any time in the near future, Terri boldly leased a 6,000-square-foot warehouse in Mesa, more than tripling her previous showroom space. "Mom was a chicken. She only wanted to take 3,000 square feet, but I told her we would grow into it. Twenty years later, we're still here!"

Terri's only concern about the new warehouse was its location. It was next door to a Costco, and while that was a plus, the warehouse district was off the beaten track between Mesa and Tempe. Terri thought about what she could do to create publicity for her new store. It was then that she remembered reading about the divorce rate in Arizona. It was the highest rate in the country. Bingo!

"Fortunately, mom had gotten a divorce," she says. "So I called the newspaper and told them our story—a mother and daughter in business. The furniture industry is predominantly run by men, and their sons, so we played up our unique angle. We got a good story in the newspaper and then one story led to several other newspapers and magazines. One Sunday our story appeared in the local newspaper and the next day 700 people came to our store! It was incredible. People were everywhere. We didn't even have room to sell."

Women especially frequented Terri's Consign & Design Furnishings. "Women shop for furniture," Terri explains, "and women brought things in for us to sell. They'd even help us decorate the store, all the while sharing stories about themselves and their families. Everyone thought I was so cute. 'You're such a good girl to your mom,' they'd say, and then pinch my cheek." Terri loved it, of course. She wasn't so dumb after all.

And the best was yet to come!

Recognizing the appeal of the mother-daughter relationship, and always searching for creativity in her business, Terri decided to use television to promote the store. "I called the television station and they told me I'd need $3,000 to air commercials on TV. I didn't have the money. So I started saving for it. Mom was against it. But I knew it was the right thing to do. Everyone in this business uses classified ads, and I wanted to be *different*. I wanted to use TV. I kept saving my money and when I finally had enough I called mom one night and said, 'I don't care what you have to do to your hair or your makeup. The TV crew is coming tomorrow to shoot the commercial. Be ready.' She was mad, but she got over it."

While the crew shot the commercial, Loretta was filmed using a feather duster on the furniture. In between takes she grumbled to her daughter, *"Everyone's going to think the place is dirty."* Her complaint fell on deaf ears. Near the end of the commercial, one of the cameramen suggested that Loretta hand the feather duster to her daughter. When she did, Terri instinctively smiled and said, "Thanks, Mom." It was a trademark moment. "Once we aired the commercials," Terri explains, "everyone started saying, *'Thanks, Mom.'*"

Best of all, business doubled within two months!

All kinds of people visited Terri's Consign & Design Furnishings. From poor to middle-class to wealthy they came looking for a bargain. Usually, they weren't disappointed. Whether they needed one piece of furniture or a houseful, they found it at Terri's.

One night, about 6:30, Terri had just closed the store when two men and a young woman came to the door. "Do you mind if we shop?" asked the lead man, who introduced himself as Vic Caesar.

"The woman looked about nineteen," remembers Terri, "and the two men were older. One guy never said anything.

He had long gray hair and looked like he needed money. I invited them in and Vic said, 'You won't regret this.' I showed them around and within ninety minutes they bought $25,000 of furniture! Vic gave me a check and he must have read my mind because I was wondering if I should call the bank to verify it. 'Look at the name on the check,' he said. It read Geordie Hormel. 'He's the heir to Hormel Meats,' Vic told me. That was good enough for me."

As the trio was leaving, Terri boldly asked her affluent customer why he was shopping at her store.

Hormel held up a chandelier and asked her, "What does this cost new?"

Terri said $4,000.

"What price are you selling it for?" he continued.

She said $200.

"Now you know why I'm shopping at your store."

Hormel became a frequent face at Terri's Consign & Design Furnishings. "We became great friends. I've helped him furnish a 55,000-square-foot mansion. I've been able to find things that are different, but classy, for him. One day he came in looking for a bed. He has a 3,000-square-foot bedroom. He said he needed a good bed. I asked him how he wanted to try it out. 'I usually jump on it,' he said. *Come on,* I told him, and we jumped on several beds until he found one he liked. He's an eccentric guy, and really a lot of fun."

Customers kept coming to Terri's Consign & Design Furnishings as Terri continued generating publicity. "That savvy part of me," she says, "told me that I needed to be in front of the public. So I took advantage of every opportunity, especially to get on television. When Barbara Bush started talking about literacy, I decided to quit hiding my dyslexia. I didn't want anyone to know about it, but for publicity, I was willing to talk about it." When the local newspaper revealed that the woman in the flashy consignment commercials suffered from dyslexia, she was nominated for a Blue Chip Award for people who succeeded in business in spite of a disability. Of course, that led to more media exposure, and attracted many more customers.

Within a couple of years, Terri's Consign & Design Furnishings needed an additional 6,000 square feet, and not long afterward 6,000 more. "Our sales were as high as $90,000 a month," Terri recalls, "but it was still a lot of hard work. One day mother decided she had had enough. 'I've lifted, I've carried, and I can't do it anymore,' she told me. Mom had a lot of typical female programming that said men are supposed to do the things we were doing. She had a lot of fear about it. So she decided to get out. The Arizona real estate boom was on and she wanted to go after it. We had numerous employees by this time, so I supported mom's decision. It was a good move for her."

It also proved to be a good move for Terri. "I was going to miss my mom in the business, but I decided to go for the gusto," she says. "I opened a second and a third store, and then I decided that I wanted a chain of consignment stores across the country." Next, she decided to franchise the business. She hired a franchise consultant. "He made promises about me making big money, buying a big house, and he'd take care of everything," she says. "But the short story is he made $80,000 and I learned how to spell the word franchise!"

Later, she hired several reputable consultants and started franchising her business in 1996. Terri's Consign & Design Furnishings franchisees have since opened fifteen stores in Las Vegas, Tucson, San Diego, and Denver. In addition to stores in Arizona, Terri's corporation owns outlets in Atlanta.

By 1997, Terri had built a $16 million corporation without borrowing a dime more than the original $2,000. "All this from a girl without a computer on her desk," she says teasingly. Franchising, as well as other new business developments, required that she borrow money, which the bank was only too happy to do. "The first time I knew I had made it," she says, "was when I had my own lunchroom. A room for nothing but eating lunch in it. The second time I knew I had made it was when the bank asked me out to lunch, just to eat!"

Nowadays, with nearly twenty years of publicity and TV commercials behind her, Terri is a celebrity in Phoenix. The fame she desired for so long is hers. Everyone knows her, including the former teachers and classmates who teased her. "But somehow," she says, "it doesn't matter so much anymore. I had always dreamed of going to my class reunion in a limousine. But when it was time to attend my twenty-year reunion, I didn't need to go in a limo. I went because I wanted everyone to know that I had succeeded. But I wasn't bitter about it. I knew that I was *okay*, and that alone was a great gift."

It has taken many years, however, for Terri to believe that she's smart. "I never send Christmas cards," she explains. "In ten years I've read only one book. It took me two and a half days to read my franchise offering circular. That tells you I'm still struggling with reading and writing. I can talk like crazy, but a pen in my hand sends up a block that I struggle to work through."

It doesn't matter, of course. As long as she can attract customers—*and she can*—the sales in her business will continue to increase. And that takes a smart woman.

CHAPTER SIXTEEN

BE PERSISTENT: DON'T GIVE UP

When Cynthia Wake had only a shelter to call home, people told her to get a job and give up her small business. Cynthia wouldn't listen. She refused to quit. That's why she's an entrepreneur today.

Persistence is probably the most important attribute leading to success. Almost by definition, if you own a business things will go wrong on a daily basis. Plans will go awry, experiments will fail, and problems will crop up when least expected. It's easy to quit, but where does that get you?

Thomas Edison was persistent. He failed 1,000 times with various experiments to invent the light bulb. Imagine how different life would be had Edison quit when his ninetieth or 900th experiment failed?

Abraham Lincoln was persistent. Before he became the sixteenth president of the United States, he was defeated eight times when he ran for public office, including four attempts to win a seat in Congress and once for vice president. Twice Lincoln failed in business. But with each setback he persevered and tried again until finally he was triumphant in the most important political bid of his life, the presidential race of 1860.

I'm sure you get the point. Never give up because you never fail until you quit.

When you start your business, you'll make plans and you'll set goals. However, no matter who you are, how much money you have, or what kind of business you begin, obstacles and problems will pop up continuously. What's important is that you're mentally prepared to meet the challenges.

Whether it's a financial crisis, a disgruntled employee, declining sales, a threatening competitor, a challenge in the production department, or . . . any number of other issues, almost every day you can expect obstacles to arise. Some small. Some big. Any one of them can discourage you, depress you, and, if you let it, force you to quit. But as long as you don't quit, you'll still be in control of your destiny. You may not arrive the way you had envisioned and your timing may be off by a year or two. You may need a second, a third, or a thirtieth plan to finally arrive at a successful destination. But as long as you persevere, and refuse to give up, you *will* have a chance to succeed.

It's easy for outsiders to look at Subway today, with 14,000-plus stores, and conclude, "They're so big. They couldn't have had many problems." But, of course, we weren't always so big, and our expansion was painfully slow in the early years. People are surprised to learn that it took ten years to build our first twenty-five stores, twenty-two years to build our first 1,000 stores, and then by 1987 we started opening 1,000 stores a year. But regardless of the year, we faced challenges each and every week and I have no doubt that we'll continue facing them for as long as we exist. For sure, challenges, headaches, problems, and difficulties come with every business.

You already know the story of how we persevered when our first store was failing. Later, one of our major challenges occurred when Subway opened in Australia in the late 1980s. For several years we tried to gain a strong foothold in that friendly market where American fast food had really taken off. We recruited some great franchisees, opened some terrific stores, and worked hard at cultivating a loyal cus-

257

tomer base, but just like our early days in the States, we never seemed to make significant progress. Sometimes we even slid backward.

It would have been easy to give up, especially in a market so many miles away from headquarters, but by then it was ingrained in us that you can never succeed at anything if you quit. After eight years of hard work we had opened only twenty-five stores in the entire country of Australia, but then the pace quickened. Today, we are expanding rapidly with more than 225 Subway restaurants there, many thousands of satisfied customers, and a corps of dedicated franchisees that are grateful that we never quit.

Throughout this book there are stories of other entrepreneurs who were sometimes close to giving up and certainly could have done so. But each one persevered and without fail they've benefited from their perseverance.

Rather than devote this chapter to someone who's made it big financially, I'd like to share the story of a persistent businesswoman who is successful in her own right. She lives in Atlanta and she's still working hard to achieve her goals. Self-employed for nearly twenty years, she's never made much money, but she refuses to give up. Working from her home selling hosiery, she expects her business to earn about $30,000 in the year 2000. Someday, however, she believes the business will produce revenues in the millions of dollars. But more importantly, she's gratified to be in business for herself, and she appreciates the dignity and self-respect that her own business has bestowed upon her and her family. Furthermore, she's convinced that her business is creating something more valuable than money. She's creating opportunities for other women who, like her, want to be both homemaker and entrepreneur. One day, she plans to oversee a national network of independent salespersons, similar to Mary Kay Cosmetics and Amway. On countless occasions, when others would have likely given up, this middle-aged woman has persevered. In times of dire need she was advised by family and friends to get a job, but she refused. She'll tell you there's nothing exceptional about her. She's a salesperson. She's a wife and a mother. She cooks and cleans. She attends church weekly with her family. But she's also a serious business-woman. And there's one more important quality about her. *She doesn't believe in quitting.* Even when everything went wrong, she persevered. Here's her story.

———

To most people who meet her, but don't really know her, Cynthia Wake is strictly business. Whether she's in a meeting or practicing for the church choir, it seems she doesn't have a moment to spare. One night, she chided the choir members during an Easter Sunday rehearsal. "Come on now," she pleaded. "We have five songs to learn in two hours and no one knows them. Let's cut out the small talk and get to work."

The seriousness of Cynthia's personality no doubt has much to do with the fact that for nearly twenty years, since she graduated from high school at age eighteen, she's been self-employed. Much of that time she worked alone as a traveling salesperson. There's also the fact, however, that she's a woman with a mission. She's set goals for herself, and she hears the ticking of the clock. "I plan to build a personal shopping network with sales representatives across the country," she explains. "My business will allow women the opportunity to work and sell products they care about. They can work full-time or part-time, and that's important because no job should come before your family. I'm building this business because I need to do it for myself and my family." In that sense, Cynthia Wake is finishing big!

Those may be the words of a woman who's strictly business, but they're not the words of a hardened woman. Up close and personal, Cynthia Wake can be as playful as Mary Poppins. "When I work, I work," she says emphatically. "But when the work is over for the day, I try to be there for my husband and my two children. I cook dinner, I watch television, I sit and talk with my family about their day. We go bowling together, we play volleyball and tennis. Every year we go on a vacation, to the beach or on a cruise, and during these times I not only don't think about business, I don't even think about how much money we're spending. And usually, we budget our money very carefully."

Cynthia admits, however, that her serious personality often overwhelms her fun-loving personality, and the result can be aggravating. "If people want to play when I have business on my mind," she says, "I'm going to stay focused on business." During committee meetings at her church she says she annoys people by always talking like a businessperson. For example, Cynthia's church sells audiotape recordings of their preacher's sermons and Cynthia believes in tracking every sale and reinvesting the money. During one meeting several committee members complained to her, "Why do you think like that? Does it really matter what we sell or how we spend the money?" She explained that church business was no less serious than other business. "You do business by doing business," she clarified.

Even at home, in spite of her best efforts, Cynthia sometimes gets caught talking too much about business. When it happens, her husband will remind her to loosen up. "What I try to do," she says, "is work between nine and five, when my husband works. And play when my husband and children want to play."

That hasn't always been possible in Cynthia's life, however. She was born into a poor, country family near Montgomery, Alabama. After her parents died when she was three, she lived with her grandmother, and half a dozen other children, some of them her aunts and uncles. One day she was adopted by a man and woman who also had two children. Her new father was a businessman. He owned a restaurant and lounge which featured live bands and attracted throngs of customers. As much as anything else in her childhood, Cynthia remembers that for as long as her father's business was good, life was good. "Since I was a young girl," she recalls, "I knew business was the way to go. I saw my father work hard and succeed. He never trained me for my own business, but I knew that a good business could pay more than a job. Ever since then, I never wanted just a job. For me, the only choice was to start my own business."

Right out of high school, Cynthia hit the streets selling magazines and books door-to-door. After three years, she switched product lines and began selling pots and pans, kitchen utensils, and housewares. "It's the hardest type of sales you can imagine," she explains. "It's not much fun, but it was a way to begin my own business. I like talking to people and getting paid for it. Plain and simple. Selling door-to-door was difficult, especially when the doors were slammed in my face, but it kept me out of an office job where I would have been tied to a desk. I like my freedom. I like to work. But I've never wanted to work just for the money. Whatever I do, I want to enjoy it. Selling door-to-door I could make $50 to $100 a day. Starting out, that wasn't so bad, although it was barely enough to pay my bills."

By age twenty-one, Cynthia married her high school sweetheart and they settled in Atlanta. For several years they both sold pots and pans door-to-door. When Cynthia became pregnant, her sales skyrocketed. "When people see you're carrying a child, and you're out trying to make a living, they can't very well be rude to you. They aren't as quick to slam the doors on you," she recalls. "They're more inclined to talk. And if they'd talk, I could sell them a set of pots and pans. It was great to be pregnant and selling, but I stopped in my seventh month. All that walking was difficult, and I wasn't about to risk my own health, or my baby's. I returned to work shortly after my baby was born, but the sales were never as good as when I was pregnant."

Several years later Cynthia gave birth to a second child, and about that time her husband, who had studied to become a draftsman, gave up selling door-to-door for a full-time job in the engineering department of a local business. Eventually,

Cynthia also gave up the rigorous life of the traveling salesperson and started selling jewelry and accessories at church bazaars, flea markets, and health fairs. "Many organizations in every community sponsor these kinds of events," she explains. "As I learned about these events in the Atlanta area, I reserved a table and displayed my products."

Cynthia sold products for several suppliers and earned up to 25 percent commission on her sales. Eventually, she discovered that she could make more money by purchasing the products at wholesale and reselling them. "At first, I was making a lot of money for the suppliers," she says. "The only thing they had to do was supply the merchandise. I was responsible for displaying the merchandise as well as developing the leads and making the sales. I figured if I had to do all of that anyway, I might as well buy the products at wholesale and keep the profits myself." Much to her advantage, the Atlanta Apparel Mart offered all the products she wanted to sell.

Many of Cynthia's customers worked full-time in corporate America, and while they appreciated Cynthia's reasonable prices, they especially valued her personal attentiveness. "My business has been built on convenience for my customers," she says. "The women who bought my products often didn't have time to shop for themselves. They worked and they had families. So they relied on me. The more they saw me, the more money they spent with me."

In fact, Cynthia's customers often didn't wait to see her to buy from her again. They started calling her at home, especially when they needed pantyhose. "That was my big seller," she acknowledges. "Many women who work in corporate America have to wear stockings, or they prefer to. My customers knew that I carried an excellent quality product and I sold it for a third of what they'd have to pay in a retail store. So naturally they, and everyone they told, wanted to buy from me."

But the customers didn't simply want to buy pantyhose from Cynthia. They hoped she would deliver the product to them on the job. That's when Cynthia recognized a void and decided to fill it. "My customers needed a delivery service. They needed someone who could keep them in stockings. So I played right into that market niche. At every bazaar and flea market that I worked, I handed out business cards to promote my free delivery service. Of course it wasn't an original idea. There were plenty of similar companies that sold vitamins and cosmetics. But my specialty was hosiery."

Specialization was a particularly smart move because Cynthia rarely had the money she needed to buy a wide variety of inventory which she was forced to do when she sold jewelry and accessories. By limiting her product line to just pantyhose she could purchase larger quantities at one time, drive down her costs, and earn a larger profit. But even at that she ran into difficulties.

Early on, she struggled to predict the timing of her customers' purchases, as well as quantity and size. One summer, either unaware or not remembering that pantyhose sales drop off dramatically during the warmest months, she purchased a large amount of inventory. Making matters worse, she charged her purchases on several credit cards. When the products didn't sell for three months, she couldn't make the credit card payments, and her credit rating was damaged.

On another occasion, she invested her limited capital in small- and medium-sized pantyhose. But for weeks the majority of her customers called to buy only queen-sized pantyhose! "I was stuck," Cynthia recalls. "My money was tied up in product that I couldn't return, or change out. Until I sold it, I couldn't buy new product, so I had to hold on as best I could. Some customers couldn't get the pantyhose they wanted, and there wasn't anything I could do about it. This isn't the type of business where you get a deposit. It's like pizza. When the customers want it, they want it now, and they pay when it's delivered."

Experience eventually helped Cynthia smooth out the operational aspects of her business. For example, in the future she would borrow money only in the fall, when sales are at their peak. And by tracking customer preferences, for size as well as color, she learned how to buy inventory in appropriate quantities. Yet, the worst was to come, although it had nothing to do with her ability to operate a business. Her marriage ended and for more than a year Cynthia endured the greatest of hardships not only to save her business, but to help provide for her children.

"I ran into one hardship after another," Cynthia recalls the story. "First thing, I didn't have any transportation. The car broke down and I couldn't afford to get it fixed. So to make my deliveries I had to use the bus. That was not only expensive, it was very inconvenient. It took extra time and energy and it made it hard to get back home for the kids when they got out of school.

"I wasn't making much money, only a few thousand dollars a year, so I had to get financial help. I found different agencies that helped me pay my bills. Different churches helped me, too. They paid my utilities. But then, we lost our home. When we could we lived with friends, but mostly we lived in shelters. I still kept delivering pantyhose, though. My customers never knew my circumstances. I never let it get me down when I was working."

Of course, the fact that she wasn't working all that often posed a problem for many of her family and friends. They urged her to give up selling pantyhose and get a real job. Her parents, and even her pastor, discouraged her. "You can't pay your bills," they would say, as though she needed reminding. "Go get a job. Your children deserve better."

Cynthia agreed that her children deserved better. That was precisely the reason she had no intention of giving up her business. Yes, there were occasions when she was tempted to quit. On days when she felt lonely and abandoned, when she couldn't see things getting better or even see straight, she considered quitting. But the moments of indecision were fleeting. "Every so often I would think that maybe I should get a job, at least for a while, and pick the business back up when I got on my feet again. But then I'd ask myself: Is it better to give up my customers now and start later from scratch, or would it be better to weather the storm? Each time, I decided to keep my customers and weather the storm.

"Once when we were living in the shelter I was at a very low point. What's the meaning of trying to build up a business, and become a successful businesswoman, if I couldn't have my family intact? What's it worth? But then I came to my senses. My husband wanted to be separated or divorced. There wasn't a thing I could do about that. Quitting my business wasn't going to help the situation. I knew I needed my business more than ever."

And so she persevered. "I stopped talking to the people who I knew would discourage me," Cynthia continues. "I kept my head up. I learned as much as I could about my business. I kept getting on the bus and serving my customers."

She talked to successful businesspeople and turned to them for encouragement. "They seemed to know what I was going through. They knew it was hard. But they gave me hope by telling me that it was worthwhile to build a business."

She talked to God. "Faith comes first," she says. "I have faith that God can do anything, including make me a success. I would have to do my part, of course, and that meant I couldn't give up."

She also talked to herself, convincing herself that she was doing the right thing. "Someday," she would say, "I'm going to make $100,000 in a year. And then I'm going to make a million dollars. This is a multimillion-dollar industry. L'eggs can do it. Amway can do it. Mary Kay can do it. And so can I."

While Cynthia didn't give up on her business, or her customers, or her children, she also didn't give up on her husband. A year and a few months after he had left, he returned to the family. Since that time, her business has continued to prosper. Not because her husband returned—although he's supportive of her business—but because she refused to quit.

In the mid-1990s, Cynthia hoped to expand her business

with the help of two other women. In her circle of bazaars and fairs she had met two other vendors who also were struggling to come up with enough money to buy large quantities of inventory at deeply discounted prices. "We got together," Cynthia recalls, "and formed a partnership. We called the business The Hosiery Stop. Our idea was to pool our money so that we could get a better deal on our product line. We were each able to spend $200 to $300 at a time on inventory. Together, if we could spend $1,000, we would be able to buy more for less. It was a good idea, but it didn't happen. We all discovered that we were used to working on our own and we didn't want to compromise to work with each other. When we couldn't satisfy everyone, the other two decided the business wasn't worth the sacrifices, and they left." As for Cynthia, considering the sacrifices she had already endured, she never doubted that it was worth it.

"So I got busier on my own. Every Saturday I rented a table somewhere. I handed out more of my business cards. I got referrals from my customers. Either they called me, or I called them. I especially made a point of calling them on the days that I knew they got paid. That's when they were more likely to buy. I would get as many orders together at once as I could, then buy the merchandise, then deliver it and collect my money. But even then it was a vicious cycle. Buy, then sell, buy, then sell. I just couldn't get ahead because I never had a large enough sum of money to buy the product."

But then one day Cynthia heard about Working Capital, the microlending organization, which had a branch in her community. "A friend at my church told me she had been hired as the director of Working Capital and she said they could loan me some money. I explained about my past credit problems and I said I didn't have any collateral. She said it didn't matter, and she encouraged me to visit her and apply for a loan."

When Cynthia arrived at Working Capital, she found more than a loan waiting for her. Following the successful formula established in Bangladesh by Professor Yunus, Working Capital introduced Cynthia to a comprehensive support system. "Working Capital has a tutorial program that's designed to help small businesses," she explains, grateful for the opportunity the organization has given her. "It's a learning process and a mentoring program. I was assigned to a group of several businesspeople like myself. We met once a week to talk about the issues involved in our businesses. A different mentor came every week to talk to us about how to build various aspects of our businesses. For example, a banker met with us one evening. When you operate a small business, you don't really understand what the banks expect from you before they'll give you a loan. We tend to think the banks ought to take a chance, but it doesn't work that way. The mentors work with us and prepare us to think like a banker so that when we're ready for that $100,000 loan, we'll be in a position to get it. This kind of training has proven to be invaluable to me and the others in my group."

Working Capital granted a $500 loan to each of the group members and held out the promise of additional loans in increments of $500 up to $10,000. No collateral was required. However, the initial loans had to be repaid in weekly installments over a six-month period of time. Larger loans could be paid biweekly and then monthly. The group members were each accountable to one another for their loans. If any one of the members defaulted on a loan, the other members of the group would be disqualified from future borrowing opportunities. The only way group members could redeem themselves would be to take responsibility for paying back the defaulted loan.

"When I joined Working Capital," Cynthia explains, "I was assigned to a group that included six other business owners, including a painter, a day care owner, a plantscaper, and someone who sold Christian literature. Three people dropped out after a period of time, but two of them paid off their loans. The third one defaulted. The four of us who remained in the group each had to pay $17 a month to pay off the loan. Since then, no one has left our group and we want to accept more members to build it up. However, we'll be very selective because we don't want to pay off defaulted loans."

After meeting weekly for several months, Cynthia's group began meeting twice a month and then once a month. "We help one another as much as possible," she says. "For example, I'm not very good at bookkeeping and so I'll take my questions to the group. A couple of them are better at bookkeeping and administration than I am, so they'll show me what to do. Or they'll recommend software for me. If I need help on my computer, a member of the group will teach me."

Not long ago, Cynthia told the group about a problem she was experiencing with an unmotivated sales representative. After joining Working Capital, she recruited four independent sales reps to help expand her business and to begin building a national network. One of the sales reps consistently missed deadlines. The group advised Cynthia to take control. "I'm an easygoing person. I can get along with people," says Cynthia. "But this lady was taking advantage of me. She wouldn't follow procedures. The group told me how to get firm with her without necessarily losing her. Now I'm doing a better job of explaining the structure of my business so there are no gray areas."

For everything that Cynthia takes from the Working Capital group, she also gives back. "What we do is share our expertise," she explains. "I'm good at sales, so many times a member will ask me how to meet people, or how to present a product to sell it. I'll teach the group about cold calling or how to put a promotional flyer into someone's hands and build rapport. Getting this kind of help without Working Capital isn't easy. So I think it's a terrific program. Over the years, many people who run small businesses will make mistakes. Like me, they might take a chance with borrowing money on credit cards, then something goes wrong, and then the credit goes bad. On paper you look like you're unreliable, but the truth is you're out there working hard and doing your best. Programs like Working Capital give you a second chance to prove yourself."

For all she's been through, Cynthia Wake shouldn't have needed to prove herself a second time, but she doesn't mind. She's constantly improving her skills and learning the secrets to her trade. "It's important to learn how to maintain a business. I could get rich overnight but I also know I can go broke overnight. By working through all the kinks, I'm learning how my business operates and how I can keep it moving forward. The more I'm out there selling," she says, "the more people see me and that creates opportunities. Many times I've discovered it's being in the right place at the right time. Or it's who you know, or who you know who will introduce you to someone who can help you. I still have a lot to learn, so I'm willing to continue proving myself. I'll need more help, and more money, to build a multilevel personal shopping network, but I'm on my way. In the year 2000 I expect to have twenty-five sales representatives working with me. Then I'll build it to 100 and beyond. I want to create as many jobs for others as I can. Especially women with kids. After going through my struggles, I know what it's like for women. We need a job where we're not out of the house all day. Kids need a mother. So I'm working for me, my family, and other mothers."

Meanwhile, she's not waiting for that elusive star to shine down on her. She's following her own game plan, building her business, and hoping for the best. And even if that star doesn't find her anytime soon, Cynthia Wake isn't likely to give up. Not now. Not ever.

CHAPTER SEVENTEEN

BUILD A BRAND NAME

The founder had curly red hair and they called him Kinko. With that nickname, Paul Orfalea created one of America's most visible brand names: Kinko's.

Consumers truly prefer to buy the brands they like. They'll often go out of their way to find the branded products they prefer, and they'll spend more money for their favorite brands.

For many years we have focused on building our brand at Subway, but it wasn't until a few years ago, when I attended the opening of our first store in New Zealand, that I realized how powerful a brand could be.

To me, few things are more exciting than the opening of the first Subway in a new country. I was traveling Down Under at the time of our debut in New Zealand, and I happily arranged my itinerary so that I could arrive at the store the day before it was scheduled to open. I arrived in plenty of time to help our franchisees, Earl Pfeifer and Mark Rutherglen, get ready. We worked through the day handling a variety of details, and at about 5:00 P.M. we sat down to discuss the plans for the next day. Our conversation was suddenly interrupted by a young businessman who wandered into the store asking to buy a sandwich. Earl apologized and explained that the store wouldn't open for business until the next day, and we watched as disappointment fell across his face. "Last week I was in Cairo, Egypt," he said, "and I enjoyed my first Subway sandwich there. When I saw your sign, I was hoping to get another."

Wow! In that instant, I got a much better picture of the power in a brand name! We had opened a store in Cairo only the month before, and here we were, a third of the way around the world, and look who comes into our store in New Zealand. A fellow who had become a customer in Cairo! Why? Simply because he remembered how much he enjoyed a Subway sandwich a week earlier, and he wanted to savor that experience again. He could have stopped at any number of other restaurants in New Zealand, but he stopped at Subway because he wanted the product offered by the brand.

When you develop a brand image for a product, service, or even a personality, you create powerful expectations in the minds and hearts of consumers. As brand strategist Scott Talgo explains, "A brand that captures your mind gains behavior. A brand that captures your heart gains commitment."

Brands are so powerful because of the power of the human mind. The memories of past experiences, the confidence in the product, the knowledge of what to expect, all become favorable impressions locked in the consumers' minds. By earning our reputation in Cairo, the Subway brand earned a position in the heart and mind of this businessman who would likely look for Subway no matter where he traveled in the world.

In recent years several good books have been written about branding and many businesspeople are either talking about, teaching, or studying the subject. In 1996, David Aaker, a marketing professor at the University of California at Berkeley, published *Building Strong Brands*, a definitive follow-up to his breakthrough book, *Managing Brand Equity*. In 1998, marketing guru Al Ries and his daughter Laura Ries further illuminated our knowledge about branding with their engaging book: *22 Immutable Laws of Branding*. Each of these titles is worth reading and together they provide a solid foundation in modern-day branding, and they explain what every business needs to know to create a valuable brand.

Branding isn't a new concept. Early merchants became known in their communities for their products and services. During the Industrial Revolution knowledge of brand names took on regional and national importance as factories produced goods for their local areas. Products became known by their quality, reliability, and sometimes even their color. You could buy a car from Henry Ford in any color you wanted, as long as it was black!

With the introduction and expansion of packaged goods, brands became even more popular. Soup, cereal, candy, soda, milk, bread, wine, pharmaceuticals, and most other products became identifiable and desirable by brand. In supermarkets and department stores shoppers still get on their knees to search the shelves for a certain brand. They ask for products by brand names: Kleenex for facial tissue, Reynolds Wrap for aluminum foil, Bayer for aspirin, Jell-O for gelatin, and so forth. Marketers and merchandisers soon recognized the importance of a brand that uniquely captured the hearts and minds of consumers. In *Building Strong Brands*, Sunkist Growers' retired CEO, Russell L. Hanlin, is quoted as saying, "An orange . . . is an orange . . . is an orange. Unless, of course, that orange happens to be a Sunkist."

More recently, in some cases branding has nearly become a substitute for selling. Often we'll buy a new product that we've never tried simply because we know the source of the goods and have confidence in what they produce. Branding is the most effective way to position a product or service so that it can be presold. Now, more than ever, it's important to create a brand that consumers will go out of their way to buy.

How do you create a brand name? Begin by narrowing the focus. The quickest way to create a sizzling brand is to make it stand for something singular. Become famous for what you offer.

A good example: Starbucks. The name has become synonymous with coffee. Unlike generic coffeeshops, Starbucks doesn't focus on other items like fried eggs, donuts, and pancakes. Starbucks means coffee and many people go out of their way to find a Starbucks while passing other coffee shops along the way. And they'll spend $3 for Starbucks coffee when they could buy coffee elsewhere for a dollar. For some, the Starbucks stop has become a daily ritual.

Even simple products can be branded, like water. Can anything be more generic, or more available, than water? Think about Evian, the world's leading brand of bottled water, selling nearly 1.5 billion liters annually in more than 120 countries. By winning the hearts and minds of consumers, Evian dominates the bottled water market and sells more than $625 million worth of water a year. Not only that, in many places Evian has increased the value of water beyond the value of branded beer, milk, and soda. By liter, Evian is 20 percent more expensive than Budweiser, 40 percent more expensive than Borden's milk, and 80 percent more expensive than Coca-Cola!

Realize the power of branding and focus on building your brand, even if yours is just a neighborhood business. Developing a good name, a good reputation, and a good brand will add value to your business and profit to your bottom line.

Among microentrepreneurs who have created great brands, few have been more successful in recent years than Paul Orfalea. You might not recognize the name but you know his brand by his nickname: Kinko.

What Starbucks is to coffee, Kinko's is to copies. A growing number of American consumers recognize Kinko's as the twenty-four-hour office away from home. If there's not a Kinko's in your neighborhood today, there may be in the near future because it's a brand that has found its niche. Kinko's is not necessarily for everyone, but whether you need to send a fax, scan a photograph, photocopy your tax return or résumé, or you need dozens of copies of a bound presentation, in color, printed from your own computer disk, and you want it quickly, Kinko's is the place to get it done. Kinko's is an extension of your office.

Interestingly, the marketplace has grown up with Kinko's, which was started on a college campus. There's an emotional connection between the brand and its customers. It's a connection that's reflective of the founder's personality. Here's his unique story.

––––––––

"I'm unemployable," says Paul Orfalea, explaining why he's an entrepreneur. "I have no mechanical ability. I'm all thumbs. I can't shift gears. I'm limited as to what I can do. Technology doesn't interest me. I don't know about computers or the Internet. People call and ask me about gigabytes and even copiers and I say I really don't know about that. And I really don't care. I don't read very well, and I have a limited attention span. I always knew I could never get a job, so I decided to have my own business. I really wanted to be a stand-up comic."

If that doesn't sound like a man capable of building a billion-dollar-plus business empire, look again. Paul Orfalea, once the self-acclaimed poster boy for insecurity, is the kingpin of the expanding Kinko's global network with locations in the United States and several other countries. It's an achievement made more remarkable by the fact that Kinko's was launched in a garage with a mere $5,000 borrowed from a bank.

At the time of Paul's youth in the 1950s, there was no term to describe the affliction now known as dyslexia. "Some people *say* they have dyslexia," Paul quips. "I've got the *real* thing." So much so, in fact, that he failed second grade. "A nun discovered that I didn't know the alphabet, so she flunked me. My parents had my older brother and sister try to teach me the alphabet by beating it into me, but it didn't work. I was sent to school with retarded kids in Hollywood because no one could understand why I couldn't learn the alphabet. I was tested everywhere, sent to a memory school, and tutored endlessly. My parents said it cost them $50 for every word I eventually could read. I visited an eye doctor three times a week to do eye muscle exercises, which had nothing to do with my problem. I went to every high school in Southern California, and when I graduated I was eighth from the bottom of my class of twelve hundred. I graduated with a D average."

Thus the insecurity.

"It was the most dejected period of my life," recalls Paul, whose estimated personal fortune was in excess of $250 million before he was fifty. "I went to a junior college to try to prove myself so that I could get accepted at the University of Southern California in Los Angeles. I remember sitting in a philosophy class and it was as if William Buckley was teaching. I didn't understand a word of it. Everyone is taking notes and during the break it's as if everything the professor talked about everyone already knew. It was like Aristotle and Plato were their friends from childhood. I'm completely dejected, a dummy, and I put down my pen and said, 'I'm never going to make it in this world.'"

But he didn't give up. "My parents, who owned their own business in the garment district of Los Angeles, always made a big deal about school. My mother motivated me to stay in college by saying that it looked like fun. It wasn't fun, but I didn't quit." He claims he got into USC because an admissions officer bent the rules. "When I was in junior college I got a speeding ticket and when I went to see the judge I looked disheveled." It was the late 1960s and Paul's hippie style of dress, accentuated by a curly reddish Afro—which earned him the nickname Kinko—wasn't all that unusual. But "the judge didn't like it and he didn't treat me very well. So when I visited the admissions office at USC I dressed up because I had learned my lesson. If you look nice, they'll treat you better."

At USC, Orfalea studied finance and business, but nothing about him had changed academically. "The USC football players lowered the curve," he explains, "so I could always get a D or a C. It didn't matter. I wasn't worried about getting a job. There was no way that anyone was going to hire me.

There just wasn't a doubt in my mind that I'd have to start my own business."

The genesis for his business was discovered at a copy machine. "We were frequently assigned to do term papers as a group," he explains. "Since I couldn't read or write very well, I always offered to do the Xeroxing [*Note the substitution of the brand name for "photocopying."*] 'You research it and write it,' I'd say to my group, 'and then I'll get it Xeroxed.' That was my contribution to the project." He spent so much time at the copy machine that he was soon intrigued by it. Not just the machine itself, but the service that it provided. "At the time," he says, "I was studying the life cycle of products in a marketing class. With a long life cycle, the Xerox was a cool little machine. The more I thought about it, the more I liked it, and I understood what it could do."

By the time he graduated from college in 1970, he was thinking about what he could do, and the only thing he knew for certain was that he wanted to live near a college campus. "It was like heaven being around a campus, so I had to figure out a way to stay there." Based on his experiences making copies for numerous student projects, he surmised that other students could be led to rely on him to make their copies. For one thing, the copying machines on campus charged ten cents per page and he thought he could cut the price in half and still make a profit. That's when he decided to open a tiny photocopy shop on Pardall Road, the main artery in Isla Vista near the University of California at Santa Barbara. For money, he asked his father to co-sign a loan at the Isla Vista branch of Bank of America, which had just been rebuilt after campus revolutionaries torched it during a protest against the war in Vietnam. "The bank was now trying to show that it was helping to support businesses in the community," says Paul, "so they were giving out money. That's how I got the $5,000."

The building that Paul selected for his first store also housed a hamburger stand, which was convenient for drawing traffic as well as feeding Paul at lunchtime. Kinko's set up shop in an eighty-square-foot space that was part of the garage. Paul consulted the Yellow Pages of the local phone directory to lease equipment, including one photocopy machine, a film processor, and an offset press. "It was sort of like a little Fotomat," he recalls. "I placed notebooks and pens out on the sidewalk and everyone going to school stopped by and bought supplies from me. Then, they'd drop off their copying projects, or their film, and I'd handle it for them."

Some days the little store packed in so many customers that Paul rolled the photocopier onto the sidewalk for self-service. He hired fellow hippies to operate the machinery while he catered to the customers and worked the cash register. At night, he filled a backpack with notebooks and pens and peddled products through the women's dorms. "I had nothing else to do," he explains, "and I wanted to meet girls."

Later, he described this experience as wandering. "Ever since I opened up my first store, I liked wandering. That's where I get my best ideas." One day, as an example, he wandered into the reserve book room at the campus library. "Students usually gathered there the night before a test," he says, "but it was difficult for them to get the materials they needed because everyone wanted them at the same time." Paul saw an opportunity. He invited professors to leave their materials on file at Kinko's as well as the reserve book room. "From that point on," he says, "the professors at UCSB supported my business."

Everyone, it seems, loved Kinko's. As much as it was a place to get a term paper or résumé copied, it was a funky place to gather, to talk, and to share ideas. For Paul, it was also a place to make money, a fact that didn't go unnoticed by his friends and co-workers. As they showed more interest, Paul offered to partner with them and encouraged them to open Kinko's in other locations. Before long, he helped his cousin open a Kinko's in Van Nuys, California, and then a co-worker, a surfer who operated the printing press, opened a Kinko's up the Pacific coast. Within five years, the company had opened twenty-four locations! Eventually, Paul would partner up with 128 individuals who owned the rights to open multiple units of Kinko's.

By 1980, the chain had expanded to eighty stores in twenty-eight states, then 400 stores by 1990, with outlets opening shortly thereafter in Japan and the Netherlands. "This collaborative format," says Paul, "wasn't a franchise. I chose to make money together with people. Grassroots ownership provided a lot of innovation and simplified the bureaucracy. Plus, it gave us the money we needed to expand."

What the partnerships didn't do, however, was unify the Kinko's system. Unlike a franchise, where every unit of the chain is expected to act and look alike, many of the Kinko's marched to different drumbeats. Few of them looked alike. "If yellow paint was on sale when we built a new store," says Paul, "that store would be painted yellow." This freedom proved somewhat problematic when Kinko's chose blue for its corporate color. "Over time, we understood some things about our customers," says Paul, who became slightly more corporatelike with each additional store. "They are uptight and confused. They don't know what they want, and they want it yesterday. We said to ourselves, if we paint the stores with a red and yellow color scheme and have loud music blaring, we are going to stress the customers out even more. On the other hand, if we paint the inside of the stores a nice, calm blue, and make sure that each store is impeccably neat and clean, our customers are going to calm down and respond better." Convincing his partners to repaint their stores blue wasn't easy, however. By the time the color decision was made, there were 120 Kinko's in various parts of the country. "That decision was the first time we said we need some strong central identity—that we're all in this together." Even so, Paul says he suspects some of the early stores have yet to convert to the official color.

Among Kinko's archetypal customers, college students, color wasn't much of an issue. To them, Kinko's would always represent a community as much as anything else. However, as

Kinko's expanded, it drifted away from the college scene. Stores planted their roots in suburbia where they attracted a corporate clientele, as well as free agents and small business owners, the refugees of downsized American corporations. Many of these customers worked from home and relied on Kinko's for a variety of professional services.

In spite of this newfound success, vindicating a former life in which he seemed incapable of accomplishing anything significant, Paul stepped into Kinko's leadership role without even a hint of arrogance. "I was blessed with the quality of knowing that anyone else can do it better," he explains. "How do you think I viewed the first worker that came to work at Kinko's? My whole attitude was, 'I'm so happy you are here. What can I do to make you happier?' I never said to myself, 'I can do it better than they can.' In my mind anybody else could do it better than I could." It's a philosophy that he has maintained through nearly thirty years of building his business.

Nonetheless, he's not a leader who abdicates authority, although he admits he's not a manager of people. "When we had seven stores I was an open-door, lay-the-turds-on-me kind of manager. Then one day a store manager came in and told me that he got a bounced check and he wanted to know what to do. '*Go after the person who wrote the check, and don't bother me!*' I said." After that, Paul became much less accessible.

However, he's never pretended to be a "one-man band." When he says that "things run beautifully without me," it's because he has surrounded himself with a team of experts. "Accountants are concerned with the past, managers are concerned with the present, but leaders must concern themselves with the future," he says. "I'm well suited because I worry about tomorrow. I don't know if I'm a leader, but since I can't do anything else well, I'm the leader today by default."

Paul may believe that, but anyone close to him doesn't buy it. They say he's a natural, intuitive leader whose genius is seamlessly connecting business and people, co-workers and customers. More than anything else, that singular quality sums up Paul's ability to build with an estimated value in excess of $600 million, with plenty of room to grow in a $100-billion-plus market.

"Paul's intuition was extremely valuable in building this business," says Bruce Humbert, Kinko's vice president of customer research and brand development since 1998. "He made several powerful decisions that were right on target for building a great brand."

What, exactly, did Paul Orfalea do to establish Kinko's brand?

First, he built his business where the competitors were not looking. "That's a smart approach for any entrepreneur, particularly when you don't have a big advertising budget," explains Bruce. "Find a niche [a potential market] and work it [pursue it]. Paul's competitors must have been thinking, 'Those college kids, they don't have any money.' But the college campus became the foundation for Kinko's business. It was a terrific jump-start for Kinko's. Colleges provided a base of customers that has lasted a very long time. Every day we hear from customers who say they discovered Kinko's at college. It may have been under stressful conditions and Kinko's rescued them. That experience, repeated countless times, created a strong emotional bond that has kept these customers loyal to Kinko's. Coming back to one of our stores reminds them of a past, pleasurable experience."

Bruce says that Paul's second "powerful decision" was labeling the business so that he could add products and services to meet the needs of Kinko's niche market. Before Kinko's, it wasn't easy to describe the purpose for a store like Kinko's. "There was no label for what we provided," says Bruce. "Paul might have been tempted to choose a name like Orfalea Office Products, or Paul's Copies, and while those are acceptable names, neither describes our business. Those names would have restricted our mix of products and services and thus limited our future."

Instead, Paul came up with a quirky label that provides a

huge umbrella under which Kinko's can sell anything that's related to copying, duplicating, and communicating. The label Kinko's defines the category just as McDonald's, Mr. Booter, and Ben & Jerry's defined their respective categories. "When you can define a category, you insulate your business from the competition. You get a head start, and that's a huge advantage. We don't have direct competitors," says Bruce. "There are other stores that do some of the things we do, but not the same way. Kinko's is unique."

Adding to the uniqueness is the mythology of the name. *The founder had curly red hair and they called him Kinko.* "Customers feel like they're on the inside when they get to know that story," explains Bruce. "Kinko's is a name with a heritage and a legacy. It's easier for customers to get closer to us when they know something about our history."

Differentiating Kinko's was Paul's third "powerful decision," says Bruce. Ever since he discovered the copy machine, Paul understood the importance of the leading-edge position. He instinctively knew to listen to his customers and respond to them appropriately. He believed in customer research, and through the years he invested in sophisticated tools to conduct this research. But even today Paul says he believes customer research is 99 percent sitting behind the counter, looking and listening. It's a practice that he continues even as chairperson of the company. At least once a year, and usually more often, Paul and other corporate executives spend a weekend working in a Kinko's store. "Every time I talk to customers," says Paul, "I learn something. I spend most of my time in the field, running the business from the bottom up."

"Paul doesn't wait for the results of a strategic analysis to determine if we can give customers something they want," explains Bruce. "If they're asking for it, and it makes sense, we do it. Passport photos are a good example. That wasn't our idea. It was the result of customers asking us for that service."

Giving customers hands-on access to machinery, providing well-lit work spaces, bringing technology to anyone who has a need to use it, introducing color copiers—each was a differentiator that contributed to Kinko's leading-edge position. That position is now firmly in the minds of customers. They know Kinko's will have the leading-edge technology, the oversized poster, or the high-quality photo printout. "We hear stories of people walking in our doors and saying, 'I don't know everything you do here, but if anyone can do *this*, you can,'" says Paul. "We have won that position in the minds of our customers and we are going to continue leveraging it."

Perhaps the most powerful of all brand decisions was the one that made Kinko's accessible twenty-four hours a day, seven days a week. "That plays into the hands of a big chunk of the population that does not work an eight-to-six schedule," says Bruce. "Paul saw that coming." Actually, he heard it coming by the mid-1980s. Across the country, stressed-out victims of corporate downsizing were searching for new jobs. They frequently used Kinko's to help them prepare last-minute résumés and presentations. Many of them begged store managers to keep the shops open so they could continue working. In 1985, a Kinko's in Chicago announced a trial twenty-four-hour routine. When it was immediately successful, other stores kept their doors open, too.

"Much of the work we do," explains Bruce, "doesn't have to be done between nine and five. We were working in the centers after hours anyway, so it was only a matter of unlocking the door and adding a couple of co-workers. It turns out the best way to offer the types of things we do, and to work closely with customers, is to be universally available and accessible when they need us." By tapping into a lifestyle change, Kinko's became vibrant all hours of the day and night.

Meanwhile, Kinko's brand became all the more commanding. "Each time you extend your brand," explains Bruce, "you establish connectors into a customer's DNA. There's no substitute for that chemistry. The brand takes away the customers' risk. They know what to expect. Our model is similar everywhere, if not identical. That's not the case with others who try to do what we do. We may not be the cheapest place to get copies made, and we like that. However, we have better and faster machines, and co-workers who are trained to deliver the results our customers want. Those are the values that matter. Without our brand, we would be reduced to one bullet to use against the competition. We'd have to compete on price. But those who play the price game never win. The business landscape is littered with price competitors, and no one wants to be in that position. Whether Paul did it purposely or not, he consistently managed to position Kinko's so that we've never worried about price."

Paul Orfalea doesn't reveal whether the positioning was accidental or by design. He does say, however, that business is more of an art than a science. That suggests the positioning was accidental. "If business was a science," says Paul, "you could rest easily knowing that two and two is four. But if something is an art, you always think you can do it better. I think that if da Vinci came back and looked at the *Mona Lisa* he probably would say something like, 'Oh, there's too much beige.' That's what art is all about. I am an artist when I go into business. Everything can be done better. It's not my nature to say, 'Everything is good. Let's join the Young President's Club and be a big shot.' That doesn't turn me on. I go to work to solve problems. Our philosophy is you have to take a risk. Our mistakes at Kinko's cost us relatively nothing."

But then he adds that Kinko's is like a mosaic, and as he speaks it's easy to imagine that Paul Orfalea knew precisely what he was doing when he laid the foundation for Kinko's brand. "Every report, every little anecdote, every piece of visual information is part of a puzzle that makes up this company," he explains. "You walk down the street and see things that you may think are unrelated to your business. But they are not. The only way you can begin to understand is to have an overall picture or context of the world where every piece of visual information fits."

That nonlinear mind is part of Paul's charm. On the one

hand, he'll give the impression that he bounces from idea to idea. On the other hand, he'll demonstrate that he's single-minded and disciplined. These very qualities made him all the more attractive to the leadership of Clayton, Dubilier & Rice, Inc., the New York investment firm that bought approximately a third of Kinko's for $219 million in 1997. With big money behind the Kinko's brand, the ultimate goal was to build a global network of 2,000 stores by the year 2000. "We're not going to make it," Orfalea said in 1999. "We've got 910 stores now, and we'll probably open another 110 before 2000. So we'll be better than halfway there."

Goals are good, says Paul, but building a brand is better. Success is not simply about the numbers. "Kinko's has never been about clicking copies and making money," he asserts. "It's always been about doing important work. It's about making sure that people's jobs are meaningful, and that they realize the emotional impact we have on society. I want our co-workers to realize what they do contributes to society. Each job that comes to us represents a vital need for someone in society. We help people get through school. We help them find new careers. We help them make winning presentations. We even help them find their lost children, and their pets. They bring us a photo, we enlarge it, and in a few moments they get as many posters as they need to spread the word. That's important. It's all about reputation. It's all about emotion."

Reputation and emotion. Those words say just about everything there is to say about branding. If you build a business that consumers like and trust, your reputation makes it easier for them to emotionally connect with your brand. And once that happens, consumers will go out of their way and pay more money to buy what your brand sells.

Get busy now and build a brand name!

CHAPTER EIGHTEEN

OPPORTUNITY WAITS FOR NO ONE

Except for a career-ending broken ankle, Mike Ilitch might have been inducted into baseball's Hall of Fame. Instead, he turned a "bad break" into a "good break" and he now owns three pro sports teams in Detroit. Oh yeah, he also taught Americans how to eat two pizzas!

That particular Monday in May 1974 didn't look like a very good day for my friend Brian Dixon. When he reported to work that morning he was shocked to discover a padlock on his employer's office door. A sheriff's notice stated that the business was closed. It was bankrupt.

Good break or bad break?

At first, Brian might have considered it a bad break. After all, even though he didn't care much for his job—he was a sheet metal installer for an air conditioning company—he and his wife depended on his weekly paycheck.

On the other hand, it's easy enough now to see that it was a good break. As Subway's first franchisee, and now one of our Development Agents, Brian's built a business that's far more gratifying and lucrative than most jobs. We don't know for sure what would have become of Brian had his employer not filed for bankruptcy, but it's a pretty good bet that he wouldn't be as well off as he is today. Fortunately, when

Brian read the sheriff's notice that morning, he didn't panic. Somewhere in that notice he saw the word "opportunity." He recognized the opportunity for him to do something different, perhaps something better. That's when he called me, and took me up on my previous offer to him to become our first franchisee.

And what a good break that was for me, and everyone else associated with Subway!

In businesses of all types, as with life in general, opportunities abound. Pete Buck offering me money to start a submarine shop was an opportunity. Leasing a location that we had previously turned down for our fifth store was an opportunity. Baking bread in our stores—an opportunity. Opening a store outside the United States—an opportunity. Franchising to Brian Dixon—yet another opportunity. In nearly four decades of developing Subway, I've experienced countless opportunities and some have turned out to be very fruitful. Those are the opportunities that some people would call lucky breaks. But in my experience, breaks are what you make of them.

As you operate your business, or as you think about your business, it's better to look for the opportunities as opposed to panicking over the problems. Every opportunity comes with pros and cons, and as a business owner, your job is to evaluate them. It doesn't matter how you evaluate them. List the pros and cons if you want to. Assign numeric values to each of them if that helps you. Do whatever you have to do. Talk them over with a partner, or an adviser. Think about it, study it, and make sense of it. But do it quickly. Opportunity waits for no one, and the opportunities you miss can haunt you forever.

Once you size up an opportunity, if the pros outweigh the cons, act on the opportunity. Be rational, be flexible, and make something of it!

No one I know practices that philosophy better than Mike Ilitch, the man who taught America how to eat two pizzas.

You know him for his "Pizza! Pizza!" advertising campaign. He's the founder of Little Caesars Pizza, the world's largest pizza carryout chain. Some people also know him as the owner of the Detroit Tigers, the Detroit Red Wings, and the Detroit Rockers. The owner of more than a dozen different businesses, Mike Ilitch has built a financial empire in his hometown. And it all started, literally, with one break. A break to his ankle. Here's an amazing story of how one man started small and continues to finish big by acting on opportunities.

When he broke his ankle playing baseball in the Detroit Tigers' farm league, Mike Ilitch could have guessed his father would throw him out of the house. To Pop Ilitch, an immigrant from Macedonia, baseball was nonsense. So were all sports, for that matter. Hard work, not play, was the only path to the American Dream. Pop Ilitch was a machine repairman for the Chrysler Corporation, and that's where he thought his youngest son ought to be employed, too. But if Mike was foolish enough to chase the elusive dream that he could become an all-star shortstop for the Tigers, then he'd have to accept responsibility for whatever breaks, good or bad, came his way.

"When I showed up at my parents' home with that broken ankle," Mike recalls, "my dad looked at my leg and said, 'What's this?' I told him what happened and he said, 'Out. Out!' The cast on my leg was all the verification that he needed that baseball was a waste of time. A son who couldn't work and pay room and board was not a good son, especially when he was in his twenties. As far as my pop was concerned, I was destined to become a bum, and he wasn't going to allow me back in the house until I could pay my own way."

Good break or bad break?

It could have gone either way. But Mike wasn't going to become a bum. His parents had set too good of an example for him and his older brother to become anything less than productive citizens. His father was gruff, but that was simply his way. Mike wanted to go home and make peace with him. All he needed was an opportunity to earn some money, or at least make it look like he was earning money.

First he needed a place to live, so he visited a friend and explained the situation. It just so happened that this friend worked in one of the few pizzerias that had opened in Detroit in the mid-1950s. "This fellow suggested that I think about getting into the pizza business," Mike explains. "I didn't know anything about pizza. Only kids were eating pizza. But I needed a job and so I asked my friend's boss if I could work for him. At the time, he didn't need anyone, so I offered to work for free until a job opened up. I had saved some money—it was part of the bonus that the Tigers had paid me to join the league—so I told my father that I had a paying job, and that's how I got back into the house. What my father didn't know was that I took money out of my savings to pay the room and board!"

Once Mike had the opportunity to make a few pizzas, he was fascinated by everything related to the business. "Within a few days, I knew I had to open a pizza shop," he says. "Not far from my parents' home, there was a nightclub that had a tiny kitchen in the back. It was only 250 square feet, but there was room for a pizza oven, a mixer, and a table. So I asked the woman who owned the nightclub if I could rent the kitchen to make pizzas. She agreed, and that's how I got started. It cost me about $3,000 to get the business open, and I took the money from my savings account, which was now close to a zero balance. That small kitchen was cramped, but it was just me, some equipment, and the cigar box I used to collect money. I was taking in $60 to $70 a night, and up to $100 on weekend nights. I hardly had any expenses. It was marvelous. At night I'd put the money in my pocket and go home." As good as it was, the money was never enough to make Mike forget about playing baseball.

All of his young life Mike Ilitch planned to play for the Detroit Tigers, and by the time he was a high school senior there was every indication that the Tigers would recruit him. The club made arrangements with Mike's high school to allow him to work out several mornings a week at Tiger Stadium. "That boosted my self-image," says Mike. "I was into sports, but not school. My grades were average because I didn't have any interest in school. My goal was to become a professional baseball player."

When Mike graduated from high school the Tigers offered him a $5,000 signing bonus to play in the organization's farm league. But Mike expected twice that amount of money and he said so. "I was a cocky kid," he says. When the Tigers told him $5,000 was their *only* offer, Mike told the club he was joining the Marine Corps. But that didn't mean he was giving up baseball. For the next four years, he played for the Corps. During the off-season he was a rifle instructor. "When the Korean War broke out, I wanted to go fight," says Mike. "My colonel told me I didn't want to do that. He knew what war was like and he said it wasn't for me. But I was a hotshot and I insisted that I wanted to fight for my country. So he sent me to San Francisco and I boarded a troopship headed out to the Pacific. We weren't on the ship for very long until guys started throwing up just thinking about where we were headed. As I looked behind the ship I could still get a glimpse of the Golden Gate Bridge and that's when I said to myself, '*Mike, what have you done?*'"

The Marines were at sea for three or four days when the ship docked and Mike thought he was in Korea. However, the ship stopped at Pearl Harbor. "Suddenly they call out three names and I'm one of them," Mike explains. "Turns out there was a Colonel Shephard at Pearl Harbor and he had heard that I was a pretty good baseball player. I was told to get off the ship and report to Colonel Shephard. I did, and that's as far as I was going. I played baseball at Pearl Harbor for the next two years. Some of my friends came back through Pearl Harbor from Korea and they told me how fortunate I was to have missed combat. I wasn't proud of it, but that's the way it happened."

After Mike was released from the Marines the Tigers had continued to follow his career and once again they offered him the opportunity to join one of their minor league teams. This time Mike accepted, even though his father urged him to apply for employment at Chrysler's tool and die shop. "My dad didn't understand sports, so he was against them," Mike says. "When he arrived in the United States he got a job at Ford, but then he went to school at night to learn about machine repair and after eight years he went to Chrysler and he stayed there for thirty years. He worked hard. He saved his money. And to him, life couldn't get much better."

But Mike wasn't ready to give up his own dream to play baseball in the big leagues. He had a good shot at it, too. He was a strong fielder and an expert at bat, averaging .315 and .349 his best seasons. The only problem was his brash attitude. One season he called the Tigers' management and demanded that they bring him to Detroit. "I'm tearing up the league with my batting," he told them, "and it's time to bring me up." That kind of behavior was unappreciated in professional baseball, and management let him know it.

"It wouldn't have been so bad," Mike says, "if I hadn't broken my ankle. Had I continued playing well, they might have still brought me up. When I went back to the minors after my ankle healed my game wasn't as good. A couple of seasons later I had to get a knee operation and then it was over. In those days, once you had a cartilage problem, it was nearly impossible to build up your leg. I lost a lot of muscle. I wasn't as fast anymore, so I had to retire."

By the time he left baseball Mike was both a husband and a father. He had married Marian Bayoff, a pretty blonde of Macedonian descent. His parents had picked her out for him at a church social in Detroit. At first, he said he wasn't going to date her, even though he had never met her and didn't know what she looked like. "I'm a baseball player," Mike told his parents in their native Macedonian language, which they spoke at home. "I'm not dating a Macedonian girl." However, a year or so later, after breaking his ankle and riling his father, Mike saw an opportunity to get back into his father's good graces by dating Marian. "My father was so excited when I told him I had a blind date with her," Mike recalls. "I scored a lot of points with him that day."

But Marian wasn't all that excited. She was expecting a tall handsome suitor and along comes Mike who's only five feet nine. Fortunately, he was driving a beautiful Olds Ninety-Eight convertible and at least that impressed Marian. The car wasn't his, but he didn't tell her that. Another baseball player had asked Mike to take the car for the winter while he played ball in South America. Mike was only too happy to oblige. He drove Marian to the local movie theater in grand style, but after the show, the car had disappeared! It turned out the Olds was repossessed because the owner had failed to make his payments while he was in South America. "I got caught," Mike says with a laugh. "Marian found out the car wasn't mine." But by that time, it didn't matter. Cupid had struck. Mike's charm and wit helped set the romance in motion.

When Mike retired from baseball, he and Marian decided to stay in Tampa, his home base during the season. The local recreation department hired him as a playground director. He worked in the evenings, when kids played baseball. During the day, he attended classes at the University of Tampa and he planned to become a lawyer. However, after eighteen months, Mike couldn't make ends meet financially. Plus, he and Marian were homesick. They missed their families, and they wanted their children to know their grandparents. So in 1958 they returned to Detroit. They moved into the upstairs of the Ilitch home where they were welcome . . . as long as they paid rent!

"I went home to look for work," Mike explains, "but I couldn't find anything. I didn't know anything, and I didn't have an education." Making pizza was something Mike knew how to do, but working in a pizza shop wouldn't have paid enough money to support his growing family. If he had the opportunity to own a shop, however, Mike was certain that he could make a good living, but without any money, he needed to find a job. "When I went for interviews I said I was hardworking and honest, but hardworking, honest people were everywhere in Detroit. Employers asked me, 'What do you know?' I had to say I didn't know anything."

One day Mike had stopped at a gas station when an old friend asked him what he was doing. Mike said he was looking for work, and the friend offered him a job on the spot. He needed someone to go door-to-door in Detroit's neighborhoods soliciting leads for his aluminum awning company. Even though Mike desperately needed a job, he wasn't interested in the offer.

"That's pretty low-grade," he told his friend. "That's not something I'd want to do."

But when the friend pointed out that he could make a lot of money, Mike relented.

"I'll give it a try," he said.

From the very first day Mike hated the job. "I squirmed before I rang every doorbell," he recalls. "What if someone I went to school with answers the door? It would be humiliating to have them see Mike Ilitch, the professional baseball player, asking if they'd be interested in an awning for their home. People slammed doors in my face all the time, and it was embarrassing. But I had no choice. This was the only job I could find. I used to pull up to a street and before I could get out of the car to start ringing doorbells I'd bang my fist on the dashboard and tell myself that I could do it. 'Come on, Mike,' I'd say to myself. 'You're great! You can do this! You're a good man. You've got a family who's depending on you, so get out there and get to it.' I'd give myself that rah-rah pep talk and then I'd go after it. After a couple of months I got pretty good at it, too. I made a small salary, but then I got a big commission for every sale that resulted from one of my leads."

Once Mike moved beyond the fear of ringing doorbells, and once he realized how much money could be made by selling and installing awnings, he made a bold decision to open his own awning business. "I got pretty good at generating leads," he explains, "and I knew there wasn't much to the installation side of the business. So I teamed up with a father and son who were great salesmen, and we went into business together. We split the company one third each. But when I went home and told Marian what I had done, she said it was a bad decision. 'What if they decide to squeeze you out?' she asked. She told me I should have kept 51 percent of the business. I said it wouldn't be a problem, but sure enough, she was right. One day my partners came to me and said they wanted to buy me out. The business had $30,000 in cash at that time, so I got $10,000."

To anyone else, the buyout might have looked like a bad break. But not to Mike Ilitch. During the last couple of seasons that he played baseball, Mike frequently thought about the nightclub and his tiny pizza kitchen. He owned that business for just one winter, and sold it when he returned to Florida for spring training. Someday, he thought, he might own a pizza shop again. "When you're in the lower minor leagues like I was, you spend a lot of time riding buses," Mike explains. "You'd play a game in one city and about midnight you'd get on a bus and ride all night to the next city where you'd play a game that evening. Every place we stopped I looked for the pizza shops. There weren't many of them, but whenever I found one I'd sample their pizza and take a look at their business. Many times I'd say to myself, 'Man, if I could open a pizza shop here, I'd make it rich.' I loved the pizza business."

The day Mike took home $10,000, he recognized a new opportunity. He told Marian, "Let's open a pizza shop." She agreed.

The people of Detroit had no idea what Mike Ilitch was really doing when he knocked on their front doors and asked if he could interest them in buying an awning to spruce up their homes. Every time he had the opportunity to deliver his spiel, he did so in anticipation of gathering more research for his big goal in life. Of course, Mike didn't know what that big goal was at the time. He only knew that it was important to watch these good people and listen to them. He was fascinated to see how other people lived and what they valued. Fascinated to watch the interaction between husbands and wives, parents and children. Fascinated to experience American families in their own domiciles. He didn't know why he was fascinated, or what he would do with his research, but he mentally recorded every nuance.

"Ringing those doorbells taught me about America," Mike reveals. "Here I was, a young man with no education, no secure job, totally sheltered all my life by sports, no clue about the real world, and suddenly I got a clear picture of what life was all about. One home would be sparsely furnished except for a beautiful organ in the living room, and a daughter who represented her parents' greatest dreams. Everything about that family revolved around the daughter, in anticipation that someday she would make good. In the next house there would be a man puffing on a pipe, a slide rule sticking out of his shirt pocket. He wouldn't say much, just puffed on his pipe, but he was the boss of that home. His wife was fearful of him, and even though she spoke to me about the awning, any decision would be made only by her husband. The next house would be friendlier. The woman would walk me outside to show me her flower garden while her husband followed quietly behind. In that home, she was the boss. Every day I watched these people and I got a sense of values and priorities and relationships. I felt good about it, too. I felt comfortable. I had higher opinions of some households than others, but I said to myself, 'If this is what it's all about, I can do okay out here in the real world.'"

What Mike didn't know, however, and couldn't have known at the time, was that he could do okay by selling the people of Detroit his own brand of pizza. Except for teenagers, and families in blue-collar neighborhoods, the pizza market wasn't very big in the late 1950s. In fact, among those who had an opinion, pizza was considered a fad, and not a product with any long-term future.

Even so, Mike was determined to open a pizza shop. His research was about to begin paying off. By all accounts, he knew the suburb of Garden City was the ideal spot for a pizza shop. "When I walked the streets of that neighborhood," Mike explains, "I discovered it was a party area. On weekends, those folks bought their case of beer and they always had something going on. That's where I wanted to be." So when Mike found a shopping center that included a barbershop, a drugstore, and a supermarket, he decided to add a pizza shop.

One night Mike and Marian, who became his business partner, sat down to consider a name for their business. "We had a list of twenty-five ideas," Mike explains. "I wanted to call it Pizza Treat, but for some reason Marian wasn't happy with that. Finally she said, 'I've got it. We'll call it Little Caesars Pizza Treat!' I said, 'Little Caesars?' She said, 'Yeah, your mannerisms remind me of a Caesar. But you haven't accomplished much yet, so you're a little Caesar.' So we decided to call it Little Caesars Pizza."

Mike had a variety of ideas about how to run the business, but when he consulted an equipment salesman he got an earful of advice. Few of Mike's ideas made sense to the salesman. For example, Mike didn't order tables and chairs for the store because he planned a take-out-only business. No one had opened a take-out-only pizza shop before. This would be the first in the state of Michigan, and one of the first in the entire country, and the salesman thought it was a crazy idea.

"How are you going to make a business without tables and chairs?" the salesman wanted to know.

"I don't want tables and chairs," Mike responded. "When I had my pizza shop at the nightclub I didn't have tables and chairs. That meant no waitresses, and no cleaning up. I bake it and they carry it. I don't want employees."

When the salesman visited Mike's proposed location, he had another objection. "Don't go in that space," he told Mike.

"It's no good. There's a golf course across the street. There should be homes across the street. Without homes, you won't have customers."

But Mike knew the area better than the salesman. After all, he had walked these streets for the past two years and he knew practically every home. True, there were no homes across the street, but Mike said there were plenty of homes behind his location and on either side. A couple of years later, when he had proved that he was right about the location, and he began scouting additional locations, Mike would always ask the Realtors, "Is there a golf course nearby?" If so, he accepted it as a good omen.

Mike was twenty-nine years old as he prepared to open his pizza shop in Garden City, and there were signs that the brash young man of the past had begun to mature. Fatherhood had sobered him. "I was grateful to be able to get into my own business," he explains. "I already had several children—we would have seven in all—and I knew what it cost to buy dresses, shoes, and food and send the kids to school and to the doctor. It was expensive, and it was hard to imagine how working families could do it. So when I opened my business, I decided that I was going to give my customers a good deal. When we opened our store, I flooded the neighborhood with coupons for 50 cents off my pizza. Some of my competitors called me and complained. 'What are you doing? You're giving the food away.' But I felt sorry for people and I wanted the price to be right. I wanted to give the customers a good deal and leave a good margin for myself. If I did that, I knew I could get people excited about my product and then they'd keep coming back."

If 50 cents off wasn't enough of an incentive, every so often Mike introduced a promotion. "I gave away ridiculous stuff, and things that had nothing to do with pizza," he explains. "I gave away lunch pails, garden hoses, fishing poles. Being a family man, if a mom came in with her kids I gave them a balloon or a top, or something to get the kids to smile."

Considering his generosity, it's a bit surprising that Mike

would earn his investment back within six months of opening the pizza shop. Actually, Marian deserves credit for the financial success. The first day the store opened for business, she stopped Mike from giving away the food. "When our first customer came in," Mike recalls, "he ordered a chicken dinner. In addition to pizza, we also had chicken and fish. So I said to the guy that his dinner would normally cost $1.59, but since he was the first customer, I said, 'Here, it's on the house.' Well, a few minutes later the second customer walks in and he orders a fish dinner. I said, 'You're our first fish customer, so here, it's on the house.' The third customer orders a large cheese and pepperoni pizza and it's going to cost $2.39 with tax. Just as I was ready to give it to the guy and tell him it was on the house, Marian grabbed the pizza out of my hand, smiled at the customer and said, 'That will be $2.39.' She was afraid I was going to give away the store."

Within three years Mike had opened three stores and he was building revenue every year. Not that he was making a lot of money, or that the work was easy. Many people still doubted that pizza was a good business, or even good food. One day Mike made a pizza for his landlord and walked it over to his office.

"Mr. Bamberg, I've got a pizza for you," Mike announced.

The landlord turned up his nose. "I can't eat *that*," he told Mike. "I wouldn't be able to sleep for three days. That food would make me sick."

Oftentimes Mike heard from family and friends who had doubts about his business. Some would say, "Mike, do you think pizza is just a fad?"

"I don't know," Mike would respond. "They're comin' in good and buying good."

"Mike," others would say, "do you think pizza is just a snack food?"

"I don't think so," Mike would answer. "A guy called me the other night and said he wasn't going to hold me accountable, but his kids drank an extra carton of milk during dinner because our pizza sauce was a little spicy."

Except for these occasional distractions, Mike liked the fact that he owned a business. There was no doubt that he preferred the pizza business to knocking on doors. "I was naive," he says, "and I never thought about the possibility of a setback. I didn't worry about failing. I was young and full of fire and I moved fast. It was a blast."

And yet, he wasn't sure how long he could sustain the growth. How many more shops could he afford to open on his own? And how difficult would it be to operate those shops if he couldn't be there to oversee them? By this time, Marian wasn't working in the business anymore. She had quit so that she could stay home with the children. That left Mike to run the business on his own.

One day in 1962 Mike met a Texas oilman during a business trip. They sat next to each other on an airplane. After Mike introduced himself and stated that he was a "pizza man," he asked his traveling companion what he did for a living. "Son," said the Texan, "I'm a royalty man. I run oil wells and I take so much money off each well. You oughta think about that for your pizza business."

Mike did think about it, and even though he knew nothing about franchising a business, the opportunity made sense to him. He would happily teach someone how to replicate his business in exchange for a fee. So he went home and looked for a franchisee. It didn't take long to find one. As Mike recalls, "This Greek fellow came to see me. He and his family owned some Coney Islands, hot dog stands, and the son wants to open a Little Caesars. I get him all excited and then he tells me I have to sell his father. So I go to see his dad and I tell him what a good deal the pizza business is, and I tell him how well I'm doing, and how good his son will do, and I'll be there to help him. But I can tell I'm not convincing the father. He just looked at me and then he asked if we sold coffee. I said no. He shook his head. 'If no coffee you can't make a good business,' he said. But I kept selling him and eventually I succeeded. Even so, I had to loan the son $900 because he couldn't get all the money he needed from his dad. But that franchisee went on to open five Little Caesars and was making $100,000 a year in the 1960s. Franchising turned out to be a pretty good deal."

On into the 1970s Mike continued opening corporate stores as well as selling franchises, and he soon discovered that he preferred franchising. "Things were going well and I decided to open a store at Michigan State, about eighty miles from Detroit," he explains. "The college store went nuts with volume, it was really popular, and I was going up there every night to work the dinner shift. After a while I got tired of that and I started telling myself that I didn't need to drive eighty miles up and eighty miles back just for the dinner period. That should have been my first inclination that the business was going to start slipping. If I owned it and I didn't want to be there, that was a problem. I was used to driving from one suburb to another to work in a store, but that 160 miles was a drag. You'd think that would have taught me a lesson, but what did I do? I got on an airplane and flew out to California to open a shop in San Jose!"

Mike figured all the college towns were hot markets, and he wanted to seize that opportunity. "But I was stupid. It made no sense to open a store in California where I had no infrastructure for the business. Worse yet, I didn't do any research on the location. I thought every university market was the same, but I opened near a halfway house that dominated the neighborhood and I was doomed. We failed in California and that's when I learned my lesson. If the business was going to be a distance away, it was better to sell it to a franchisee. But even then, I never opened another store outside the state of Michigan until 1980."

As with any business, Mike ran into his share of challenges. His pizza network numbered close to eighty stores in the early 1970s, and just when it looked like he was on top of the business, the business suddenly sputtered. A sluggish economy made it difficult to borrow money, and he was having trouble juggling all his responsibilities. The growth caught up with him and started to overpower him. Once again, Marian, his relief pitcher, came to his rescue. All seven of the Ilitch children were in school by this time, so Marian returned to the business. While Mike had mastered marketing, product development, and recruiting franchisees, his weaknesses were finance and administration, two areas that Marian had mastered. "Once Marian came back to the business," Mike says, "we got on track again, and she's been working with me ever since." It's hard for him to imagine that he didn't even want to date Marian, let alone marry her.

The business got back on track for several years, but by 1977, it showed signs of financial trouble once again. "We were doing okay," says Mike. "We had 150 stores throughout the state, but our margins were getting too tight. We weren't making the money. Something was wrong, and I couldn't put my finger on it. I needed to make a change, but I didn't know what to do. So I got in my car and I started driving. When pressure builds up, I go for a drive. That's where I get a lot of my ideas. I'm not the type of guy who's going to sit down and stew and give up. That's the worst thing in the world. You sit down and start thinking about all your problems and that only makes it worse. I won't accept that. I'm going to consider my options, look at every opportunity, and come up with a solution."

Oddly enough, he found the solution on Telegraph Road, a commercial highway that divides Detroit from its suburbs. Mike knew that his stores needed to sell more pizza. But he didn't know how to make that happen. Then he saw a sign that promoted a two-for-one sale on paint. "As soon as I saw that sign," he says, "I started thinking about the offer. *Why not two? Why can't we sell our customers two pizzas instead of one?*"

The next day he met with a friend who was good at math and he asked him to calculate the margin on selling two pizzas for the price of one. If he were to do that, he wanted to know what size of a pizza he should sell, and at what price. "As it turned out," Mike continues, "I could give my customers a better value by selling them two small pizzas for the price of one large pizza. And when we figured the food costs, the paper goods, and the packaging, my margin on that sale was better, too! It was a tremendous value, and I decided to do it."

Of course, everyone told him he was insane. "No one will buy two pizzas," they said. "They just want one pizza."

"Yeah," Mike responded, "but when we started this business everyone said pizza was a trend. They said only kids eat pizza. But then we discovered people in their twenties and thirties ate pizza, too. And the day a forty-year-old came into the store we nearly threw a party we were so happy. And remember we thought only the blue-collar neighborhoods would buy pizza! But then we succeeded in a semi-affluent neighborhood, and now look at how well we're doing in the affluent neighborhoods. Don't tell me people won't buy two pizzas. Everyone loves pizza."

But no one believed Mike. So he tested the concept on his own. All through 1977 he sold two small pizzas for the price of one, and his customers eagerly responded. The next year, he expanded the offer to include medium and large pizzas, and by then, the now famous "Pizza! Pizza!" campaign was perfected. "It took me more than two years to convince people that this was a great opportunity," Mike says, "but once the stores took action, we had a huge marketing advantage."

Then, about the time Mike was back on top of the world, another kind of pressure started nagging at him. As Mike tells the story, "I had 200 stores in the network by 1980 and I'm living a great life. It's beautiful. I've got plenty of money. My kids can go to private schools if they want to. I have a nice home. I don't need a thing. I'm so happy. I came from nothing and ended up with all this. But then I got to thinking. *What if another pizza company comes in and knocks me off?* We're still just a regional chain. For a couple of months I thought about that. I looked for ideas, weighed the options, considered the pros and cons, and finally I decided to go national. That was the best way to protect what we had already built. We started advertising for franchisees from all across the country. A few years later we put the Pizza! Pizza! campaign on television, and that's when our chain went wild. We started building 400 to 500 stores a year!"

By this time, Mike and Marian began surrounding themselves with other talent. But Mike retained the one responsibility that he identified as the key to success in the Little Caesars Pizza chain: site selection. "After the mistake in California, I developed a great eye for locations," he explains, "and we didn't have any bad sites because I picked them all in those early years. When I went out to inspect a site, I'd get the Realtor and my guys around me and I'd put my foot down on the dirt and push some of it to the side. 'I want to make sure I see gold under here,' I'd tell them. Every location had to be a ten, or I wouldn't approve it. I'd drive up and down every street looking for the right spot. I didn't have any demographics to rely on. I looked at the neighborhoods. I wanted to see two cars in the driveway and bikes in the yard. I wanted to see houses that were maintained with nice-looking yards. If I could find 5,000 solid homes in a square mile, I called that a parachute. I wanted to land my store in the middle of those houses because if there were houses, there had to be sales."

Mike also befriended the franchisees, although he admits he couldn't always satisfy them. He loved helping people develop their businesses, but he also realized that business wasn't for everyone. If a married man wanted to buy a franchise, Mike insisted on going to dinner with him *and* his wife. Once again he fell back on the research he had gathered working door-to-door. "I knew all the combinations between husbands and wives," he explains. "I wanted to see if the marriage was solid, if the couple was a good team, and if they could work together. I wanted to know all about them, how they made decisions, and could they stand on their own feet and work long hours? Could they handle the physical and mental aspects of a business? I had a rule that if they weren't suited for business, they couldn't become franchisees."

As a result of Mike's and Marian's dedication, Little Caesars

Pizza flourished and that allowed them to broaden their business interests. Even though he hadn't played ball for many years, Mike never tired of the sport scene, professional and amateur. Little Caesars sponsored countless community ball teams. "One year," he recalls, "we made $100,000 in our business and Marian was upset with me because we should have made more. 'You gave it all away sponsoring sports teams,' she said. I couldn't help it. I'm a sports guy. My kids and my nephews were playing baseball and hockey, and it's good business to support those teams."

Sponsoring youth teams was a drop in the bucket, however, compared to what he was about to spend. In 1982, the Detroit Red Wings was a sorry hockey franchise. The locals had nicknamed the team the "Dead Wings." Mike was a fan, and when he heard the franchise was for sale, he acted quickly on the opportunity to buy it. "I got it cheap," he says. "The timing was just right, and it was a lucky situation." That may be one of the all-time greatest understatements in sports history. The Detroit Red Wings organization is now consistently rated one of the National Hockey League's most valuable franchises. The team won back-to-back Stanley Cups in the late 1990s. As long as Mike owns the team, no one will call them the "Dead Wings" again.

But the Red Wings wasn't the only sports franchise Mike wanted to buy. In fact, if he could own only one team, his choice would have been the Detroit Tigers. Ironically, the Tigers were owned by another Michigan-based pizza entrepreneur, Tom Monaghan, the controversial founder of Domino's. In 1992, when the Domino's chain fell on hard times, Monaghan decided to sacrifice the Tigers to save his business empire. Who stepped up to the plate to buy the franchise for $85 million? None other than the former minor leaguer Mike Ilitch. To this day Mike has to pinch himself to be sure he really owns the Tigers. "My whole life I dreamed about playing for the Tigers," he says, "and now I own them."

Then he also bought the Detroit Rockers, in the pro soccer league, and that rounded out his sports portfolio. However, there was more to Mike's entrepreneurial interests than sports and pizza. In 1987 he purchased Detroit's historic but neglected Fox Theatre and restored it to its original splendor. The 5,000-seat Fox has since become one of the top-grossing theaters in the country. In 1996 it ranked second only to Radio City Music Hall. The Ilitches also created Olympia Development to focus on projects in downtown Detroit. The company managed the $295 million Comerica Park, the new home of the Detroit Tigers, and a $15 million entertainment complex next to the Fox Theatre. In 1999, Mike and Marian formed Ilitch Ventures, Inc. to oversee their numerous investments. The company's consolidated revenues exceeded $800 million.

It's an amazing story for a guy who just wanted to play baseball. For years, Mike Ilitch had focused only on sports. There were no alternative plans in his life. And yet, when things didn't go his way, he was forced to look elsewhere to take advantage of the opportunities that others might easily have seen as obstacles. As a result, he has become one of the giants in American entrepreneurism.

"Marian and I woke up one morning," Mike explains, "and realized that our little business had outgrown us. It was too much for us to oversee. So we brought in experts to help us. Since then, I've realized that if you bring in the right people, bright people, business becomes so much easier." Not that he or Marian plan to retire, however. Along with three of their children, they remain active in the business. "I'm still looking for opportunities," Mike says. "If you hear of a good one, let me know."

CHAPTER NINETEEN

TAKE THE FIRST BOLD STEP

Armed with these Fifteen Key Lessons, you're ready to start small and finish big. The journey begins here!

Now that you've read the Fifteen Key Lessons and the stories of our microentrepreneurs, one point must be glowing obvious: *There is no master plan to success in business!* Getting started is what really counts. It's the step that separates the millions of people who dream about owning a business from those who actually start one. Far too many people wait too long to get going. They wait for the timing to be exactly right, the plan to be perfect, the vision flawless, and they wait to have more than enough money in place before they take any step at all, and as a result, many of them never get started.

Armed with these fifteen lessons, you're wiser than I was when I started Subway. I'm sure most if not all of the twenty-one other microentrepreneurs whose stories you've read in this book would say the same thing. But even wisdom doesn't matter nearly as much as getting started. When you take that first bold step, that's when your business, that journey of a thousand miles, really begins.

By following these lessons there's no guarantee that your business will succeed, or that it will become everything you'd want it to be. These lessons are simply guideposts to help you keep your priorities in check. Starting a business can be confusing, especially when it's your first one, but now you should have a little better idea of what to do.

On those days when nothing seems to work and you're thinking about quitting—and you can count on those days occurring—return to this book and reread the struggles and challenges faced by some of the microentrepreneurs you met here. If their stories aren't enough to inspire you, look around for other examples. There are scores of them.

Bill Gates dropped out of Harvard and started a small company that we know today as Microsoft. Gates has become the world's wealthiest person and he started as a microentrepreneur.

Wayne Huizenga, the founder of numerous enterprises, including Blockbuster Video, and the owner of the Miami Dolphins, borrowed $5,000 to start his business career in the sanitation industry.

With an eighth-grade education, Bill Rosenberg had less than $2,000 to start a chain of donut shops now known worldwide as Dunkin' Donuts.

Michael Dell began assembling computers in his dormitory room at the University of Texas and bootstrapped his way to the creation of Dell Computer, one of the largest and fastest growing companies of the last fifteen years.

Kemmons Wilson dropped out of high school, made a start in the vending machine industry with little money, and eventually founded Holiday Inns.

Looking for a way to pay for his college education, Tom Monaghan borrowed $500 and started making pizzas in Michigan. He called the business Domino's Pizza.

Frank Carney had about $600 when he started Pizza Hut.

John Schnatter, the latecomer in the pizza industry, and the youngest of the pizza microentrepreneurs, launched Papa John's in a broom closet with $1,600!

Jim McCann, a former social worker, borrowed $10,000 to buy a flower shop in New York. He built a chain of fourteen shops before he acquired 1-800-FLOWERS to distribute his products worldwide.

Leslie Wexner borrowed $5,000 from an aunt to get a start in the retail clothing business. Today he's the chairman of The Limited, Inc., which owns several of the world's top fashion retail chains such as The Gap and Banana Republic.

As a young woman, newly married, Lillian Vernon spent $2,000 of her wedding gift money to promote monogrammed handbags and belts in *Seventeen* magazine. Today, her mail order catalogue company, Lillian Vernon Corporation, tops annual sales of $240 million.

A young Texan in San Antonio, Elmer Doolin, borrowed $100 to create a corn chip and launched an entirely new industry dominated by the Frito Company, which he founded.

At about the same time, Henry Lay borrowed $100 in Nashville, Tennessee, to start a delivery service for a potato chip company based in Atlanta, Georgia. When the potato chip supplier ran into problems, Lay purchased the company. Eventually, Doolin and Lay teamed up to create Frito-Lay, Inc.

J. W. Marriott spent $5,000 to open a curbside restaurant in Washington, D.C. That was the beginning of Marriott International, a $12 billion company.

J. C. Penney lived with his young wife and their baby in an attic above their dry goods store in Wyoming. He started with $500 and today there are more than 1,300 Penney's stores in the U.S.

With a $1,000 loan from his wife, Ross Perot started a one-man data processing company that he called Electronic Data Systems. Perot eventually sold EDS, now a multibillion-dollar corporation employing 70,000 people.

Rich DeVos and his high school buddy Jay Van Andel launched several small businesses before they invested $49 in a sales kit for a vitamin supplement. That investment led to the creation of Amway.

When Mary Kay Ash attended a direct sales convention at a hotel in Dallas, Texas, she couldn't afford to buy food, so she brought along her own cheese and crackers. In 1963, she invested her life savings, $5,000, in a little company that she called Mary Kay Cosmetics. The company now has more than 500,000 independent sales representatives in twenty-nine markets worldwide.

Don Dwyer was a college student in search of tuition money when he borrowed $2,000 from his future father-in-law to purchase a newspaper route in Brooklyn, New York. He was soon earning $1,000 a week delivering the *New York Daily News*! He later sold his route and purchased a Success Motivation Institute franchise. Ultimately, he started a franchise company and built a conglomerate of home service businesses under the name The Dwyer Group, now a publicly traded company.

None of these microentrepreneurs had master plans when they started their businesses. They simply got started, they persevered, and they built their master plans step by step as they built upon the success of their enterprises.

If you aspire to become a microentrepreneur you may still need encouragement or resources to take that first bold step. I want to assure you that in most every community there are people to help. The U.S. Small Business Administration (the SBA) does a terrific job helping small businesses get started, and they provide guidance, as well as experienced mentors. They also guarantee loans. Their free mentor program is called SCORE. That stands for the Service Corps of Retired Executives. Many communities also have Small Business Development Centers (SBDCs) that are usually associated with colleges and universities. You'll also find chambers of commerce, local business networking groups, and private business coaches and mentors working in almost every community. Search for these resources on the World Wide Web, or look for them in your local Yellow Pages.

There's yet another resource. Today there are about 100 microenterprise lending organizations in the United States that provide small loans to people in need. These neighborhood microenterprise lending groups are just starting to appear in the U.S. and I expect hundreds more of them to pop up across the country in the next several years. Perhaps one of these programs will help you or one of your neighbors. There's a partial list of these organizations in the Appendix of this book.

Or possibly, if a microenterprise lender doesn't exist in your community, you will be instrumental in helping to establish one of these programs. You will find details in Appendix I.

As I explained in the first chapter of this book, my interest in microenterprise lending began in the late 1980s when *60 Minutes* delivered a story about Professor Muhammad Yunus and his accomplishments in Bangladesh. In the years that followed, I reached out to learn more about the movement and the people involved in it.

As you can imagine, I immediately felt an affinity to microenterprise lending because of my humble start with a $1,000 loan. From there I was able to build a good business for my family, and then I was able to franchise the business and help others get started, too.

That's why I started a local microenterprise program and why I now see a chance to use the franchise model that I understand so well to help others bring microenterprise lending to their communities.

I like the experience of helping people to help themselves. It's gratifying to watch a new microentrepreneur take his or her first small steps and to be able to contribute in some small way to their earliest attempts at business.

My early interest in the microenterprise movement led me to a remarkable woman who established America's first successful microenterprise lending program modeled after the Grameen Bank. Connie Evans is the executive director of the Women's Self-Employment Project (WSEP) in Chicago, Illinois. By the time I met Connie, she had already helped establish 400 new businesses that created jobs, improved self-esteem, and reduced poverty among poor women.

I first visited WSEP in 1992 to learn more about the organization and microenterprise in general. During that visit I was able to meet on site with several small businesswomen that were being helped by WSEP, and I was able to attend a center meeting with about forty enthusiastic new business-women.

The next year, my wife and I visited WSEP's offices to spend a few more days learning about their operation and providing some organizational advice and ideas to Connie and her employees. For example, WSEP was struggling with communications so I gave them some simple pointers to help launch and easily maintain a weekly newsletter. On a much larger scale, I developed a broad plan for WSEP to expand its services nationally.

WSEP had a professional office and a talented staff focusing on microlending in Chicago. Their offices reminded me of Subway's headquarters and I thought they had the administrative capabilities to help people in other communities offer microenterprise services locally. As I considered this further I envisioned a central office that could support over 1,000 neighborhood chapters run by local volunteers. Overhead at the chapter level would be minimal and all local resources could be devoted to helping those in need.

This was akin to franchising except for the volunteerism at the local level. I've since come up with the term "public service franchising" to describe this approach. It's a nonprofit model for franchising. The American culture includes many fine examples of volunteer organizations such as the Jaycees, Kiwanis, Rotarians, the Knights of Columbus, and many others. Why not rely on volunteers to bring microenterprise lending to those in need of assistance?

After suggesting my ideas to Connie I then underwrote a comprehensive research study so that WSEP's board of directors could explore the feasibility of adapting the franchise model as a method for expansion for WSEP's program.

Connie had already created the operating system for a thriving organization. If she and her staff could show other people how to use WSEP's system and expertise throughout North America, that would be the fastest way to bring microenterprise lending to the people. Local chapters would cover their own costs while gaining access to an established microenterprise program.

From my vantage point, franchising and volunteerism was the way to go. WSEP's directors, however, voted against the idea. The staff was already busy enough meeting the needs of the Chicago market, and there was still plenty to do. If they branched out it might have been overwhelming, and the burden may have limited WSEP's already potent effort in Chicago. I accepted the board's decision, but I remained convinced that franchising was the way to expand the microenterprise movement. If the opportunity arose to implement my idea, I would pursue it.

That opportunity appeared a couple of years later. Occasionally, I join many of the Subway staff at a local bar for Friday Happy Hour and during one such occasion I met a young woman who worked for the Federal Housing Authority. When I told her that I had once lived in public housing she immediately said, "You should do something to help support public housing," almost making me feel guilty that I hadn't already done so. She then handed me a business card and told me to call Karen DeVito, coordinator of the Milford Housing Authority Section 8 Program. I buried the card in my pocket, as I had done so many times after meeting someone who thought that I ought to get involved in this or that. However, for some unknown reason this time was different.

A few days later, I found myself sitting in Karen DeVito's office. I told her I didn't really know why I was there, or what I could do to help. But I felt compelled to contact her because I wanted to give something back to my community and to society in return for the benefits that I've enjoyed as a business owner. As Karen told me about her responsibilities, I found it most interesting when she said a large part of her job was to help people become self-sufficient. That's when it occurred to me that she might be interested in microenterprise, even though it had nothing to do with public housing.

After telling her about the Grameen Bank and WSEP, I suggested that with her help, and seed money from me, we could establish a national program to assist microentrepreneurs. Initially, of course, we would start a pilot program in Milford.

Karen immediately accepted my offer and in 1996, after several months of collaboration, we established the nonprofit Micro Investment Lending Enterprise, Inc. (MILE), modeled after the Grameen Bank but specifically designed to expand via public service franchising. We also announced the formation of MILE's first local chapter in Milford, and we invited a few members of the public housing community to join us if they were interested in starting a small business with our assistance.

I pledged a no-interest loan of up to $100,000 to fund the initial microloans that would be granted to the borrowers who joined our chapters and also agreed to pay the expenses of MILE's national office for at least the first three years. The purpose of the national office, which was based at Subway's headquarters in Connecticut, is to help individuals and groups from around North America start local chapters in their own neighborhoods, to share our system and expertise, and to be the collective clearinghouse for new learning from our chapters.

By the fall of 1996, the Milford chapter of MILE was in operation. Several local businesspeople volunteered to serve as mentors and I participated in some of the meetings. Starting MILE has been a little like starting Subway. With each passing month we learn more and make improvements to the system, but we're still in our early development stages.

As people join a local chapter they're introduced to the organization's rules. For example, five nonrelated persons make up a "Borrowing Circle" and a chapter is designed to support eight circles. People join the chapter, get to know each other, and when five people feel comfortable with each other they form a circle to provide peer support.

During a circle meeting, members discuss their business ideas and ultimately each member presents a brief business plan and requests a loan. Circle members critique, help improve, and actually approve loan requests before passing them on to the chapter chairperson for a final decision.

No collateral or guarantee is required for any loan, since all lending decisions are based solely on the character and honor of the circle member and the feasibility of the business plan. Loans may be as little as $100 or as much as $1,500 and are repaid in fifty-five weekly installments at 2 percent of the loan value each week. The chapter uses the interest earned to cover its operating expenses, which are minimal due to volunteerism. In addition, borrowers pay 5 percent of each loan into the circle's emergency fund, which is the property of the circle and may be used to make emergency loan payments at the members' discretion.

A borrower may apply for additional loans prior to the current loan being paid in full, but all loan payments due from a circle must be current before additional loans are granted to any circle member.

These chapter rules are similar to those established and proven effective by the Grameen Bank and adapted in Chicago by WSEP.

Members of MILE's first circle also created the Ten Disciplines patterned after the Sixteen Decisions of the Grameen Bank. As Alex Counts explains in *Give Us Credit*, his informative and entertaining book about Professor Yunus and the Grameen Bank, the Sixteen Decisions provide a social constitution for the bank's members. As Counts explains, "It was the bank's attempt to respond to the social dimensions of poverty, a series of rules to ease the workings of the bank and help borrowers help themselves out of poverty." The decisions included limiting the size of the family, educating children, not accepting or giving dowry, planting vegetable gardens and fruit-bearing trees, and building sanitary pit latrines. Many of the bank's Decisions were not relevant in the United States, so our members created the Ten Disciplines, consisting of the following rules.

1. We are honest, trustworthy, hardworking, and conduct ourselves as professionals.
2. We build our businesses and treasure our customers.
3. We seek greater challenges for ourselves and our businesses each day.
4. We are positive role models for our family and friends.
5. We support our chapter members and are open to support and guidance from them.
6. We openly rejoice in the successes of others.
7. We value education and will educate ourselves and our children.
8. We live in housing which provides our families with security and a clean environment.
9. We eat nutritious food, balanced meals, and provide a healthy lifestyle for our families.
10. We balance our lives with work, education, thought, and play.

Soon after we established the MILE chapter in Milford, one of our board members, Mary Anne Beecher, who had a job similar to Karen's, decided she wanted to open a second chapter sixty miles away in Torrington, Connecticut. I agreed to provide the lending capital for that chapter, too. Since then we've established a third chapter in Hamden, Connecticut. So far our expansion has been slow, but we're making steady progress.

As is usually the case when you start a new venture, things take longer than expected, so I started thinking of ways to speed up MILE's development. First, I decided to write this book with John Hayes. He helped convince me that my Fifteen Key Lessons would be of interest to readers, and to the media, and he enthusiastically brought together the people and the stories to create this book.

Secondly, I decided to form a strategic alliance with the Grameen Foundation USA, the recognized brand name in microenterprise. After teaching himself Bengali, Fulbright scholar Alex Counts spent several years working in Bangladesh with Professor Yunus. By 1998 he was well grounded in Grameen's policies and procedures, and Yunus asked him to return to America to start and oversee the Grameen Foundation USA with the mission to advance the microenterprise movement in the United States and Latin America. In addition to raising money and building public awareness for microenterprise, the foundation establishes educational and technical assistance programs to provide training and support for microenterprise organizations. It also facilitates joint ventures between microenterprise programs and the private sector. Essentially, the goals of the Grameen Foundation USA and MILE are very similar.

We don't care who has the most chapters or the biggest chapters, but we do care about the goal of 1,000 chapters of all types in operation by 2005.

Our objective is to promote microcredit lending so that more people, especially impoverished and low-income people, can start their own businesses and be more successful. To me, this is an exciting and worthwhile cause. It's a way to give people a chance to improve their lives, build their self-esteem, and fulfill their dreams. Part of my plan for writing this book is to attract readers who want to join a microenterprise chapter to borrow money and build a business.

Also, I'm hoping to hear from people throughout North America who think a neighborhood microenterprise chapter is needed in their area. We'd love to work with individuals, civic organizations, banks, businesses, churches, or government agencies and we'll be happy to help in any way possible. If you see a need in your area just give us a call. Also, you'll find additional information about how to get involved in Appendix I of this book.

Whether you get involved in the microenterprise movement or not, if you want to own a business I wish you well. Perhaps you'll take that first bold step and get started soon. If you do, please allow the Fifteen Key Lessons to help guide you, but rely on yourself, your hard work, and the great people around you to get the job done.

Go forth, start small, and finish BIG.

In closing, I want to thank you for taking this journey with me. I appreciate the time you invested in reading this book, in studying the Fifteen Key Lessons, and particularly the time you invested in learning about microenterprise. I hope to hear from you, and to work with many of you as we spread the good cause of microenterprise.

APPENDIX I

———

Information About Starting
a Local MILE Chapter
Micro Investment Lending Enterprise
Attn: MILE Administrator
C/O Subway World Headquarters
325 Bic Drive, Milford, CT 06460
Telephone 800-888-4848 extension 1636
Web site: http://www.mileloans.org
E-mail: mile@mileloans.org

The following information will be useful to anyone interested in participating in the Micro Investment Lending Enterprise. Starting a local MILE chapter, or contributing time as a
mentor, can be a richly rewarding and emotionally gratifying
experience. If you want to begin a local MILE chapter, the following information will be helpful.

CHAPTER ORGANIZATION

MILE's national headquarters provides guidance to local chapters and serves as an information clearinghouse. MILE chapters can be established by any interested person, civic

organization, business, or government agency. The purpose of a chapter is to lend money to people who do not have access to credit so that they may start their own small businesses. MILE provides educational information about microlending and assists chapter leaders in every facet of chapter development and operations. All chapters fall under the organizational umbrella of MILE headquarters.

TRAINING

MILE's staff will provide two days of training to chapter organizers. Training will occur the second weekend of every month in Milford. Attendees are responsible for their own travel and lodging expenses. The details of how to establish and operate a MILE chapter are taught during this initial training. Additional training is provided through newsletters, manuals, and the Internet.

LOAN CAPITAL

MILE national headquarters will train you to pursue local sources of funding to grant loans to borrowers and to pay expenses. If necessary to help a chapter get started, MILE may loan the chapter a small amount of money. However, every community includes businesses and entrepreneurs that will be willing to provide a loan to the chapter. Or, they'll agree to guarantee a bank loan. In-kind donations (such as meeting space, printing donations, computer support) will also contribute to the chapter. MILE will provide additional information to help local organizers spread the word about their chapters.

LOCAL BANKING ASSISTANCE

Traditional banks rarely grant microloans because the process is time-consuming and expensive. It takes as much time to process a large loan as it does a small loan, and the smaller the loan, the smaller the profit to the bank. In addition, traditional banks often believe there's more risk in granting loans to tiny businesses or start-up entrepreneurs. The banks fear not being able to collect their money. All of that is understandable. However, there are local banks that will be willing to provide assistance to a MILE chapter, either by mentoring the lenders, or by providing free banking services, or both.

RECRUITING MENTORS

Community mentors are a key resource to running a successful MILE chapter. Mentors work with the borrowers by offering their expertise and moral support and they assist the chapter leadership. Mentors volunteer their time and do not pay any dues. Businesspeople frequently love to mentor others who are starting businesses, so the recruitment effort should not be very challenging. You can attract mentors by networking with bankers, accountants, lawyers, and other business leaders, including members of the Chamber of Commerce, as well as local colleges and universities.

RECRUITING BORROWERS

After establishing a chapter and lining up funding and mentors, it will be time to recruit borrowers. Government agencies, civic groups, and religious organizations will be instrumental in helping the chapter recruit borrowers. Again, MILE will provide information about how to recruit borrowers.

The borrowers will participate in Borrowing Circles of five members each. Borrowers attend circle meetings and support other members. A borrower will be required to submit a business plan (not to exceed four pages) to apply for a loan. All loans are approved by the borrower's circle and the chapter. Approval is based solely on the character and honor of the borrower, and the borrower's overall business plan. Borrowers do not pay fees to join the chapter, but they are required to pay off their loans with interest in fifty-five weekly installments. Borrowers may apply for additional loans before their existing loans are repaid.

CHAPTER MEETINGS

Meetings are conducted at least monthly for approximately two hours for borrowers and mentors. The first half hour of the meeting is devoted to chapter business. Then the circles meet. During this time the circle members receive support from each other as well as from mentors. Loan applications are also discussed during the circle meetings.

COMMUNICATIONS

All chapters, as well as MILE's national headquarters, will communicate via e-mail and the World Wide Web. MILE will publish a newsletter to share information among the chapters.

PUBLICITY

As a nonprofit, community service franchise, a MILE chapter serves a valuable purpose in any community. Consequently, it's not difficult to generate media publicity about the chapter's purpose and mission. MILE's national headquarters will be instrumental in teaching chapter leaders how to pursue local publicity and benefit from it.

Sponsoring a chapter, or volunteering to help a chapter, requires mostly time. It's a meaningful way to contribute to the community. Anyone interested can contact MILE's national headquarters or visit www.mileloans.org and request information and an application for a chapter charter.

Appendix II

Microcredit Lending Programs
in the United States

Anyone interested in contacting a microenterprise organization, or volunteering time to help a microenterprise organization, can call the Grameen Foundation at 202-628-3560, or send an e-mail to: info@grameenfoundation.org. Or contact the Micro Investment Lending Enterprise (MILE) at 800-888-4848, extension 1636.

According to the Aspen Institute, the premier research organization for microcredit in the U.S., there are several hundred microenterprise development agencies in the country, but only about 100 of them offer loans. Some are engaged only in training and education. Following is a partial list of microcredit lenders in the United States. This list is expected to expand dramatically in the next several years. Keep in mind that many of these associations, such as ACCION International, support microlending programs in other countries. For additional listings, contact the Aspen Institute at 202-736-5800.

ARIZONA
P.P.E.P. Microbusiness and Housing Development Corp.
   (MICRO)
802 East 46th Street
Tucson 85713
Phone: 520-622-3553 Fax: 520-622-1480

Self-Employment Loan Fund, Inc.
201 North Central Avenue, Suite CC10
Phoenix 85073-1000
Phone: 602-340-8834 Fax: 602-340-8952
E-mail: self-employment@juno.com

ARKANSAS
Arkansas Enterprise Group: Good Faith Fund
2304 West 29th Street
Pine Bluff 71603
Phone: 870-535-6233 Fax: 870-535-0741

CALIFORNIA
ACCION San Diego
1250 6th Avenue 1000
World Trade Center San Diego
San Diego 92101
Phone: 619-685-1380 Fax: 619-685-1391
E-mail: 76463.2222@compuserve.com

Arcata Economic Development Corp.
100 Ericson Court, Suite 100
Arcata 95521
Phone: 707-822-4616 Fax: 707-822-8982

Economic and Employment Development Center
241 South Figueroa Street, Suite 240
Los Angeles 90012
Phone: 213-617-3953 Fax: 213-617-3341

Pomona Inland Valley Microenterprise Loan Fund
363 South Park Avenue, Suite 104
Pomona 91769
Phone: 909-868-7303 Fax: 906-622-4217

West Company
306 East Redwood Ave., Suite 12
Fort Bragg 95439
Phone: 707-468-3553 Fax: 707-468-3555

Women's Initiative for Self-Employment
450 Mission Street, Suite 402
San Francisco 94105
Phone: 415-247-9473 Fax: 415-247-9471
E-mail: wilsf@igc.org

CONNECTICUT
Micro Investment Lending Enterprise (MILE)
c/o 325 Bic Drive
Milford 06460
Phone: 203-877-4281, extension 1636 Fax: 203-876-6674
Web site: www.mileloans.org
E-mail: mile@mileloans.org

Micro Investment Lending Enterprise of Hamden
c/o Grove & Associates
2839 Old Dixwell Avenue
Hamden 06518
Phone: 203-248-7562 Fax: 203-248-8706
E-mail: jcwiertniewicz@snet.net

Micro Investment Lending Enterprise of Torrington
c/o 325 Bic Drive
Milford 06460
Phone: 203-877-4281, extension 1636 Fax: 203-876-6674
E-mail: mile@mileloans.org

DISTRICT OF COLUMBIA
FINCA USA, Inc.
1101 14th Street NW, 11th Floor
Washington 20005
Phone: 202-682-1510 Fax: 202-682-1535

Grameen Foundation USA
1709 New York Avenue NW, Suite 101
Washington 20006
E-mail: info@grameenfoundation.org

DELAWARE
First State Community Loan Fund
100 West 10th Street, Suite 1005
Wilmington 19801
Phone: 302-652-6774 Fax: 302-656-1272

Working Capital
233 King Street
Wilmington 19801
Phone: 302-658-7161 Fax: 302-658-7457

FLORIDA
Tools for Change
6015 Northwest 7th Avenue
Miami 33127
Phone: 305-751-8934 Fax: 305-751-1619
E-mail: tfc@tfc.org

Working Capital Florida
3000 Biscayne Boulevard, Suite 101A
Miami 33137
Phone: 305-438-1407 Fax: 305-438-1411

GEORGIA
Quality Care for Children
1447 Peachtree Street, Northeast, Suite 700
Atlanta 30309
Phone: 404-479-4200 Fax: 404-874-7427
E-mail: info@qualitycareforchildren.org

Micro Enterprise for Greater Atlanta
250 Auburn Avenue
Atlanta 30303
Phone: 404-688-6884 Fax: 404-688-4009

HAWAII
Immigrant Center & Pacific Gateway Center
720 North King Street
Honolulu 96817
Phone: 808-845-3918 Fax: 808-842-1962

ILLINOIS
ACCION Chicago
3245 West 26th Street, 2nd Floor
Chicago 60623
Phone: 773-376-9004 Fax: 773-376-9048
E-mail: lpacheco@accionchicago.org

Women's Self-Employment Project
20 North Clark, 4th Floor
Chicago 60602
Phone: 312-606-8255 Fax: 312-606-9215
E-mail: loan-dir@wsep.com

IOWA
Institute for Social and Economic Development
1901 Broadway, Suite 313
Iowa City 52240
Phone: 319-338-2331 Fax: 319-338-5824
E-mail: jfriedman@ised.org

KENTUCKY
Community Ventures Corporation
1450 North Broadway
Lexington 40505
Phone: 606-231-0054 Fax: 606-231-0261

LOUISIANA
Catholic Social Services
1220 Aycock Street
Houma 70360
Phone: 504-876-0490 Fax: 504-876-7751
E-mail: casaucier@aol.com

Louisville Central Development Corporation/Business Plus
1015 West Chestnut Street
Louisville 40203-2048
Phone: 502-589-1173 Fax: 502-583-8824

MAINE
Women's Business Development Corporation
P.O. Box 658
Bangor 04402
Phone: 207-947-5990 Fax: 207-947-5278

MARYLAND
Women Entrepreneurs of Baltimore, Inc. (WEB)
1118 Light Street, Suite 202
Baltimore 21230
Phone: 410-727-4921 Fax: 410-727-4989

MASSACHUSETTS
Greater Holyoke, Inc.
57 Suffolk Street, Suite 101
Holyoke 01040
Phone: 413-536-4611 Fax: 413-538-9716

Valley Community Development Corporation
16 Armory Street
Northampton 01060
Phone: 413-586-5855 Fax: 413-586-7521

Working Capital
99 Bishop Allen Drive
Cambridge 02139
Phone: 617-576-8620 Fax: 617-576-8623

MICHIGAN
Detroit Economic Entrepreneurship Institute
455 West Fort, 4th Floor
Detroit 48226
Phone: 313-961-8426 Fax: 313-961-8831

Northwest Michigan Council of Government
P.O. Box 506
Traverse City 49685
Phone: 231-929-5028 (800-692-7774 inside Michigan)
   Fax: 231-929-5012
E-mail: mmay@nwm.cog.mi.us

MINNESOTA
FINCA Minnesota
1885 University Avenue, Suite 190
St. Paul 55104
Phone: 888-287-1032 Fax: 612-645-1327
E-mail: 102336.3176@compuserve.com

Neighborhood Development Center, Inc.
651½ University Avenue
St. Paul 55014
Phone: 651-291-2480 Fax: 651-291-2597
E-mail: windndc@mtn.org

Northeast Entrepreneur Fund, Inc.
Olcott Plaza 820 Ninth Street North, Suite 200
Virginia 55792
Phone: 218-749-4191 Fax: 218-749-5213
E-mail: info@entrepreneurmn.org

Northwest Minnesota Initiative Fund
4225 Technology Drive
Bermidji 56601
Phone: 218-759-2057 Fax: 218-759-2328
E-mail: nwmf@nwmf.org

Women Venture
2324 University Street
St. Paul 55114
Phone: 651-646-3808 Fax: 651-641-7223

MISSOURI
St. Louis Reinvestment Corp.
P.O. Box 4558
5000 Washington Place
St. Louis 63108
Phone: 314-367-3075 Fax: 314-367-2494

NEBRASKA
Catholic Charities Juan Diego Center
5211 South 31st Street
Omaha 68107
Phone: 402-731-5413 Fax: 402-731-5865

Center for Rural Affairs (REAP)
P.O. Box 406
Walthill 68067
Phone: 402-846-5428 Fax: 402-846-5420

City of Lincoln Economic Development
P.O. Box 82043
Lincoln 68501
Phone: 402-441-8218 Fax: 402-441-7734
E-mail: rickwallace@juno.com

Northeast Nebraska Economic Development District
111 South 1st Street
Norfolk 68701
Phone: 402-379-1150 Fax: 402-379-9207
E-mail: rrobschr@ncfcomm.com

NEVADA
Nevada Self-Employment Trust
560 Mill Street, Suite 260
Reno 89502
Phone: 702-329-6789 or 800-337-4590 Fax: 702-329-6738
E-mail: nemploy198@aol.com

NEW HAMPSHIRE
New Hampshire Community Loan Fund
7 Wall Street
Concord 03302-0800
Phone: 603-223-0634 Fax: 603-225-7425

NEW JERSEY
Camden Community Credit Union
423 Market Street
Camden 08102
Phone: 609-964-2228 Fax: 609-963-1835

New Jersey Community Loan Fund
16-18 West Lafayette Street
Trenton 08608
Phone: 609-989-7766 Fax: 609-393-9401

Trenton Business Assistance Corporation
P.O. Box 245
Trenton 08608
Phone: 609-989-3600 Fax: 609-989-4243

NEW MEXICO
ACCION New Mexico
219 Central Avenue, NW, Suite 620
Albuquerque 87102
Phone: 505-243-8844 Fax: 505-243-1551
Web site. http://www.accion.org
E-mail: 7643.2305@compuserve.com

Women's Economic Self-Sufficiency Team
414 Silver, SW
Albuquerque 87102
Phone: 505-241-4758 Fax: 505-241-4766

NEW YORK
ACCION New York
235 Havemeyer Street, 3rd Floor
Brooklyn 11211
Phone: 718-599-5170 Fax: 718-387-9686
Web site: http://www.accion.org
E-mail: loans@accion/newyork.org

Church Avenue Merchants Block Association
885 Flatbush Avenue
Brooklyn 11226
Phone: 718-287-0010 Fax: 718-287-7119

Project Enterprise
2303 7th Avenue
New York 10030
Phone: 212-690-2024 Fax: 212-690-2028
E-mail: pe@projectenterprise.org

Rural Opportunities, Inc.
339 East Avenue
Rochester 14604
Phone: 716-546-6325 Fax: 716-546-7337
E-mail: jdallisl@aol.com

The Target Exchange, Inc.
203 Champlain Drive
Plattsburgh 12901
Phone: 518-563-0701 Fax: 518-563-0701

Trickle Up Program
121 West 27th Street, Suite 504
New York 10001
Phone: 212-362-7958 Fax: 212-877-7464
Web site: http://www.vita.org/trickle
E-mail: 73444.557@compuserve.com

NORTH CAROLINA
Eastern Carolina Microenterprise Fund
400 Front Street, Suite 15
Beauford 28516
Phone: 919-504-2424 Fax: 919-504-2248

Good Work, Inc.
115 Market Street, Suite 470
Durham 27701
Phone: 919-682-8473 Fax: 919-687-7033
E-mail: gwinfo@goodwork.org

Mountain Microenterprise Fund
29 Page Avenue
Asheville 28801
Phone: 704-253-2834 Fax: 704-255-7953
E-mail: mmf@circle.net

North Carolina Rural Economic Development Center, Inc.
  (REDC)
4021 Carya Drive
Raleigh 27610
Phone: 919-250-4314 Fax: 919-250-4325
E-mail: ckperry@ncruralcenter.org

Self-Help
301 West Main Street
Durham 27701
Phone: 919-956-4400 Fax: 919-956-4600
Web site: www.selfhelp.org
E-mail: lyle@selfhelp.org

PENNSYLVANIA
Kutztown University Entrepreneurial Development and
  Global Education Center (EDGE)
P.O. Box 253
Reading 19603
Phone: 610-375-4220 Fax: 610-375-4229
Web site: http://www.kutztown.edu.acad/cab/edge
E-mail: mahon@kutztown.edu

Philadelphia Development Partnership
1334 Walnut Street, 7th Floor
Philadelphia 19107
Phone: 215-545-3100 Fax: 215-546-8055
E-mail: JWHITE5117@aol.com

Rural Enterprise Development Corporation
238 Market Street
Bloomsburg 17815
Phone: 570-784-7003 Fax: 570-389-4221
E-mail: lind@bloomu.edu

RHODE ISLAND
Greater Elmwood Neighborhood Services
839 Broad Street
Providence 02907
Phone: 401-461-4111 Fax: 401-461-2210

SOUTH DAKOTA
The Lakota Fund
P.O. Box 340
Kyle 57752
Phone: 605-455-2500 Fax: 605-455-2585

TEXAS
ACCION El Paso
7744 North Loop Road
El Paso 79915
Phone: 915-779-3727 Fax: 915-779-3966

ACCION Texas
109 North San Saba
San Antonio 78207
Phone: 210-226-3664 Fax: 210-226-2258
Web site: http://www.accion.org
E-mail: 75607.2152@compuserve.com

FEFA (Federación Ecuménica de Fey ACCION)
211 North Park Boulevard
San Antonio 78204
Phone: 210-222-1955
E-mail: fefa@connecti.com

The PLAN Fund of Dallas City Homes
729 North Bishop Avenue
Dallas 75208
Phone: 214-943-9007, extension 12 Fax: 214-948-4830

VIRGINIA
Ethiopian Community Development Council
1038 South Highland Street
Arlington 22204
Phone: 703-685-0510 Fax: 703-685-0529

Virginia Eastern Shore Economic Empowerment and
    Housing Corporation
P.O. Box 814
Nassawadox 23413
Phone: 757-442-4509 Fax: 757-442-7530
E-mail: ee@esva.net

WASHINGTON
Washington Community Alliance for Self-Help (CASH)
7755 45th Avenue, NE
Seattle 98115
Phone: 206-729-8589 Fax: 206-729-8589
E-mail: washcash@nwlink.com

ACKNOWLEDGMENTS

———

This book would not have been possible without the support of my parents, who encouraged me in my first microbusinesses: collecting deposit bottles and delivering newspapers, and without the encouragement of Pete Buck, my business partner. I also appreciate the support of my wife, Liz. We've been together since even before Subway, and in her own right she's become an important part of the Subway family.

I also want to thank the folks at *60 Minutes* for broadcasting their story about Dr. Muhammad Yunus, who founded the Grameen Bank; and the *Wall Street Journal* for early reporting about the microcredit movement in the United States. My primary motivation for authoring this book is to help promote the microcredit movement wherever possible, and all money that I earn from this book will be contributed to the Micro Investment Lending Enterprise (MILE), a nonprofit organization.

I want to thank Connie Evans, who so graciously took much of her time to show me how the Women's Self-Employment Project (WSEP), a microcredit organization, worked in Chicago; Alex Counts, who became my link with the Grameen Bank; and Karen De-Vito, who worked unselfishly to start the first chapter of MILE and who serves on its board of directors. I also want to thank other members of MILE's board of directors: Mary Anne Beecher of the Torrington Housing Authority; Barbara Bourdeau of RM Bourdeau Financial Services; Steve Grove of Grove & Associates; Gary Johnson of the United Way of Milford; Paula Murphy of Mary Kay Cosmetics; Patricia J. Rooney, R.S.M. of Yale Divinity School; Richard Roy of The Write Choice, and a state representative from Milford; and Michele Klotzer, Subway's Director of Public and Community Relations.

Acknowledgments

I also want to acknowledge the International Franchise Association based in Washington, D.C., and its many members, some of whom through the years have taught me about franchising and frequently lended a helping hand to our endeavor.

Of course, I particularly want to send a huge thank-you to all of Subway's franchisees, Development Agents, and corporate employees. Without them, and their belief in Subway, this book would not have been possible.

In addition to thanking each of the twenty-one microentrepreneurs who contributed time to be interviewed for this book, John Hayes and I want to thank several people who introduced him to microentrepreneurs and in several instances arranged interviews. We appreciate the help of Renee Allen, Program Manager at Working Capital Atlanta; Bonnie Cronin, Director of Development and Public Affairs, Working Capital National Office; Robin Ratcliffe, Vice President Communications, ACCION International; Mandy Smith, Director of Communications, ACCION International; Timothy Freundlich, Program Associate, Calvert Community Investment; Laurie Magers, Zig Ziglar Corporation. Also, Leslie Enright, at the Grameen Foundation USA, for providing information related to the microenterprise movement. We acknowledge the support and interest of Sam Daley-Harris, Executive Director, Microcredit Summit, and Terry Mollner, Co-Chair of the Calvert Foundation.

Thanks to Michelle McEvoy, Michele Klotzer, and Kathy Bonetti, all at Subway headquarters, for their dedication to reading and improving the manuscript.

We also appreciate the enthusiasm of our literary agent, Bob Diforio, and the commitment of our editors, Rick Wolff and Dan Ambrosio.

To these and others who supported our efforts, we remain grateful.

Fred DeLuca
John P. Hayes

INDEX